INTRODUCING SIGN LANGUAGE

INTRODUCING SIGN LANGUAGE LITERATURE

FOLKLORE AND CREATIVITY

RACHEL SUTTON-SPENCE AND
MICHIKO KANEKO

 palgrave

First published 2016 by
PALGRAVE

Palgrave in the UK is an imprint of Macmillan Publishers Limited, registered in England, company number 785998, of 4 Crinan Street, London, N1 9XW.

Palgrave is a global imprint of the above companies and is represented throughout the world.

Palgrave® and Macmillan® are registered trademarks in the United States, the United Kingdom, Europe and other countries.

ISBN 978-1-137-36381-7   ISBN 978-1-349-93179-8 (eBook)
DOI 10.1007/978-1-349-93179-8

A catalogue record for this book is available from the British Library.

A catalog record for this book is available from the Library of Congress.

For Bencie Woll

Contents

List of Figures

Acknowledgements

This book would not have been possible without the participation of four British deaf poets (in alphabetical order): Richard Carter, Paul Scott, Donna Williams and John Wilson. We worked with them especially closely for three years during the life of a project entitled 'Metaphor in Creative Sign Language' funded by the Arts and Humanities Research Council at the University of Bristol (Ref: AH/G011672/1) between 2009 and 2012. Their participation in this and various poetry-related teaching and research activities over the last few years, and their generosity in sharing access to their work, have made the world of difference to our understanding of sign language literature and poetry. We are very grateful to them for their involvement and for their kind permission to draw so extensively on their work in this book and to use illustrations from it. Donna West was a key member of the team during the research project with us and her contributions to the collection, analysis, preservation and promotion of BSL poetry are woven throughout the pages here.

We also thank Johanna Mesch, poet and researcher at Stockholm University, for permission to use her poems and for her involvement and contributions to this study.

The following poets also kindly gave permission to draw on examples from their work: Atiyah Asmal, David Ellington, Kabir Kapoor, Fernanda Machado, Modiegi Moime, and Nelson Pimenta. SLED (Sign Language Education and Development) in South Africa gave permission to use the poems of Atiyah Asmal, Brian Meyer and Modiegi Moime created for their workshops.

In addition, several participants in poetry festivals held between 2006 and 2012 have provided material for our analyses here: Penny Beschizza, Vitalis Katakinas, Penny Gunn, Siobhan O'Donovan, Nigel Howard and Maria Gibson.

Anna Mothapo modelled examples in Figure 6.1, and Tim Northam modelled our examples in Chapter 18.

The late Don Reed, owner of Dorothy Miles' estate, gave his kind permission for us to use her work.

Images of Wim Emmerik's work are drawn from the European Cultural Heritage On-Line website and we are grateful for his kind permission to use them.

Chris John and Rob Nagy provided technical support in editing and converting video clips. The photos of the handshapes were taken by Naomi Janse van Vuuren. Martin Haswell provided invaluable professional support for photos and videos and generally kept things going when they wobbled.

Part of this book was written during periods of study leave for Rachel, funded by the visiting professorships of the Julien and Virginia Cornell fund at Swarthmore College, Philadelphia, USA and CAPES (Coordenação de Aperfeiçoamento de Pessoal de Nível Superior), at the Federal University of Santa Catarina, Brazil (BEX 17881/12-9). Michiko also wrote part of this book on a writing retreat sponsored by the University of the Witwatersrand.

We would like to thank Merrilee Gietz, Isabel Hofmeyr, Victor Houliston, Donna Jo Napoli, Gillian Rudd, and Donna West for their comments on earlier drafts of this book.

Finally, we would like to thank all the members of the deaf community who have discussed sign language poetry with us, and all the students we have taught sign language literature courses to over the years for their input, suggestions and comments.

All the errors, of course, are our own.

Conventions

'Deaf' and 'deaf'

It has become a convention in some situations to use a capital 'D' ('Deaf') to refer to a cultural, social and linguistic minority, as opposed to a small 'd' ('deaf') which simply refers to an audiological condition of deafness. However, the distinctions are not always clear between these two concepts, and the two terms 'deaf' and 'Deaf' in the context of a book such as this can create unintended divisions that become unnecessarily distracting. In this book, we focus on the sign language literature and language art forms of deaf people and their cultures and communities that encompass the experiences of many people with many identities. We will use 'deaf' to refer to all deaf people, unless it is part of a quotation drawn from another source where the author has made a distinction.

Glossing

When we refer to signs in this book, we use sign glosses.

Following the convention in sign language linguistics, each sign is glossed or translated using an English word or words (in small capitals) that best correspond to its meaning – for example, BOOK, HOUSE, DOG, EAT, THINK.

In sign language, especially in creative sign language, which we will be looking at in this book, a great deal of information can be packaged simultaneously rather than sequentially. Information expressed through several separate lexical items in English is often expressed in one sign. Thus, in many cases, one sign corresponds to several English words. A hyphen connects these English words in the gloss. For example, CAR-CRASHES-INTO-WALL translates a visual, simultaneous, and coherent representation of the scene in one sign, not four separate lexical items.

Readers should be aware that in creative sign language, signs can have various meanings, and each gloss we offer is just one of many possible interpretations.

Abbreviations

The following national sign languages commonly appear in this book and are often referred to in abbreviation:

ASL (American Sign Language)
BSL (British Sign Language)
LIBRAS or Libras (Brazilian Sign Language, *Língua Brasileira de Sinais*)
SASL (South African Sign Language)

A note about the sign language literature we discuss in this book

This book aims to introduce the general features of sign language literature, which we believe are applicable to literature in many sign languages. However, we, the authors of this book, are most familiar with British Sign Language (BSL), having studied it for many years, and many of our examples will come from BSL work. In particular, we will highlight the work of five British deaf poets: Dorothy Miles (who also composed work in American Sign Language), Paul Scott, Richard Carter, John Wilson and Donna Williams. In addition, the work by a Swedish deaf poet, Johanna Mesch, will be mentioned frequently as she has worked closely with the British poets.

Michiko has also worked with the South African Sign Language (SASL) work of South African deaf poets and Rachel with the Brazilian Sign Language (Libras) work of Brazilian deaf poets, and we will include examples from these two national sign language literatures where we hope readers will find them interesting.

We will also refer to examples from American Sign Language (ASL) as most research so far about sign language literature comes from the USA. The ideas developed there are extremely helpful to anyone who wants to understand literature in the visual languages of deaf communities around the world. Where we know of examples of sign language literature from other countries, we will occasionally use them too.

The visual nature of sign language literature (and the fact that it uses more productive signs than those from the established lexicon, which is language-specific) makes it more 'transparent' and accessible to audiences who are not familiar with that particular sign language. It is possible to watch poems in sign languages we don't know, and still enjoy them. However, it would be a mistake to assume that all sign language literature will be the same in all countries. Literature and culture are closely connected, and American, British, Brazilian or South African deaf cultures, or the culture of other deaf communities around the world, are not the same. We caution readers to test whether what is reported for a particular sign language will hold for other sign languages.

List of Handshapes

Each handshape has a symbol that is conventionally used to describe it, and we will use the following handshape symbols to refer to a particular hand configuration in this book:

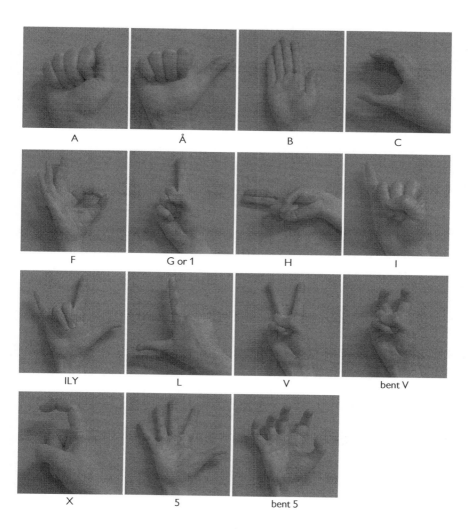

A Å B C

F G or 1 H I

ILY L V bent V

X 5 bent 5

What is Sign Language Literature?

A superhero runs in slow motion to catch an assassin's speeding bullet, a sunbather grabs the fading sun to make it shine again and Father Christmas converses in sign language with his reindeer. Cleopatra's headpiece becomes a living snake that bites her and Macbeth encounters three witches plotting to teach deaf children using a form of language they do not understand. A person becomes a cat, a tortoise or a doll. A jilted woman stabs herself with the bread knife, before apparently miraculously returning to life and throwing the knife away in delight. Two men play at swapping identities until they find what they have in common, and a woman seeks to understand her identity as a deaf person moving in the hearing world.

All these scenarios have been played out visually, in artistic sign language, as we will see later in this book. The deaf performers presenting their work do so as part of a long heritage of visual creativity within the deaf community. The stories they tell, the riddles they set, the poems they perform and, above all, the language they use to produce it, show many aspects of the potential and pleasure of sign language literature.

This book is about sign language literature – a body of creative and artistic sign language (such as poems, stories and jokes) composed and performed by deaf people. It will explore the extended use of sign language and language creativity in deaf communities. We will describe and discuss a range of stories, jokes and poems from sign languages around the world to understand how they create the effect they do.

Sign language literature is the literature of deaf people in the language of deaf people. This much is clear, but beyond that, it is hard to define succinctly or exactly. It is literature created in a visual gestural language and it only exists when someone performs it. This means that sign language literature is different in many ways from the written literature that most of us are familiar with. Sometimes it seems to have more in common with painting, dance or film than written literature. Although it frequently uses sign language vocabulary, it builds on these signs to create something far more visually powerful and innovative, so that it seems to have moved beyond the boundaries of a language.

Defining sign language literature

The word 'literature' is perhaps problematic for an unwritten art form such as this, because it is derived from the same Latin word that gives us the word 'letter', and has long been associated with the written word. It is also a value-laden word: people expect to value and respect something called 'literature' more than something that is not. Earlier meanings of the word related it to the idea of education gained through reading and referred to the technical skills of reading and writing. Since then, it has also come to mean the body of writing produced during a certain period (for example, 19th century literature) or aimed at a particular group (such as children's literature), produced by a particular group (women's literature or French literature) or produced on a particular topic (travel literature). It has also taken another meaning as a special way of working creatively with written language. In literature, the form of the language often comes to the foreground, calling attention to itself in a way that everyday language does not.

None of this can be directly applied to sign language literature, which is produced live in sign performances. However, contemporary under-standings of the word 'literature' have come to include more than the written word so that even in languages that do have a written literature, there is scope to use the word to mean a special way of working creatively with language in any modality (written, spoken or signed). It is within this understanding that creative sign language, respected and valued within deaf communities as an art form that represents their culture, can be called literature.

The language used in signed literature is particularly aesthetic, that is, it appeals to the senses, especially to the sense of beauty. Aesthetic language aims to do more than simply communicate information. It allows signers to increase the significance or communicative power of the message.

Often we think of literature as a 'thing' and sign language literature has rightly been described as an important artefact of deaf culture. However, sign language literature is a process as well as a thing. People perform and take part in sign language literature, and we should remember that it is an activity that people do (both performers and audiences 'do' sign language literature), as well as a collection of artefacts. It is also a body-centred art form. Sign language authors compose using their whole body, including facial expressions, not just their hands, as many non-signers expect. This makes sign language literature highly performative, and is one of the ways in which it is closer to dance than written literature.

In the light of these thoughts, we can work with a definition of sign language literature proposed by the American researcher Heidi Rose (1992) that it is 'a union of language and gesture that results in linguistically organized aesthetic movement' (p. 157). It is a 'literature of the body' (Rose, 2006, p. 131) that shows deaf people's views of their place in the world. It prioritises the visual image. Importantly, it often plays with sign language, exploring its creative potential, primarily for aesthetic pleasure. Put simply, a great deal of sign language literature is beautiful and fun.

Many frameworks for understanding written literature have been developed and refined over the years and they can help us considerably as we use them and their terminology to understand and explain sign language literature. However, they can also limit our understanding of this visual, body-centred, signed art form because they were not designed for it. For this reason, although in this book we treat creative sign language primarily as a language art form, we also treat it as a visual art form, most especially a moving visual art form. Ideas developed for understanding the grammar and impact of cinema (as developed by Dirksen Bauman (2006) in the USA) can provide different but very enlightening ways to approach these visual, moving performances.

'Deaf literature' or 'Sign language literature'?

The scope of deaf literature can include work written in the majority language of the hearing society that surrounds a deaf community. A piece of literature written by a deaf person could be considered part of deaf literature, but so too could a piece of literature written about a deaf person (or deaf people). Some hearing authors with extensive knowledge of sign language and deaf culture have written about deaf people to show deaf people's experiences in a way that many deaf people find credible. Examples include *Ancestors* by the Zimbabwean author Chenjerai Hove, *Apple is My Sign* by Mary Riskind in the USA and *Tibi and Joca* (*Tibi e Joca*) by Cláudia Bisol in Brazil. Although these could come into the category of deaf literature because of their content, there is an understanding that works produced by deaf authors form the main canon of deaf literature (although some deaf authors and illustrators work in partnership with hearing people to create deaf literature).

It is not enough that the authors should be deaf, however. Readers often expect deaf literature to concern itself in some way with the lives or experiences of deaf people, so a book written by a deaf author that does not address these topics is not considered central to deaf literature.

The *Tales From Signtown* series by the British deaf author Nick Sturley is a good example of deaf literature, written by a deaf person and referring to deaf culture. In this playful series, Sturley uses written English to retell a range of fairy stories, filled with deaf characters and references to deaf history, deaf culture, deaf behaviour and sign language. The *Inspector Morse* series by Colin Dexter, on the other hand, is also written by a deaf person but with no mention of deafness (with the exception of *The Silent World of Nicholas Quinn*) and is not usually considered to be deaf literature.

Sign language literature may be considered part of deaf literature, but the term specifically refers to pieces that are performed in sign language and are almost always produced by deaf people. It includes faithful signed translations of written pieces of literature, and detailed representations of a film, in sign language. In such cases, the signing will be valued because it is especially visual and aesthetically very satisfying, but the content does not relate to the lives and experiences of deaf people. Other pieces have been adapted in their translation, so that the basic story has its origins in a non-deaf setting, but is retold in sign language with deaf characters. Original sign language literature (the focus of this book) is composed in sign language by culturally deaf members of the deaf community, and comes from a deaf perspective.

Types of sign language literature

Perhaps the peak of sign language literature is the highly polished, original, signed performance art sometimes called sign language poetry, where deaf artists can present new ideas in new ways, using original forms of signing. Community members recognise it as an art form, displaying the fullest potential of their language. It is usually strongly visual and carefully constructed for maximum impact on the senses. As an expression of the community's sense of deaf identity, it is an art form with its own rules and patterns.

Folklore (which includes traditional narratives, jokes and language games) is sometimes seen as a contrast to literature but we will see in Chapter 4 that there is good reason to include performances and texts that are usually called folklore in a study of literature.

Many people think of fiction when they think of literature, and plenty of sign language literature is fiction, but non-fiction can also be sign language literature. Nancy Frishberg (1988) was one of the first researchers to note this as she identified different forms of sign language literature. *Oratory*, or making speeches, is a way of using language to catch people's attention and deliver more than simply a message, as speeches use many of the same language devices as poetry or theatre, such as repetition, timing and rhythm, to generate emotions in their audiences. Frishberg noted that sign language oratory occurs at banquets or formal occasions, in sermons and at political rallies and campaigns. Political works form part of literature, especially those that highlight social injustice and fight oppression, and we will see that political expression occurs in a range of signed art forms. It may present a deaf perspective on politics generally. For example, many poems in South African Sign Language (SASL) deal with racial segregation and apartheid. Alternatively, it may address specific deaf-related political issues, such as provision of services for deaf people or access to education. Autobiography is a common form of literary non-fiction and we will see that narratives of personal experience are a central part of sign language literature that emerges in stories and poems, and even in jokes and theatre. Chronicles are critical descriptions and narratives of people, events or daily life, sometimes in other societies or in other times. When we see sign language stories about deaf history (such as the BSL piece *Three Queens* by Paul Scott), we are seeing deaf chronicles, which may take the form of a creative story or a factual account of events or people. Political literature, autobiography and chronicles, whether written or signed, are often valued as literature, and can be funny, ironic or lyrical as they comment on the events they describe and often seek to change them.

Signed religious literature is important for many signers. For years, churches were some of the very few places where people used sign language in a formal situation. Signing ministers (many of whom were deaf or were the hearing children of deaf parents) were widely respected in their communities for their signing skills. Churches today are still places where sign language is recognised and promoted. Much of signed religious literature is translated as faithfully as possible from written religious literature, especially the Bible or hymns in the Christian religion, but when the translation is done with careful attention to the form of the signed language, it can create a signed art form in its own right. There are also examples of adapted religious stories. For example, the British signer Penny Beschizza retold the Old Testament bible story of Moses and the parting of the Red Sea, to include some deaf characters in her BSL translation. Deaf people who saw her adaptation said afterwards that it helped them feel that the Bible was more relevant to them.

In this book, we have chosen to include creative pieces from a range of genres, all produced by deaf signers and all with some aesthetic aspects. We will think about what they say and how they say it, focusing on the language they use, other elements of performance and the structure of the texts. We will also consider the people who create and perform it and the audiences who watch it.

The content of sign language literature – it's what you say

Anything that is presented in sign language carries a mark of being deaf simply because it is signed, even when deafness or deaf people are not the focus. However, a good deal of sign language literature does address deafness in some way because it represents the views of the deaf community. The importance of focusing on deafness in sign language literature varies according to time and place. In the USA, for example, researchers such as Stephen Ryan (1993) and Ben Bahan (2006a) suggested that in the 1980s and 1990s ASL poetry was expected to address the idea of deafness directly, but two or three decades later it rarely does (according to a review by John Lee Clark, 2009). In South Africa, racial and political issues can be prioritised over deafness as a topic for sign language literature, due to its complex historical background. In Britain and Brazil, deafness is still considered a suitable topic for sign language poetry.

Sign language literature often celebrates deaf people's lives and experience, and focuses on what is valued about the deaf community and its language, so it rarely describes deafness as a loss. Much of the early written literature by deaf people addressed the oppression of deaf people and their culture by hearing society. These themes still occur in sign language literature, although Karen Christie and Dorothy Wilkins (2006) have shown that sign language poetry often includes themes that show deaf resistance to this oppression. It often shows the sensory experience of deaf people, celebrating a world understood through sight and touch (and even occasionally taste, for example, in a sign language poem about jam by Richard Carter). We will explore this more in Chapter 9.

The form of sign language literature – it's how you say it

The form of sign language literature refers to how it is delivered through the visual, spatial and kinetic (moving) modality of sign language. Whereas written or spoken forms use a string of words in sequence, signed forms utilise both sequential and simultaneous combinations of manual components (what the hands are doing) and a variety of non-manual components (what other parts of the body are doing – such as the eyes, mouth, head and torso). The space surrounding the signer can also be an essential part of sign language literature.

Cynthia Peters (2000) has observed that much of the cultural meaning and value of sign language literature comes from the way it is signed, and from the fact that it is signed at all. These aspects are often more important than what is signed. Most deaf people growing up in hearing families without access to deaf culture and sign language have never learned about the possibilities of sign language nor how to perform it. This means that when they finally do see creative sign language they often value it more for its fluency and expressive potential than for its message.

The form of language often highlights the importance of linguistic play in literature. Some playful language is only possible in writing, such as crosswords or graffiti. On the other hand, tongue-twisters, puns and mimicry are language games that can be played in speech or sign language as they rely on live language play. A lot of sign language literature has the important function of being for enjoyment, and much of it includes an element of playing with language. In fact, even though we can talk specifically about deaf humour (see Chapter 18), humorous language is valued in many sign language poems and stories, even ultimately serious ones.

What sign language literature has that spoken language literature has not

Whereas most spoken or written literature relies heavily upon the established words of a language, sign language literature uses many productive signs, which are basically new signs, created *ad hoc* to describe a particular scene. They often use so-called classifiers – signs that are shaped to provide an accurate visual description of objects and people. For example, a closed fist represents spherical objects (rocks, heads, balls), whereas an extended index finger can represent a long thin object (a pencil, a piece of string, an upright human being). Although everyday signing makes use of classifiers, they are particularly relevant in creative signing, as poets constantly seek new and productive ways of saying something, without relying on existing signs. For example, instead of using an existing sign CAT and adjectives such as SMALL, CUDDLY and SOFT to describe a cat, signers can use classifiers to illustrate the details of the cat (its size, the shape of its ears, tail and paws, the texture of its fur, and how it behaves), while indicating the cat's expressions on the face. (See, for example, Dorothy Miles' *The Cat*, Donna Williams' *My Cat* and John Wilson's *For Two Special People*.)

Sign language literature also consists of elements that do not occur in written literature (although there may be some parallels with spoken performance literature). As we explore sign language literature throughout this book, we will see that signers draw on a range of language devices to create extra enjoyment or new meanings. They can vary the speed at which signs are made, to be unusually fast or slow. They can place signs in different parts of their signing space and move them through the space. They can select and repeatedly use specific handshapes for the signs. They can show multiple perspectives at the same time. For example, a signer can use the hands to represent a child holding a doll ('I am holding a doll') while the face simultaneously expresses the emotion of a personified doll being held ('I am the doll you are holding'). (See Paul Scott's *Doll*.) Signers can take on the role of humans, animals, plants and inanimate objects by mapping the physical features of these referents onto their body, so they seem to become the referent. In all these examples, the signers are drawing on the options available in their bodily language to create powerful visual images with movement, in ways that words in a spoken language cannot do.

This means that to understand what deaf people value in sign language literature we must see it in its original form. Thus, we strongly encourage readers to view original performances by deaf performers (either live or video-recorded) to appreciate fully their aesthetic values. The pieces we cite in this book are all available either on commercial DVDs or on Internet sites.

Why should we study sign language literature?

When we study sign language literature, we aim to understand what drives it and what deaf audiences appreciate in it. Careful study will allow us to understand what makes some pieces 'work'. However, different people respond to different pieces differently at different times, and a performance that is appropriate in one situation may not work in another. We will not make value judgements on the examples we describe here but rather will attempt to describe and explain how they achieve a certain literary effect.

Sign language literature can change people's attitudes about deaf people and sign language. Hearing people have often labelled deaf people as disabled rather than members of a community that uses a different language. For many years, neither deaf nor hearing people believed that sign languages were real languages or that they were capable of expressing complex ideas. Sign languages were certainly not acceptable languages for literature. These attitudes have now changed considerably but there is still a long way to go before wider hearing society stops seeing deaf people as disabled. Study of sign language literature shows clearly that members of a deaf community have a rich language heritage, and that we should give sign languages the same respect as any spoken or written language for the beautiful, elegant and ingenious ways they can express ideas. For many deaf people, studying sign language literature gives a sense of pride in their language, heritage and sense of identity.

We would encourage people learning sign language to study sign language literature. Learning about literature is one of the most exciting aspects of learning a new language. Students can watch sign language literature for enjoyment, but studying it also helps them to become more aware of the language, and thinking about the themes and meaning contained within the literature helps students understand deaf culture. When students of sign language have enjoyed and studied sign language poems by established poets, they can create and perform their own sign language poetry. When deaf children do this, it helps them to express their emotions, developing confidence in social and linguistic interactions, taking pride in self-expression and developing their sign language skills further (Scott, 2010).

Summary

In this introductory chapter, we have thought about what sign language literature might be and what it might include. We have seen that it is created by members of deaf communities for other community members to enjoy. It is characterised by the ideas it expresses and, perhaps more importantly, by the way it expresses them. We have seen that sign language literature is a linguistic art form that can be compared to written literature but that it has many different aspects, caused by its unique visual, moving nature. We have noted that it is hard to categorise and that it has many different genres and styles but that anyone who studies it will increase their understanding of sign language and deaf culture. As we work through our exploration of sign language literature, we will expand on these key points, providing more in-depth examples and considering the significance of many of these aspects for an overall understanding of the area.

Further reading

Bahan, Ben (2006) 'Face-to-face tradition in the American Deaf community' in H-Dirksen Bauman, Jennifer Nelson and Heidi Rose (eds) *Signing the Body Poetic* (California: University of California Press).

Bauman, H-Dirksen (2006) 'Getting out of line: toward a visual and cinematic poetics of ASL' in H-Dirksen Bauman, Jennifer Nelson and Heidi Rose (eds) *Signing the Body Poetic* (California: University of California Press).

Frishberg, Nancy (1988) 'Signers of tales: the case of literary status of an unwritten language', *Sign Language Studies* 17(59), 149–170.

Peters, Cynthia (2000) 'The deaf oral tradition' in Cynthia Peters (ed.) *Deaf American Literature: From Carnival to the Canon* (Washington, DC: Gallaudet University Press).

If you are interested in finding out how deaf people have been portrayed in written literature, read:

Krentz, Christopher (2007) *Writing Deafness: The Hearing Line in Nineteenth-century American Literature* (Chapel Hill, NC: University of North Carolina Press).

Activities

1. English literature includes literature written about deaf people, usually written by hearing people, who frequently use deaf characters as a specific plot device. We don't cover that in this book, but it is an important topic in its own right. There is also literature written by deaf people, which shows the perspectives of deaf writers and their view of the world. Find some examples of poems or stories that are about a deaf person or the idea of deafness written by hearing people and by deaf people. What similarities or differences do you find in the way that deafness and deaf people are shown? As an example of a hearing poet, the South African Anthony Delius wrote a poem titled *Deaf-and-dumb School*, which 'presents an unusually sensitive attempt to observe and enter the world of hearing-impaired and mute children' (Moffett, 2014, p. 180). (Note that today we do not use the word 'dumb' to refer to deaf people.) Examples of work by deaf people are *To a Deaf Child* by Dorothy Miles and *On His Deafness* by David Wright.

2. Find an example of creative sign language that you do not consider to be fiction (for example, an autobiography of a deaf person). How would you justify calling this piece 'sign language literature'?

3. Find an example of a piece of literature translated directly into a sign language that you know. Find another piece that has been adapted so that it includes deaf characters or references to deaf culture. What elements make you think they could be part of sign language literature? BSL users can use Carolyn Nabarro's *The Boy Who Cried Wolf* (available from the European Cultural Heritage Online website) for the first example, and Jerry Hanifin's adaptation of *Little Red Ridinghood* (in Chapter 14 of the DVD accompanying Sutton-Spence and Woll, 1999) for the second example.

4. How would you reply to someone who says, 'Sign languages can't have a literature. For a start, they aren't written down'?

2 Sign Language Literature in Context

In this chapter, we will consider the context in which sign language literature is produced and consumed. We will look at where the literature is performed and watched, and think about who created it, who is performing it and who is in the audience, to understand how these aspects might affect its form. We also ask why people sign stories or recount other forms of sign language literature, and try to show why access to sign language literature is so important for deaf children.

Any description of sign language literature will almost certainly include a description of the text, detailing its content and form. However, it should also ideally include the following:

- Where and when the piece is told.
- Who tells it.
- Whether it is privately owned, or generally part of the cultural heritage.
- Who the audience is, and the extent and type of audience participation.
- Why the piece is told.

Although this chapter is dedicated to exploring these aspects, we will bear them in mind throughout this book in our consideration of a wide range of creative sign language texts because they can influence our understanding.

Where and when we see sign language literature

Historically, creative sign language has been performed live. Deaf people have told stories and jokes, and performed poems and skits to school friends, to audiences at deaf clubs, on social nights, at weddings and funerals, and at parties and sporting events (Bahan, 2006a; Ladd, 2003; Peters, 2000; Rutherford, 1993; Hall, 1989). Some communities arrange formal literary performances, and there may be competitions of storytelling and poetry. Live storytelling to friends and other community members is still an important part of deaf community life, but recorded stories, jokes and poems are now often watched on DVD or the Internet.

Recorded performances create a distance between a signer and the audience, which means they can be watched almost anywhere and at any time (for example, at home, in a café, on a bus or in a classroom). This has freed sign language literature to occupy new spaces in place and time. To this extent, video recordings of sign language literature are more like written literature. There is some concern (see for example, Krentz, 2006) that recording, preserving and promoting literature through digital media separates signers from their audiences, breaking a crucial link between them. However, recordings allow many more people to see the work and audiences can watch signed performances repeatedly. We will discuss this more in the next chapter.

The relatively small percentage of deaf children born to deaf parents (usually, up to about five per cent of in many deaf communities) learn sign language from their parents, and sign language stories often form part of their upbringing. In the past, most deaf children from hearing families where sign language was not used learned sign language stories and story-telling skills at residential deaf schools. Young deaf people growing up today in a mainstream school system without the company of other deaf people found in residential schools do not have the same peer groups to learn from. Instead, they may have access to sign language literature performed live by adults (deaf or hearing) who teach at or visit their school. They may also see it in recorded collections specially made for education. Examples include the CHASE videos (Culture, History, Arts, Sign and Education), made by the Royal College for the Deaf in Derby in the UK, those made by INES the Brazilian National Deaf School in Rio de Janeiro, or educational materials on sign language poetry created by SLED (Sign Language Education & Development) in South Africa. Some people may attend special deaf cultural events organised by community members and their hearing allies who want to promote sign language literature. Young deaf adults who have grown up without access to deaf culture also learn it from their signing peers when they join the deaf community, perhaps at college or university or when they join a deaf club. The deaf club has long been the place where deaf adults pass on sign language storytelling traditions. In many cases, this remains the case, although increasingly stories are passed around in other meeting places, or on the Internet, especially through social media.

Who produces the literature and tells the stories?

To appreciate better the context of sign language literature we need to know who tells the sign language stories that form the basis of literature in signing communities. At one level, we all tell stories because they are a way to express who we are. However, in a more formal sense, many communities identify particular people who have the job of storyteller. In the past, in many oral societies where writing was unknown (or at least not used for their language and culture), a chosen person learned the unwritten stories about the history of their community from an older 'master' through apprenticeship. Everyone in the community was expected to be familiar with their community's traditional stories in order to appreciate the tales told by the storytellers. This situation still occurs in present-day oral societies and there are parallels in many deaf communities where deaf people with deaf parents hold the stories of deaf history for their community and pass them on to the next generation. In contrast to the traditional stories and histories in oral societies, most literate societies expect their storytellers (for example, novelists, poets and playwrights) to create new stories and not repeat old ones (unless they tell a traditional story in a new way).

In addition to the specially marked out storytellers in deaf communities, however, everyone can tell sign language stories. It is understood that deaf people can express themselves and tell stories in sign language in a way that they often cannot in spoken language. A well-known leader in the British deaf community mentioned to us that, 'Stories start from when you start signing'. He added that the moment deaf children learn sign language, after only having experienced spoken language, 'they're off telling stories'.

The core sign language storytellers are deaf people. Susan Rutherford, an American researcher of deaf folklore, found that deaf people usually reported that only members of the deaf community should tell traditional sign language stories (Rutherford, 1993). They have the language and culture skills to produce cultural art forms and want to share their experiences with other community members. Hearing learners of sign language may learn sign language storytelling techniques to focus on specific elements of the language but they do not tell stories for the reasons that deaf community members do. Exceptionally, hearing people who have grown up with deaf family members (as siblings or children of deaf signers, for example) may be respected as storytellers in their own right.

Although any community member can take part in sign language storytelling, there are a few acknowledged 'masters' (male or female) of the genre. For example, Rutherford found that although most adolescents discover the ASL genre of ABC stories (we will talk about them more in Chapter 5), and plenty of young adults tell them, only a few adults who have a reputation for skills in the genre perform them at parties. They need to have good signing skills in general, a reputation for skilled storytelling, and a strong deaf identity. Rutherford calls these skilled sign-ers people who have 'the knack'. They are 'often sought out and coaxed again and again to perform' (1993, p. 55). Ben Bahan (2006a) calls them 'smooth signers'. Charles Reilly and Nipapon Reilly (2005) refer to them as 'master signers'.

Thus, some stories are prepared and performed formally, and others are more spontaneous and performed informally; they may be told by signers from deaf families as well as by signers from hearing families. These two sets of distinctions can influence the pattern of storytelling traditions in different deaf communities. For example, the stories that are often described in research about ASL story traditions are formal, prepared performances, and many of the 'masters' of these narratives are from deaf families where they learned the stories and traditional storytelling skills, or from hearing families but learned sign language and these stories at an early age at school. Narratives that are part of informal, spontaneous social situations are more commonly described in other countries. They have been described in UK traditions, where the 'masters' of these narratives are often signers from hearing families who learned to see and describe the world around them without help from a ready-made language passed on by their families. Without a model of sign language to follow at an early age, they had to rely on their visual experiences and they developed storytelling styles that are valued for their powerful visual images. In this case, the stories may not be the traditional ones, but they are told in a highly valued visual signing style that audiences enjoy and appreciate.

Many people are used to the idea that there is only one storyteller at any one time. In this single-floor approach, the storyteller has the audience's full attention and can usually continue signing without interruption. However, in jointly constructed storytelling, everyone is the storyteller and everyone is the audience. These group narratives, which are strongly theatrical, have been noted in many countries. Susan Rutherford (1993) described the group narratives of deaf children in America but the jointly constructed group narrative genre is also described in the UK, in Brazil, in Thailand and is seen in many other countries. It occurs in many forms of sign language literature, created by adults as well as children, and the boundary between these sign language narratives and signed theatre is unclear. Topics highlighted by Rutherford's research on the group narratives by children include life experiences (such as expecting a baby) but also often come from films or television programmes. The more visual and action-packed the film, the better it is for creating visual stories full of action in sign language, and with many characters in the story, all the children can be involved. These children's stories use mime and exaggerated performances. Rutherford described how deaf children worked in a group in a visual modality, with a lot of cooperation and simultaneity to create a rich visual picture in a way that parallels the creation of a film. Clive Mason (cited in Smith and Sutton-Spence, 2007) described a group narrative concerning a battle scene constructed when he was at a residential school for deaf children in Glasgow in the 1960s. Each night, in the dormitories after bedtime, the children would take turns to be the 'director' of the stories. The director would allocate roles to each child, and then invite them all to contribute to his story as he controlled it.

The question of who tells stories is especially relevant to the live, face-to-face tradition of sign language storytelling because anonymity of the author or performer is not an option. Sign language literature cannot be produced under a pseudonym, as written literature can be. This puts the personal identity of the signing performer more centrally into the spotlight, and deaf audiences often have a strong sense that the performer will own what they are saying. The relationship between the signer and their signed performance has parallels with spoken performance slam poetry. Like deaf performers, slam poets frequently come from less socially powerful minority groups. Boudreau (2009) has shown that audiences of slam poetry usually assume that the words of the poet-performer represent that person's views. Although there are many differences between signed performances and spoken slam performances, the live, personal performances mean that deaf audiences often expect sign language literature to represent their beliefs and experiences.

Who is the audience?

Any literature, written or signed, needs an audience. The nature of the audience can influence both the form and content of the performance. The relationship between storytellers and their audiences is complex, but it is generally accepted that a story is the result of the joint participation of storyteller and audience. When the story is performed live, the presence of the audience can be very influential but even in recordings of sign language stories, the literary event is only complete when the audience has seen it and responded to it.

Traditionally, sign language stories have been directed at deaf people who have acquired certain expectations about the performances. Bahan (2006a) mentions an elderly deaf storyteller who knew what to expect of his deaf audience and they of him, saying, 'It was as if the audience was in him and he was in the audience' (p. 44).

All communities teach their members to understand stories in a particular way and deaf audiences learn to respond to sign language literature in ways that are different from people who are conditioned to written literature. Historically, deaf people have not learned to read by using sign language at school, and they very rarely have the opportunity to learn formally about literacy processes in sign language (Kuntze et al., 2014; Arenson and Kretschmer, 2010).[1] For example, although hearing children are often taught to link rhyme or rhythm in conversational spoken language to what rhyme and rhythm look like on a page, very few deaf children are shown how to link rhyme or rhythm in conversational sign language to what rhyme and rhythm look like in poetry. To reduce the difficulties that deaf audiences may have with some sign language literature, they need to learn it, ideally at school (Sutton-Spence and Quadros, 2014).

Master signers understand the expectations of their audiences, having lived very similar experiences to their audiences, and they will often change the story to suit each one, in order to provide the best entertainment. Audiences can vary by age, gender, region or language and education experiences, for example and each one will bring a different set of expectations, experiences and abilities to the process. Bahan (2006a) explains that a storyteller must choose:

1. The right elements of language to suit the language skills of the audience (signs, nonmanual elements, grammar).
2. The right way to perform it to generate the right emotions (rhythm, speed, nonmanual elements).
3. The right story to suit the natural views of the audience.

If the audience of a live performance does not react in the right way (for example, if the audience does not understand or laugh in the expected way), a skilled storyteller will modify all these during the performance. Audiences watching recordings, however, make different demands upon the storyteller. Although they can see the storyteller's performance, which still has a personal touch (that is not present when readers read a story in a book, for example), there is no chance for interaction, so the storyteller has to make all the decisions on language, performance and content that will best satisfy an imagined audience in advance.

Another challenge is made when the audience contains a mixture of deaf and hearing people. Hearing people who come to sign performances often know some sign language and may have some knowledge of deaf culture, but their life experiences are very different from those of deaf people, posing a challenge to them as well as to the deaf performer.

The American deaf storyteller Stephen Ryan (1993) listed several tips for good sign language storytelling in a public performance that show how important it is for the performer to work with the audience:

- Generate rapport, especially via eye-contact with the audience.
- Allow the live performance to affect the story.
- Create strong visual images.
- Use gestures with signs.
- Vary gestures with signs.
- Use pauses to allow the signs to sink in.
- Celebrate the Deaf Heritage.
- Hook the audience in from the start.
- Be selective and know how little you need to tell.
- Empower the audience to imagine things from the story.
- Respect and like both the audience and the story.
- Be prepared and practise the sequence of events but remain spontaneous.
- Be enthusiastic.
- Consider the age and interest of the audience.

Why sign language literature is important

Stories and other forms of literature are usually highly entertaining. This is as true for sign language literature as for any other, but literature has functions beyond enjoyment. In any community, stories help to store, organise and pass on tradition, culture and folklore, so deaf storytelling can be an opportunity to repeat stories that are part of the deaf cultural heritage (Peters, 2000). The traditional stories told by a community may act as a metaphor for the community's experience, and transmit the cultural values of the community, although they can sometimes be used to challenge or question those values. At an individual level, personal stories created and told by individuals can help a person to understand who they are and show this to other people.

As well as often being good entertainment, traditionally stories have helped to:

- Help people to make sense of the world.
- Teach people facts about the world and life in it.
- Teach people about their culture.
- Create and maintain the identity of the community.
- Give authors/tellers opportunities to develop or show off their linguistic skills.
- Give authors/tellers opportunities to show who they are.
- Allow people to explore and develop their language, pushing its boundaries (Ryan, 1993; Bascom, 1965).

In order to explore the reasons behind sign language storytelling in more depth, we will take as an example the popular genre of sign stories in which signers represent non-humans as though they were human, using the device of anthropomorphism. We will consider anthropomorphism in detail in Chapter 7, but for now we will use it as a way to illustrate why sign language storytelling is important.

Anthropomorphism is a favoured literary device for several reasons. A simple but very important reason for so many non-human characters in sign language literature is that it is great fun to see them behave like humans. However, it also allows storytellers to provide a new perspective on life. When we anthropomorphise a non-human, we can put ourselves in its place and this reversed perspective allows us to see the world in a new way, and think how we should feel if we were in their place. The non-human characters can also observe human behaviour (and especially the behaviour of the deaf community members or hearing people's behaviour) from an outsider's viewpoint, and they may challenge this existing behaviour.

Moreover, taking the perspective of non-humans is to present a story from a minority viewpoint. Any story featuring non-humans as central characters can upset traditional hierarchies between humans and non-humans. This can be liberating for oppressed minorities, including deaf people, at least within the story world. Non-humans in sign language literature may be especially popular when they don't communicate using a spoken human language. Deaf people may identify more closely with these non-speaking non-human characters than with speaking human characters, although, as we will see in Chapter 7, there is extra pleasure to be had when they are portrayed as using sign language.

Sign language storytelling to teach children in the classroom

Cultural and anthropological research studies of sign language storytelling have usually looked at adult literature. However, sign language storytelling is also very important for the social and linguistic development of deaf children. Ladd (2003) described in detail the importance of conversational storytelling for many deaf children at residential school in the past. According to Lane et al. (1996), storytelling developed early in residential schools for deaf children when children signed stories to each other, teaching sign language and helping them to learn about life, both generally and as a deaf person. Children with access to deaf clubs and deaf adults would tell the other children stories they had learned there. There are very few accounts of deaf teachers telling sign language stories in the classroom because such events have been comparatively rare. However, where deaf children are lucky enough to be taught by deaf teachers, storytelling is an important part of their education (Sutton-Spence and Ramsey, 2010).

Teachers use sign language stories in the classroom to teach children sign language. They can teach very basic sign language to children with minimal sign language skills (many deaf children arrive at school with limited language because their hearing parents cannot sign) and encourage older deaf children to extend their existing signing skills to become more adult-like. When hearing children tell their own stories in speech, or they read and write stories, it all helps to stimulate their imagination and memory skills. Sign language stories allow deaf children the same benefits without having to struggle with the written language. Sometimes stories are a good way to help children learn facts, especially when they help to engage their interest in a subject.

Sign language stories told by deaf teachers also help children learn how to tell stories. Younger children learn to tell stories by watching and copying the teacher's story, and teachers can explicitly teach story techniques to older children. Deaf teachers may encourage a story from a child and ask other children to watch, support and comment. This helps children learn the social skills that accompany storytelling, such as supporting peers, negotiating meaning and understanding how and when to take the floor. It also introduces them to the important social activity of building stories collectively, and we have already seen in Chapter 1 that this is an important part of deaf culture in many deaf communities.

Storytelling to build and develop identity

Although it is clear that sign language storytelling is an important way to pass on deaf identity at a collective level, it is also important to build and develop identity at a more individual level, as each deaf person can build and show their own linguistic, social and cultural identity through creativity. For many deaf people, the act of signing stories is part of what makes them 'a deaf person'. Smith and Sutton-Spence (2007) quote a deaf man who explained that when he was a child at a residential deaf school, signing stories after a day in the classroom where only oral communication was allowed changed who he was. In the daytime he was one person – 'oral deaf'; by night signing stories, he became another person – 'deaf deaf'.

Signers can use stories to express powerful feelings that they cannot easily express through spoken language, so encouraging children and young people to tell stories and create poems in sign language is a positive, creative way to help them express sometimes complicated and difficult emotions. Stories further help young people build a confident sense of identity because, when a person tells a story – whether their own or a story about, or by, another person – the audience pays attention to them. Too often hearing non-signers ignore deaf people (especially deaf children), so storytelling in sign language is an opportunity to be truly noticed by people who understand.

Summary

In this chapter we have considered the 'where, who and why' of sign language literature, especially sign language stories. The extra information about the context in which the literature occurs is inextricably linked to the texts and their performance. We have seen that stories were traditionally told as live, interactive events by children to each other at deaf schools and by adults in deaf clubs. In some remaining deaf schools, deaf teachers now tell stories to children. Deaf gatherings are still venues for live storytelling, but as deaf people's social patterns change, stories are increasingly recorded and posted on the Internet. All deaf people enjoy telling stories informally but in any deaf community there are storytellers who are master signers (male or female), 'smooth signers' or people who have 'the knack'. They know how to encourage their audiences to respond best to the performances. Sign language stories are important for all signers to express who they are but they also form part of the folklore tradition that passes on the cultural knowledge of the deaf community.

Note

1. We know of a few schools that are beginning to use ebooks with sign videos in them to help teach deaf children how to read, but this is not the experience of most deaf children.

Further reading

Arenson, Rebecca and Robert Kretschmer (2010) 'Teaching poetry: a descriptive case study of a poetry unit in a classroom of urban deaf adolescents', *American Annals of the Deaf*, 155(2), 110–117.

Bahan, Ben (2006) 'Face-to-face tradition in the American Deaf community' in H-Dirksen Bauman, Jennifer Nelson and Heidi Rose (eds) *Signing the Body Poetic* (California: University of California Press).

Ryan, Stephen (1993) 'Let's tell an ASL story' in Gallaudet University College for Continuing Education (ed.) *Conference Proceedings, April 22–25, 1993* (Washington, DC: Gallaudet University Press).

Sutton-Spence, Rachel and Claire Ramsey (2010) 'What we should teach Deaf children: Deaf teachers' folk models in Britain, the U.S. and Mexico', *Deafness and Education International*, 12(3), 149–76.

Sutton-Spence, Rachel and Ronice Muller de Quadros (2014) '"I am the Book" – Deaf poets' views on signed poetry', *Journal of Deaf Studies and Deaf Education*, 19(4), 546–558.

Activities

1. Select a variety of sign language stories or poems that you consider are aimed at different audiences (for example, younger children, sign language learners, fluent adult signers) and think about the following:

   ■ Who are the stories for? Keep in mind that a given story/poem can fit into one or more (or none) of the categories we have discussed in this chapter. Why do you think this?

   ■ Do they signal that they are stories for the deaf community? (If so, how do they signal this?)

   ■ Who is telling the story, where is the story being told and why is the story being told?

   (BSL users may like to look at the poems and stories included in the DVD accompanying Sutton-Spence and Woll, 1999.)

2. Select a sign language story and identify who it is aimed at. Think of a different audience. How would you change the story if it were aimed at this other audience?

3. Ask a deaf signer to tell you about a sign language storyteller they like. Find out from them what they like about the way this person tells stories. Ask a hearing person to tell you about a storyteller (who tells stories in either written or spoken language) they like. Find out from them what they like about the way this person tells stories. What differences can you see between the answers of the deaf and hearing person?

3 Oral Literature and Performance

In this chapter, we will describe the features of sign language literature that are related to it as a type of non-written literature. The fact that sign languages do not have widely used written forms makes their literatures closer to so-called 'oral' literature – despite the fact that a sign language is obviously not 'oral', as it is not spoken. We will explore some definitions of oral literature and see how sign language literature can fit them. Then we will discuss how the advance of video technology has altered the status of sign language literature and how the weight has shifted from performance to text.

Definitions of oral literature

Oral literature is a body of non-written work that forms a community's cultural and linguistic heritage. It includes stories, folk songs, poetry, prayers and legends, which are passed on from person to person, through repeated performances and retelling. It exists in people's memory and in the performance space, rather than on paper. The word 'oral' is related to the mouth, so it would seem an odd word for describing sign languages.[1] However, the term makes a distinction between things that are written and things that are not, so here we use 'oral' to mean 'non-written', which makes it applicable to the body of sign language literature.

There has been a long debate whether the term 'oral literature' is best suited to describe the body of any culture's oral heritage. As we saw in Chapter 1, the word 'literature' mostly refers to written work, so it contradicts the notion of an oral (non-written) medium in which these stories and poems are transmitted. Several alternative suggestions have been made, including *epos*, which is the Greek word for 'song' or 'speech'. This might work well for unwritten spoken languages but not for describing unwritten sign languages. The Ugandan scholar Pio Zirimu coined the term 'orature' to avoid referring to 'literature' (Wa Thiong'o, 1998). It was later adopted by Cynthia Peters (2000) to describe the ASL literary tradition and the way it has been passed down in the American deaf community. Ben Bahan (2006) has used the phrase 'face-to-face tradition' to cover the artistic and creative signing of ASL. This might be a useful term for us to use, although we also need to define a 'tradition'.

The term 'oral literature', unsatisfactory as it is, is useful because of the theoretical understanding that comes with the term. We suggested in Chapter 1 that we can disregard the linguistic link between the word 'literature' and any idea of reading, and then use the word to mean a body of language-based work that is considered socially, historically, religiously, culturally or linguistically important for the community (that is, the 'canon'). However, we still need to determine what parts of the definition of oral literature are applicable to sign language.

There are many definitions of oral literature. Some are very precise but not may not be very useful because we can always see exceptions to the narrow definitions. Others are much broader but can be so broad that they become very woolly. Ruth Finnegan, one of the leading scholars in the study of oral literature, warns us that oral literature 'is inevitably a relative and complex term rather than an absolute and clearly demarcated category' (1977, p. 22).

The most basic definition is that it 'circulates by oral rather than written means' and '[d]istribution, composition and performance are by word of mouth and not through reliance on the written or printed word' (Finnegan, 1977, p. 17). Clearly, we need to alter this definition to allow for sign language literature using signs rather than word of mouth, but it does not rely on the written or printed word.

Another traditional view is that oral literature is 'composed in oral performance by people who cannot read or write' (Lord, 1965, cited in Finnegan, 1977, p. 7). We will return to the idea of 'composition in performance' later, but the idea that the artist cannot read or write needs addressing here. This requirement seems to suggest that the default of artistic activities is to read and write, and that only those who cannot will use the oral channel. It establishes the written form as normal, and makes oral literature highly marked (that is, unusual). However, oral literature may not be for people who *cannot* read and write, but for those who *choose not to*.

This question has significant implications for sign language literature, as most deaf people who compose and perform sign language literature are also literate in another language – mostly the spoken language in their community (for example, English for British deaf people or Portuguese for Brazilian deaf people). In multilingual countries like South Africa, deaf people often know more than one spoken language (such as English and Zulu, or Afrikaans and English). Although the level of command of written language varies among individuals, the option to use written language as a means of expression does exist for deaf people. For example, Dorothy Miles originally composed her poems in English, and later shifted to using sign languages (both ASL and BSL) as her main medium of creativity. It was her choice to create oral literature. Therefore, it is not accurate to say that oral literature is for those who cannot read and write, even just seen from the context of sign language. In fact, knowledge of another language and its literature has significantly influenced sign language literature. The influences from spoken languages have not always been recognised, perhaps because of the need to emphasise that an independent sign language literature exists. However, now that we have a clearer understanding of sign language literature (and confidence that it certainly does exist), we cannot ignore the influences from the literature of hearing communities which are evident in the works of signing poets and storytellers.

Oral literature is seen in societies around the world, both literate and non-literate. Even the most literate societies enjoy live storytelling, poetry readings and so on. Unfortunately, however, oral literature has been generally less valued unless it is either ancient such as Homer's *Iliad* or exotic (from the European scholars' point of view) such as Zulu praise poems. This places sign language literature in an unusual position for theorists as it is not ancient or exotic. Researchers are coming to understand that sign language literature can guide the way we think about any literature – spoken or written. However, the number of mainstream literary scholars who know anything about sign language literature is still extremely small.

A canon of oral literature

The canon of oral literature is hard to identify, perhaps because the original idea of a canon of any form of literature originated in written literature. However, in terms of genres of oral literature, we can see that any canon will include traditional stories, spoken poetry (from ancient epics to slam poetry), jokes, riddles and urban legends. Many of these are seen within the creative sign language of deaf communities. Songs are often passed on in unwritten form, so oral literature can include folksongs, pop songs, hymns and psalms, drinking songs, work songs, war songs and lullabies, as well as children's chants and sports songs (for example, football and rugby songs, which are frequently quite rude). There are far fewer original examples of songs in sign language literature, although they feature in the creative repertoire of some signers (see Chapter 5). Some do not find a cultural parallel in deaf communities, for example, signed lullabies are not going to work if the baby has closed its eyes, but others do, for example Peters (2000) and Bahan (2006) note rhythmic signed pieces that are similar to drinking songs or sports songs.

In terms of length, oral literature ranges from short jokes to very long epics. Some of them exist nowadays in a written form (for communities which have a written form of their language), but they are still termed 'oral' because they have their main impact through oral circulation.

Composition, distribution and performance

As described in Finnegan's definition above, oral literature can also be defined with respect to composition, distribution (mode of transmission) and performance. We can see if these apply to sign language stories and poems.

Composition

Composition in oral literature is closely tied with performance. Totally oral literature does not exist unless it is being performed, unlike written literature, which can wait inside a book even if no one is reading it. One defining feature of oral literature used to be that the stories and poems were composed as the teller performed them. The basic idea of the very long story or poem was in the poet's mind, but as he went along (and it was often he not she), he used a series of formulae to help him build up a version of the poem. Each time the result came out slightly differently, according to the circumstances. We saw in the previous chapter that this also happens in sign language storytelling, when signers work with their deaf audiences to create the exact form of the story.

Although 'composition through performance' is still relevant, there are other ways to compose oral literature, however. Classic rhetoric, which focuses on the live delivery of speeches, assumed that the speech would be composed in advance and memorised either in whole or in part (for example, its headings) before its live delivery (Leith, 2011). In some cultures, poets are expected to compose orally but can write the text later. For example, Inuit poets have been reported to compose for hours before they perform, compose further while they perform, and modify it after-wards (Finnegan, 1977).

Sign language pieces might be fully memorised in advance or their approximate form can be memorised and the signer will make the rest of it up during the performance according to the circumstances. Signed texts are often composed without any writing, although there can be a written English *aide memoire* or drawings, or even recorded video notes, but any of these records are put aside once the signer starts to perform in front of the audience.

In oral literature, even if the stories or poems are memorised there is greater opportunity to change them. Changing a piece of written literature makes it something that literate people consider different and maybe even wrong. Changing an oral poem or story to fit a new circumstance is not only not wrong, but is also perfectly acceptable and maybe even expected. In many cases, there is no exact written text to deviate from. For example, we could not expect a storyteller to tell *Sleeping Beauty* word-for-word because there is no single reference text whose words they could repeat. Instead, we expect them to include the essential points of the story and, beyond that, the pleasure comes from a good story-teller performing the story in their way, adding details or changing the tone of voice, rhythm, pace, and so on, to keep the audience engaged. The same is true for most jokes. In all these cases, creative deaf signers work to similar rules and expectations as creative oral language performers.

Distribution and performance

If a story or poem is transmitted by oral means, it may be considered a piece of oral literature. If performances of the literary form are only live and face-to-face, then they are definitely oral. However, writing can be involved at some stage. For example, something may have been composed in writing but is passed on orally. Alternatively, it might have originally been passed on orally but was written down later (like Homer's epics). Sign language literature in this sense is oral literature, as it is essentially performed and distributed visually. Sign languages do not have a widely used written form, so when a signed work is written down, we read a translation in another language, and not the original composition. We might assume a video recording would not be a translation, but, as we will see later, when creative sign language is recorded on video, certain features associated with spoken oral performance diminish.

Features of oral literature

Oral literature comes with a set of characteristics which are different from those of written literature, due to the fact that it is composed and trans-mitted orally. One fundamental feature is repetition (Finnegan, 2012), which has aesthetic and practical functions in oral transmission of stories. Repetition helps performers to remember and organise certain elements in oral performance and it helps the audience to remember important parts of the story (such as characters, places or events in the past). After all, the audience cannot go back and look for information which has already been presented, unlike a reader reading a book. In written literature, on the other hand, excessive repetitions appear redundant, as the readers can always look for information by themselves. In other words, in oral literature the performer is more responsible for ensuring that the audience can follow their stories, while in written literature the reader is expected to share this responsibility.

Repetition includes verbal repetition (including characters' names, place names, key words and phrases), repetition of incidents (events may be retold to remind the audience of what happened previously) and rhythmic repetitions (linguistic or thematic units recur with a rhythmic pattern). All of these elements of repetition are seen in sign language literature (see Chapter 13, especially).

Embodied rhythm is another feature which is shared by oral and signed performances. Signers perceive and produce rhythm in a spontaneous way using their body. This often resembles the beats of drums. Bauman (1998, p. 138) analyses Peter Cook's ASL poem *Poetry*, and finds a strong connection between the signing and the physical rhythmic body movement:

> He [Peter Cook] begins by stamping his foot repeatedly signing POETRY ... Cook retains an almost primordial connection to an embodied oral tradition through keeping rhythm by the tapping of his foot.

Oral literature also exhibits a clear and relatively uncomplex structure. This helps the poets and storytellers to perform and the audience to follow. Stories told orally, regardless of their length, tend to have clear beginnings and ends, and events often unfold in a logical, chronological order. In a written novel, writers can present a series of events in more innovative ways. An event which chronologically comes last can be presented at the beginning, and the novel unpacks past events which have led to the conclusion – often moving back and forth between past and present. This happens far less often in oral literature as it can confuse the audience and even the performer telling the story. These features occur in sign language literature, too, where the structure of sign language stories is relatively straightforward, and they usually have clear beginnings and endings (see Chapter 8).

Text and performance

As sign language literature has traditionally been composed, distributed, and performed without relying on writing, the notion of performance as opposed to text becomes very important, especially as the two are so tightly linked in sign language literature. The American researcher Heidi Rose has undertaken seminal work in this area. She suggests that ASL literature is 'a literature of performance, a literature that moves through time and space' (2006, p. 131).

Rose provides helpful definitions that show how the two concepts are separate but closely related in sign languages. She writes, '[a] text can be viewed as "the original words of an author" (Grambs 367) whether printed, spoken or performed. In a spoken or performed text, text would include all the aspects of articulations, gesticulation, and mise-en-scène' (1992, p. 23). She goes on to use Richard Bauman's definition of performance as 'an aesthetically marked and heightened mode of communication, framed in a special way and put on display for an audience' (1992, p. 24).[2]

The word 'text' can be traced back to a word meaning something woven. Words that are carefully chosen and inscribed on a piece of paper possess a certain texture and become a material, like a woven cloth, which is now visible and exists independently of the creator. The following quote from the Canadian poet Robert Bringhurst explains this well:

> An ancient metaphor: thought is a thread, and the raconteur is a spinner of yarns – but the true storyteller, the poet, is a weaver. The scribes made this old and audible abstraction into a new and visible fact. After long practice, their work took on such an even, flexible texture that they called the written page a *textus*, which means cloth.

> (Bringhurst, 1992, p. 25)

Whereas a performance cannot be separated from the circumstances in which it was created and performed, a text can be seen as more fixed, static, completed and independent from when, where, (or even by whom) it was created. It is possible to read and enjoy a novel knowing nothing about the author, or the place or time in which it was written. There was no true 'text' in sign language literature before the 1970s because the oral tradition of storytelling in the deaf community made it impossible to separate a piece of creative signing from the contexts in which it was performed, including the place, time and audience. This changed, however, with the invention of video recording.

Impact of video technology

Although there are a few films of sign language stories in ASL dating back to 1913, recording signed materials became widespread only after the 1970s. In contrast to the history of written languages and literate cultures, where for many years the social and intellectual elite of societies could read and the rest of the community could not, video recording very rapidly became accessible to everyone. This wide accessibility has meant that sign language literature, previously unrecorded, is now recorded for the purposes of composition, distribution and performance. In fact, it is an even closer record of the story or poem than we see in a written version because the written version does not contain the details of the performance and the performer.

Heidi Rose (1992) and Christopher Krentz (2006) have investigated the impact of video technology on ASL literature. Rose (1992) applied a concept of pre- and post-videotape literature to the categorisation of sign language art forms. Pre-videotape literature refers to all materials passed down 'orally' and 'face-to-face' – and therefore shares many features of oral literature as mentioned above. Post-videotape literature, on the other hand, refers to literature produced after the spread of video (later DVD and other electronic forms) and now can be recorded, distributed and preserved. In the era of post-videotape literature, new types of creative sign language texts have emerged. Rose argues that sign language poetry (and some narratives that we now consider to be part of the canon of sign language literature) could not exist as they do now without the use of video to record and distribute material.

Christopher Krentz has written extensively about the impact of the camera on sign language literature. His work in 2006 made an explicit analogy between the effect of the printing press on spoken language literature and the effect of filming on sign language literature. He provides a list of ways in which filming has influenced sign language literature, as it:

1. Makes performances static and certain stories become fixed 'texts' with a particular form.

2. Frees texts from constraints of time and place (so more people can see them at any time).

3. Preserves forms that might otherwise disappear (such as the one-two, one-two-three 'chants' in ASL popular in the mid-20th century).

4. Can distance performers from their audiences (raising the possibility that people might no longer go to see live performances of stories).

5. Commodifies literature (so signers and distributors can make money by selling recordings of sign language literature).

6. Helps performances reach mass audiences (so people with little access to live sign language can still watch the videos).

7. Increases recognition of some deaf artists (leading to more stories, or forms of stories, being recognised as belonging to specific people).

8. Allows artists to become more experimental with their work.

9. Makes audiences more analytical (because there is the opportunity to review work many times to see things that were not obvious on the first viewing).

As a result of video recording, deaf artists may become more conscious of their performance, elaborating the language and the theme. Although the main purpose of pre-video literature was to entertain the live audience and therefore did not carry so much literary weight, post-videotape literature has a thematic complexity which requires more than one viewing. In this aspect, the transition between pre- and post-videotape literature is where the notion of 'text' emerges. Cynthia Peters observes that the textualisation of ASL literature has led to an 'increase in aesthetic play' (2000, p. 189), which, in essence, is the development of poetic language.

However, the influence of performance is still very strong even in modern sign language literature. Whether live or recorded, the fact that someone is signing a text foregrounds the role of the performer. As Rose says, the text of sign language literature is on the body of the signer, and is 'a four-dimensional literary text' (Rose, 2006, p. 140).

Summary

We have seen in this chapter that many cultures have a body of important language works that are not written down, and this has been termed 'oral literature'. Despite the unsuitability of the word 'oral' for sign language, its literature shares many characteristics with spoken language oral literature, as it is essentially composed, performed and distributed without relying on writing. The development of video recording has changed the potential for sign language literature, allowing us to preserve texts and performances and making it easier to distribute signed work much more widely. Although recording cuts the traditional links between the signer and audiences, there is still a strong link between text and performance because the audience can always see the performer.

Notes

1. The word 'oral' also has negative implications in the deaf community due to its association with oralism, a philosophy of education that denies deaf children an education in sign language. See Ladd (2003) for a thorough introduction to deaf people's critiques of oralism.
2. Rose is quoting from David Grambs (1984) *Words about Words* (New York: McGraw Hill).

Further reading

The following three chapters from Bauman, Nelson and Rose's *Signing the Body Poetic* (2006) are highly relevant to this chapter:

Bahan, Ben (2006) 'Face-to-face tradition in the American Deaf community' in H-Dirksen Bauman, Jennifer Nelson and Heidi Rose (eds) *Signing the Body Poetic* (California: University of California Press).

Krentz, Christopher (2006) 'The camera as printing press; How film has influenced ASL literature' in H-Dirksen Bauman, Jennifer Nelson and Heidi Rose (eds) *Signing the Body Poetic* (California: University of California Press).

Rose, Heidi (2006) 'The poet in the poem in the performance: the relation of body, self, and text in ASL literature' in H-Dirksen Bauman, Jennifer Nelson and Heidi Rose (eds) *Signing the Body Poetic* (California: University of California Press).

If you want to know more about oral literature, you could read the following books:

Finnegan, Ruth (1988) *Orality and Literacy* (Oxford: Blackwell).

Barber, Karin (1991) *I Could Speak Until Tomorrow: Oriki, Women, and the Past in a Yoruba Town* (Edinburgh: Edinburgh University Press) – a good book on Yoruba oral poetry.

Activities

1. Consider the effects of digital technology on sign language literature, asking the following questions (you may wish to do this in a group/pair):

   ■ What changes does it make for the poet?
   ■ What changes does it make to the viewer (audience)?
   ■ Does it change the relationship between the poet and the audience?

- What are the implications in terms of distribution?
- Does it affect the notion of 'ownership'?
- Has filming changed the status of creative sign language as 'literature'?

2. Watch Wim Emmerik's *Growth* (www.youtube.com/watch?v=MGLKN MepUIU) or another sign language poem that has been filmed with extra production, and discuss the following questions:

    - Imagine you saw the same poem performed live on the stage. Would it be the same experience? Or very different? Why/how?
    - What is the role of the camera in this poem? What is it doing for the poet? What is it doing for the audience?
    - Whose poem is this? Does it entirely belong to the signer?

4 Folklore and Deaflore

In this chapter, we will consider folklore and how it relates to deaf culture and sign language literature. We will explore how far we can distinguish between sign language literature and sign language folklore, introducing the concepts of 'deaflore' and 'signlore' suggested by the deaf anthropologist Simon Carmel.

What is folklore?

Folklore is often thought to have three key characteristics: it is traditional, it is anonymous and it is variable. The word 'tradition' is not easy to define, but there is a general understanding that most traditions have existed for a long time, and are passed down through generations. As the folklore researchers Iona and Peter Opie noted, the generations that pass on folklore may not refer to parents and children, but to older children and younger children in school (Opie and Opie, 1959). Traditions in schools develop very quickly, often without any input from adults, and folklore passed on in school forms a vital part of many people's early learning. Given this, we can see the importance of deaf schools for the development of sign language folklore because, while the majority of deaf children did not receive their deaf cultural education from their parents, they learned it rapidly from their deaf peers in school.

Webster's Dictionary also defines 'tradition' as 'a characteristic manner, method, or style', which is helpful to understand how folklore can be traditional, even when elements of it are new.

Folklore is often seen as knowledge that is transmitted face-to-face rather than learned through formal education or reading (Dundes, 1965). This means that most deaf community knowledge can be called folklore, because it has not been written down and has been transmitted face-to-face, outside formal schooling (Bahan, 2006a; Rutherford, 1993). Deaf folklore, like folklore in many communities, has traditionally been a group activity, shared when deaf people meet. Even when folklore is written down, it is still folklore because it was transmitted face-to-face originally. Today a lot of deaf folklore is recorded on video and made available on the Internet, or is included in books, so it is not transmitted face-to-face. This may reduce the sense of being part of a group that shares the experience of telling the folklore, but its origin, form and function mean it is still part of folklore.

Jokes are a good example of folklore because some of them have been passed down through the generations and new ones follow traditional formats. In addition to this, most jokes are anonymous because they do not have an identifiable author and they are variable because the same joke is rarely told in exactly the same way twice. For example, within some deaf communities there are some jokes with a format that involves three characters: a blind man, a man in a wheelchair and a deaf man. One joke with this structure (from Sutton-Spence and Napoli, 2009, p. 21) runs like this:

> A blind man goes to a barber for a haircut. The barber cuts his hair and refuses payment, saying he's doing community service for the handicapped this week. The next morning the barber finds a thank you card and a dozen roses at his shop. Later a man in wheelchair comes in for a haircut. The barber cuts his hair and refuses payment, saying he's doing community service for the handicapped this week. The next morning the barber finds a thank you card and a box of a dozen muffins waiting at his shop. Later a Deaf man comes for a haircut. The barber cuts his hair and refuses payment, saying he's doing community service for the handicapped this week. The next morning he finds a dozen Deaf people waiting at his door.

The origin of this joke is unknown (at least to the people we have asked, who have told us the joke) but it is well-known in many deaf communities and forms a part of their folklore. We have seen it told in Britain, the USA and in Brazil. We have seen it told live and on video. The details vary, and each signer brings their own style to it, but the basic plot is the same.

We have already seen in Chapter 1 that there are various types of creative sign language produced in deaf communities: traditional sign language stories and jokes, pieces translated and adapted from films and written texts created by non-deaf people, and original creative pieces composed and performed by deaf people. As well as sharing aspects with other kinds of written or spoken literature, each of these can show some of these folklore characteristics of tradition, anonymity and variability.

Some signed translations of stories, films, jokes and poems come from the folklore traditions of the wider hearing society, so that they form a specific part of that national deaf culture's folklore. It is important to remember that deaf people in each country have their own national heritage as well as their own deaf heritage, so their folklore develops as a result of the fusion of the two. For example, Japanese people traditionally tell ghost stories in summer (to 'get a chill' in intense summer heat), and this is also a popular practice among deaf schoolchildren in Japan. Signed adaptations of traditional pieces make them more deaf-focused when they are translated so, for example, children's stories that form part of the folklore of hearing society can be adapted to include deaf characters, sign language and other behaviour in deaf culture. For Peters (2000), these adaptations are examples of the deaf storyteller as a 'trickster' who mixes elements of deaf and hearing culture, and signed and spoken language traditions.

In a signed adaptation of *The Pied Piper*, the child left behind is not lame but deaf and in the retelling of *Little Red Riding Hood*, all the characters are deaf (sometimes except for the hearing wolf). We have seen stories in Brazil of a deaf Rapunzel who has very long arms to sign with from the top of her tower and deaf Cinderella loses her gloves (which draws attention to her signing hands) at midnight when she flees the deaf prince's party. The deaf wolf in *The Three Little Pigs* signs so fast that the wind generated by his hands blows down the first two houses. Although the wolf is deaf in this example, many deaf adaptations of fairy stories make mischievous fun by presenting deaf heroes and heroines, and hearing villains. Not all deaf cultures make these adaptations and some have only occurred recently, as deaf people have become more confident in their challenges of dominant hearing society (Smith and Sutton-Spence, 2007). As we noted in our definition of tradition, the popular idea that folklore must be old to be traditional needs to be refined: the format has to be old, but the content may include new views on the traditional elements, or even completely new material.

Even where signed texts are not considered central to deaf folklore because their content is not traditional, the practice of translating them and the style in which they are performed is folkloric. Signed translations and adaptations of original 'single authored' works from hearing society whose author is known (and so would not be considered folklore in the source language) use a form of sign language and other devices that are part of deaf folklore. In the same vein, original pieces created by individual deaf people (and, therefore, not anonymous) often draw on and incorporate many aspects of deaf folklore, and they may vary greatly between each performance. Thus, we can see that discussion of folklore can help us to understand a range of aspects of sign language literature.

Deaf folklore – deaflore and signlore

The American deaf researcher Simon Carmel (1996) suggested the terms 'deaflore' to refer to deaf folklore generally and 'signlore' to refer to deaf folklore that makes sign language its focus. Although it is not always easy to distinguish between them, we can use the term deaflore to refer generally to what the signers say about their traditional knowledge. It includes the content of creative signed language forms such as knowledge, values, beliefs, behaviours and habits expressed in sign language poetry, deaf jokes, legends, riddles, stories and personal experience narratives, and the contexts of their performance. In contrast, signlore brings language to the foreground and draws attention to the way the signs are used specifically to reflect deaf culture. Thus, signlore is how signers say deaflore.

Much of our discussion here will consider elements that deaf communities around the world share in their folklore because they share a visual outlook on the world and often have similar life and language experiences of belonging to an exceptional language and cultural minority. Susan Rutherford's *Study of American Deaf Folklore* (1993) is the classic text for folklore research and much in it can apply to other countries. However, ideas about American deaf folklore should not be applied uncritically to other sign languages because each deaf community has its own characteristics and influences from its own national heritage (see Smith and Sutton-Spence, 2007, and Paales, 2004).

The function of folklore

Folklore has the important function of teaching people the knowledge of a community and is usually entertaining or enjoyable in some way because that makes learning easier. For communities that are non-literate it is the main way of transmitting knowledge and even for literate societies it is a way of teaching young people about cultural values and rules of behaviour. Sign language folklore helps new members of the deaf community develop a sense of deaf identity and learn about their cultural heritage. It also helps hearing people who want to learn about deaf culture. We can see the educational function of folklore in deaf communities in the stories told of deaf lives in the tradition of 'narratives of personal experience' because they show young people and new community members how other deaf people faced the problems experienced in their lives, and how they solved these problems. Deaf jokes that are so central to deaf folklore may not immediately seem educational (maybe they are too much like fun) but they allow community members to bond and enjoy themselves while learning about deaf cultural values as the jokes sanction or challenge them.

Structure of folklore texts

Folklore texts often have noticeable forms that set them apart from other uses of language. As with the unwritten literature we considered in Chapter 3, much of the language used in folklore is designed to be easy to remember and the rhythm or repetition built into its structure is one way to do this. Structures using three-fold repetition are particularly common in folklore of European origin, and occur in a lot of deaf folklore. Jokes and poems, for example, are often told so the climax occurs in the third part. The earlier example of the barber joke recounts the events involving the blind man and the man in the wheelchair, and the deaf man appears in the third part of the joke, carrying the punchline. We will explore this three-fold structure in more depth in Chapter 13.

The sort of language used in folklore is often less erudite than the language used in literature, in that it is less influenced by the study of written forms that are valued by literary cultures (creating a somewhat circular process). Nevertheless, while the syntax and vocabulary may differ from that of the more socially prestigious written language, community members often feel that the form of the language used represents their culture at a deep level. Many deaf people see their folklore as being a truly deaf way of using language. In this way, signed folklore, stories and jokes can be seen as 'cultural artefacts' that represent the deaf community.

Folklore or literature?

Clearly, much of what we have been describing as folklore here also readily applies to the oral literature described in Chapter 3. Indeed, literature is strongly influenced by folklore because folklore is our original framework for creating and understanding any form of language art. When we look at sign language poetry or stories, it is hard to say where folklore ends and literature begins. Sometimes, simple snobbery suggests literature is better and more respectable because it is associated with high culture, education and being aware of itself as art which addresses a defined (usually elite) audience, whereas folklore is simple, uneducated (and thus accessible to all) and has no direct links to high culture, although it may well contain direct social comment. We will not make these value judgments in relation to sign language literature and folklore because we consider that all deaf language art forms have value, but it is worth noting that carefully crafted, single-authored, highly aesthetic signed work is valued in the deaf community in a similar way that works of literature are valued in other cultures. If we had to make a distinction, we might say that folklore uses conventional themes and devices without trying to hide them, while literature tends to pick up conventions only in order to develop or refine them with some new twist.

Collecting, preserving and promoting folklore

Many folklorists try to find out where a folkloric text or belief comes from, which is a challenge because folklore is unwritten so it is often hard to determine these origins for sure. However, beliefs about folklore are an important part of understanding the folklore itself, so knowing 'the truth' about its origins might be less important than what people believe the origin to be. Simon Carmel began his research into deaflore because he noticed deaf jokes and stories spread nationally and internationally and now it is hard to tell where the ideas and forms began.

Collecting and preserving folklore is especially important for deaf communities where very few deaf children are born to deaf parents who can pass on their cultural heritage and where it is constantly threatened by education policies that keep deaf children from learning from deaf adults. Even the long-standing channel of passing deaflore from older to younger deaf children in deaf schools is under threat with growing mainstream education for deaf pupils. It is increasingly important that hearing people are also aware of deaflore so that they understand the richness of deaf culture. In this way, they can help to preserve and promote it and do not accidentally destroy it.

Anyone wanting to collect information on deaflore must think carefully about how to do it and examine the motives for any research into it. This is especially true for community outsiders, such as hearing researchers who are interested in folklore.[1] Some folkloric information might be sensitive and community members may not want outsiders to know it. Questions such as the following need to be asked and the answers carefully considered before any folklore is collected:

- Should outsiders collect 'off-colour' or obscene folklore from deaf informants who may not want to share it with outsiders?
- What should we do if the folklore is considered offensive according to the social norms of outsiders, but not according to deaf cultural norms?
- What should we do if the folklore directly attacks outsiders (for example, many deaf jokes show hearing people in a very unflattering light) and could offend them?

- If insiders of the community who know this folklore want to share it with outsiders, what are their responsibilities? What will anyone do with this information? Would other community members want outsiders to know?

- If stories are usually told in a certain situation, what happens if we collect them for research in a different situation? For example, if deaf jokes are told directly to a camera for research, not to a group of friends late at night at a party, are we collecting 'folklore' or just a part of it?

Another very important question is what we should select and what we should leave out from a description of folklore. Some people believe deaflore should be 'Strong Deaf' folklore so any signed folklore that appears to be a copy of the folklore of the surrounding hearing society is not relevant to deaflore. However, this might mean we ignore large parts of deaf folk wisdom; after all, what is shared between deaf and hearing cultures can be as important as what is different.

Canons of deaf folklore and sign language literature

When we collect folklore, we create a canon so we can say, 'This is the folklore of this community'. Canons of folklore are collections that are generally accepted as being representative, and are understood to be central examples of folklore, judged 'the best' by a community. Thus, a sign language folklore canon is made up of the sign language folklore that is judged to be the knowledge that is most valued by community members as their folklore. This definition is not perfect and who has the right to decide what is canonical is often contested, so that it can change or have different contents at the same time. However, many items are understood in a community to be part of their folklore canon. For example, asking members of a deaf community for a traditional signed joke often results in people choosing from a small group of jokes that they consider canonical.

The deaf storyteller Stephen Ryan (1993) suggested that all stories that are part of a canon of sign language literature have certain elements in common (and we are arguing here that there is no clear difference between Ryan's canonical stories and deaflore). They are expected to:

- Show the deaf perspective.
- Inform us in some way about the concerns of the deaf community and its relationship with the hearing world.

- Increase signing skills (including for second language learners).
- Increase cultural sensitivity.
- Teach cultural values.
- Be good entertainment.

Sometimes the cultural 'elite' of a community decides what makes a good representation of the community's culture to select what goes into the canon, and sometimes outsiders such as academic researchers make that judgement. Canons are an idea rather than a concrete reality, although they are often represented by collections and anthologies containing real examples. As the study of sign language literature and deaflore grows in schools and universities, the canons and any anthologies or collections that are created will influence what is considered worth studying. Deaf teachers who teach deaflore to deaf children will be part of the creation of canons of deaflore as they control what will be passed to the next generation.

Depending on a particular interest, there can be any number of canons, and canons within canons. We could devise a canon of deaflore and one of hearing folklore, or one of British deaflore and another of American deaflore (or South African, Brazilian, French, Indian, Estonian or Swedish folklore and so on). We could have a canon of folklore that is known by older signers and one known by younger signers. We can divide canons by genre to look at canons of signed jokes, stories or poems, and even create sub-canons within them.

Summary

We have explored here some of the main characteristics of folklore and deaflore. We have seen how deaflore can be understood in terms of its origins, form, ways of transmission and functions. We have also seen that it is hard to separate forms of sign language folklore from sign language literature and how both literature and folklore may be part of any number of canons that represent the rich deaf cultural heritage of creative signing.

Note

1. This is true for outsiders collecting any folklore in any community.

Further reading

Dundes, Alan (1965) 'What is folklore?' in Alan Dundes (ed.) *The Study of Folklore* (Englewood Cliffs, NJ: Prentice Hall).

Opie, Iona and Peter Opie (1959) *The Lore and Language of Schoolchildren* (Oxford: Oxford University Press).

Paales, Liina (2004) 'A hearer's insight into Deaf sign language folklore, *Electronic Journal of Folklore.* www.folklore.ee/folklore/

Rutherford, Susan (1993) *A Study of Deaf American Folklore* (Silver Spring, MD: Linstok Press).

Smith, Jennifer and Sutton-Spence Rachel (2007) 'What is the Deaflore of the British Deaf community?', *Deaf Worlds,* 23, 44–69.

Activities

1. Find an example of a signed adaptation of a traditional 'hearing' story, a sign language joke and a sign language story told about an older deaf person's life experiences. Suggestions for BSL users are *Little Red Ridinghood* by Jerry Hanifin (in Chapter 14 of the DVD accompanying Sutton-Spence and Woll, 1999), the joke of the Four Deaf Yorkshire Men (available on YouTube), and John Wilson's *For a Deaf Friend* (about a deaf man who lived during the war and the post-war periods in the UK, posted on the YouTube channel that accompanies this book).

   - What criteria do you use to decide whether they can be called 'folklore'?

   - What elements of deaflore and signlore do you see in them? (You can use Steven Ryan's criteria outlined in this chapter to help you think about them.)

2. We know that canons of sign language folklore should contain pieces that community members think are good representations of deaf culture. Consider some of the following and discuss them with other members of the deaf community.

   - Who are the community members who decide?

   - What can deaf community members do to choose the canon of their folklore?

   - Why are certain examples central to a canon?

   - How do we judge what is 'major' or 'the best'? How do we even decide what is 'good'?

3. Alan Dundes (1965 p. 3) defines folklore for 'the beginner' using an item-ised list. Much of this simply has not been researched in any sign language yet. Look at this list and find some examples in your sign language of any of these types of folklore. Is this folklore shared with hearing people in the surrounding community, or is it unique to the deaf community?

- Myths, legends, folktales, jokes, proverbs, riddles, chants, charms, bless-ings, curses, oaths, insults, retorts, taunts, teases, toasts, tongue-twisters, greeting and leave-taking formulas (for example, 'see you later alligator').

- Folk songs (including lullabies) speech (slang), folk similes (for example, 'blind as a bat') folk metaphors (for example, 'paint a town red') and names (place names and nicknames).

- Folk poetry including oral epics, autograph book verse, latrinalia (writing on toilet walls), ball-bouncing rhymes, skipping rhymes, finger and toe rhymes, dandling rhymes, counting-out (to see who is 'it' in a children's game) and nursery rhymes.

- Games, gestures, symbols, prayers, practical jokes, folk etymologies, calls to summon animals and traditional comments after body emissions (e.g. burps, farts and sneezes).

- Major forms of festivals and special day customs, for example, Christmas, Halloween and birthdays (this implies that we describe what people do and why, but language is used for these too, for exam-ple, signing 'happy birthday').

4. In this chapter, we asked the following questions without providing detailed answers, simply as a way to show what questions we need to ask. What do you think the answers could be and why?

- Should outsiders collect 'off-colour' or obscene folklore from deaf informants who may not want to share it with outsiders?

- What should we do if the folklore is considered offensive according to the social norms of outsiders, but not according to deaf cultural norms?

- What should we do if the folklore directly attacks outsiders and could offend them?

- If insiders of the community who know this folklore want to share it with outsiders, what are their responsibilities? What will anyone do with this information? Would community members want outsiders to know?

- If stories are usually told in a certain situation, what happens if we collect them for research in a different situation? For example, if deaf jokes are told directly to a camera for research, not to a group of friends late at night at a party, can we be sure we are collecting 'folk-lore' or just a part of it?

5 Story Types

Stories are the foundation of sign language literature and folklore, and they are told in many different forms – perhaps as narratives, poems or as dramatic theatre pieces. This chapter will look at a range of types of sign language story that we can categorise depending on their origin, form and general content. We will see that some of these story types have parallels with European-heritage written literature and some are similar to other types of literature around the world, but others seem specific to sign languages and deaf communities. Working with ASL, Susan Rutherford, Cynthia Peters and Ben Bahan have all explored different types of signed narratives and their work will form the foundation of what we discuss here although we must remember that what is seen in North America may not be repeated in other deaf communities.

The extent to which a story has a plot and character who is the focus of the action (the protagonist) may vary along a scale, where at one end there is a clear plot and easily identifiable protagonist, and at the other end there is no identifiable plot and no easily identifiable protagonist. Many folkloric stories have a protagonist and a plot in which there is some sort of problem or conflict that the protagonist must resolve before the story can end. This type of plot will be most familiar to readers from European storytelling traditions and there are many signed examples, too, as we will see in Chapter 9. However, in other stories, there is little sense of plot, as a string of apparently unconnected things happens to the protagonist (or there may not even be an identifiable protagonist). For example, a British deaf friend told us a story about a group of swimmers with different swimming styles. Each swimmer was introduced and described in great detail and a few things happened to each one, but there was no pattern to the events and no swimmer was more important than any other, as the shared pleasure in the variety of signs was more important than finding out the end of the story. The key to this story was to enjoy the signer's representations of the different swimmers. This form of storytelling is probably less familiar to many readers but is common in sign language, as signers add copious details which may seem unnecessary from the Western literary perspective, and may go off at tangents, from which they never return. A South African signer we know told a well-known joke about a newly wed deaf husband in a motel car park, hooting his car horn in the middle of the night in an attempt to know which room his deaf wife is in. The punchline of the joke is that the lights go on in the rooms of the hearing people woken by the hooting, so the husband knows that his wife must be in the only darkened room. The signer started this joke by telling how the couple met and fell in love, where their wedding was (and what dress the bride wore, and the food and cake), where they decided to go on honeymoon (where this incident happened) and so on. None of it was remotely relevant to the punchline of the joke, but it made excellent entertainment as she told it.

Whether they are literature or folklore, poems or prose, all sign language stories that are told by members of deaf communities can be regarded as part of the wider category of sign language literature. Ben Bahan (2006a, 2006b) reviewed a large number of sign language stories in ASL to create a system of categorising them. He observed that, amongst other things, signers tell of their personal deaf experiences and general deaf experiences, retell jokes and scenes from movies as well as ghost stories, and create stories simply to play with signs, including ABC and number stories. It is significant that his approach started with the stories and led to his creation of categories, rather than starting with existing categories created from patterns in mainstream literature and trying to fit sign language stories into them, so that he did not constrain himself to supporting existing categories. We will consider some of these categories, keeping in mind the idea that they may be determined by their content, form, origin or audience.

Narratives of deaf experience – defined by content

Narratives of deaf experience are categorised by their content as they all relate something of deaf people's lives. Some are narratives that tell of the experience of the 'Deaf Everyman' – an ordinary character that the storyteller hopes the audience can relate to – and others are more directly personal life stories that may be considered a type of memoire. Memoire is an established form of literature in many cultures, in which people tell stories of their own life, often so that other people can learn from their experience. While memoires usually take the written form, people also frequently recount stories about memorable things that happened in their lives. Narratives of personal experience are central to the storytelling of many deaf communities, and deaf people tell them so that other deaf people may learn from the life experience of 'someone like me'. Because these are stories of things that could have happened to the signer or someone like the signer, they offer insight to deaf people's experience and ways to discover a deaf identity.

Most narratives of personal experience are short accounts in which the signer tells a story of 'an event that happened to me' or 'an event that happened to someone like me', with the implication for the audience that it is 'an event that could happen to someone like you'. Longer narratives of personal experience as biographies even say 'this is my life story'. In our experience, most of these longer life narratives by deaf people are found in written form, while the shorter accounts are more likely to be signed.

Many signed narratives of deaf personal experience inform deaf audiences about the challenges of life as a deaf person, and ways to overcome them. Personal narratives do not need to be entirely 'true' to be meaningful, remembering the old rule: 'Never let the facts get in the way of a good story'. It is more important that the ideas behind the story are meaningful, and provide important cultural information and cultural reinforcement. Stories may be about school days, work experiences, travelling (especially about meeting other deaf people while travelling), family life and encounters with hearing people.

Bahan (2006b) found that many of the characters in the stories were based on stereotypes because they made the narrative easy to understand and so more enjoyable and interesting. The characters in many personal experience stories fall broadly into 'deaf' (shown in the stories as 'Us') and 'hearing' (shown as 'Them'). Often, just being deaf or hearing is all that identifies a character, because when the storyteller says 'There was a deaf woman...' or 'There was a hearing man...' audiences will draw on their cultural experiences to know what this means. Deaf characters, who are 'us', are generally portrayed as people who experience the world through sight and touch, and use sign language. Speech is often mentioned; perhaps referring to deaf people's speaking skills. Unsuccessful attempts to speak to hearing people can create conflict (for example, getting the wrong drink at a bar) but successful 'deaf speech' can be very effective (for example, a bus driver ignores hearing passengers shouting 'stop!' but quickly stops when he hears the unusual voice of a deaf person shouting).

Many stories refer to the deaf person's lack of hearing. This can lead to some sort of conflict that needs to be resolved. Sometimes the stories focus on the problems of not being able to hear, in order to show how deaf people's resourcefulness found ways to solve the problem. For example, a British story from the Second World War tells how a deaf person who could not hear air-raid sirens at night tied a piece of string to his toe and hung the string out of the window when he went to bed. Neighbours heading to the shelter in an air raid would pull on the string to wake him up. The stories can also be moral tales to teach deaf people to accept their deafness and not try to pretend they are hearing. An example is a story of a young deaf man trying to be cool, cruising round town with his car radio turned up loud, believing it was playing hip-hop music. He was embarrassed when his hearing friend told him that it was a gospel preacher's station. Another story tells of a man on an aeroplane who pretended he was foreign rather than admit he was deaf. He missed some crucial information during the flight as a result and humiliated himself. Other stories show the benefits to not being able to hear, such as renting a flat in a busy area for a very cheap rate because it is too noisy for a hearing person to live there, or the pride of deaf shipbuilders who had important jobs that would have damaged the hearing of anyone else.

Sometimes the stories may be serious warnings to others (for example, there are many tales of deaf people who were injured or killed because they did not hear something), but often they are very funny, and show deaf audiences that they are not alone in their life experiences and that is it good to live a deaf life. Audiences can laugh with the storyteller, with shared understanding.

Hearing people, who are 'them' in deaf narratives may be portrayed in a variety of less than flattering ways. They may be characterised as ignorant, patronising, bullies who oppress deaf people, or as fools. 'Hyper-hearing' people who react nervously to sound (especially sounds made by a deaf person) are frequent butts of deaf narratives and deaf jokes and their poor signing skills may be ridiculed. Bahan (2006b) found that hearing people who are colleagues or allies rarely occur in sign language stories. These people are acknowledged and respected in deaf communities but they tend not to appear in narratives because they do not contribute to the conflict needed to make a good story.

As many original fictional sign language stories arise from the personal experience of their creators, there is no clear division between genuine, accurate narratives of personal experience and clearly fictional narratives that have a deaf protagonist and so are narratives of 'The Deaf Experience' in general that tell of the experiences of the Deaf Everyman. The characteristics that Bahan identified are similar across the types because they are all told from a deaf perspective, but their form can vary. The stories may be told in a traditional narrative form, but they can also be told in a more poetic form or as a theatrical drama because their content is the key focus and how they are told is less important for their categorisation.

Cinematic stories – defined by origin and signing style

Bahan (2006a) proposed a category of sign language stories based on films retold in ASL, and these stories are also popular in many other deaf communities around the world. The stories are translations of the films, but they are not translations between two languages. Instead, they translate from one non-verbal system that uses visual symbols (the 'language' or 'grammar' of film) into a verbal system that uses visual symbols (a sign language). Unlike narratives of deaf experience, which share similar themes even when their form is very diverse, cinematic stories have varied themes but their similar origin unites them in a category and it determines the language form used. The content in the cinematic stories is determined by the makers of the film (and rarely contains reference to deaf people because of this) but signers choose specific films for retelling in sign language. Action films are the most popular choice because dialogue is far less important than visual impact and the skill and enjoyment in these stories comes from the way the signer reproduces the visual impact of the film in sign language. Jerry Hanifin's BSL performance of the film *Speed* (released in 1994, starring Sandra Bullock and Keanu Reeves) is a sign language story that presents selected scenes from the film, reflecting its fast pace and reproducing in BSL the visual effects we see in film (such as close-ups, fast-cutting sequences or slow motion). We will see in Chapter 6 that cinema has been an important influence on sign language storytelling of all types, but it is particularly noticeable in this genre, where the signer represents the cinematic devices in films through artful sign language. Thus, the key feature of these stories that makes them a part of sign language literature is the way that they are signed.

Stories with constraints – defined by form

Like cinematic stories, these stories are grouped by their form rather than by their content. The constraints on the form of these stories come from rules that are outside the story structure. The category includes ABC stories and worded handshape stories, where the constraint is imposed by some form of the surrounding written language, and number stories that are constrained by the order of numbers. Single handshape stories (also called set handshape stories) are constrained simply by rules occurring within a sign language requiring the signer to use a particular handshape (for example, stories told with only signs that use the full open-hand '5' or the 'ILY'[1] handshape).

ABC stories are especially well-known in North America although they also occur in other countries, possibly because the concept has spread from North America. Susan Rutherford reports that American deaf community members believe the ABC story genre is as old as sign language, with a deaf person reporting that her mother told such stories, which placed it at least to the early 1900s. Rutherford explains that the genre of the ABC story is also the 'mediation between the two poles of linguistic identity – external English control and internal ASL affective expression, simultaneously' (1993, p. 68).

In ABC stories, the storyteller creates a story (or retells a classic) in which each successive sign uses the handshape of letters from the manual alphabet, running from A to Z. An example here from Libras (Brazilian Sign Language) should make this clearer for readers who are unfamiliar with these stories. In Libras (and also in ASL), the manual letter 'A' is made with a closed fist, 'B' is made with all the fingers extended but together to make a flat hand, 'C' is made with all the fingers curved making a 'C' shape, and 'D' is made with the index finger extended while the other fingers form a circle with the thumb. So the first sign of the story must have a fist handshape, the second sign has a flat handshape, the third has a curved handshape and the fourth sign must have an index finger extended while the other fingers form a circle with the thumb. The story progresses with each sign sharing the same handshape at the next letter of the alphabet. In Nelson Pimenta's ABC story of *The Painter from A to Z (O Pintor de A a Z)* (shown in Figure 5.1), the painter adjusts the canvas with the fingers held lightly into fists (letter A) and then represents the artist's palette with a flat hand (letter B) on his left hand, before picking up a spray can with a curved right hand (letter C) and thinking what to do (letter D).

These rules constrain the signer so that the person who can succeed in making a story that gets all the way to 'Z' shows considerable signing skills. Creating a story that uses signs with the right handshapes is more important than telling a profound, tightly plotted story, although traditionally many of them have been on topics that appeal to their mainly adolescent tellers, such as sex, drugs and other unconventional behaviour.

FIGURE 5.1   AN EXAMPLE OF ABC STORIES – *THE PAINTER FROM A TO Z* BY NELSON PIMENTA

According to the deaf educator and storyteller Ben Jarashow (2006), the skill of creating ABC stories lies in the signer being able to follow the following rules:

- Succession (appropriate alphabetical order; consistent rhythm; transition between letters; combination of letters).
- Minimal deviation (not changing the manual letter to fit the sign or changing the sign to fit the manual letter).
- Use of cohesive devices (role shift, space, gaze, pacing, pausing and phrasing).
- Integrity of story line (a good story makes sense, has a plot and has a conclusion).

Although ABC stories can be categorised as 'stories', their use of action and dialogue, nonmanual elements and role shift, all within a rigidly disciplined form, makes it hard to put examples in an existing literary category. Peters (2000) asks if an ABC story is a story, a poem or theatre, suggesting it defies any existing categorisation.

In 'fingerspelled/signed word characterisations' signers make signs with each handshape related to the meaning to show the character of the word spelled. In an example from ASL, for the English word 'golf', the handshape for the American manual letter -g- is used in the sign for a golf tee, the -o- is the handshape showing the golf ball in the tee, the -l- is the swinging golf club that strikes the ball and the -f- shows the ball flying out of sight. Rutherford notes that this form of language play probably dates from the 1960s, and is performed by younger people. Sometimes the word characterisations take the form of humorous skits and sometimes they form part of carefully constructed poetry that parallels the acrostic form in some written traditions. The ASL poet Clayton Valli created many poetic works using signs with the handshapes of letters of words to create extra meaning. The handshapes in his poem *Something Not Right*, for example, spell out the word 'education' while signing things that are wrong with deaf education. Another ASL poet Debbie Rennie composed a poem *Veal Boycott* in which the handshapes repeatedly spell out the word 'calf' while describing the cruelty behind the farming practices that produce veal.

Paul Scott's BSL poems *Cat* and *Deaf* (performed as one poem entitled *Acronym*) are a rare example of this language game played with a two-handed alphabet. Figure 5.2 shows how the word 'deaf' is spelled using the two-handed manual alphabet letters of BSL. The brief poem about being deaf uses the signs EARS, CLEAN-EARS, AGREE and DEAF. The

'd'   'e'   'a'   'f'

FIGURE 5.2 MANUAL LETTERS FINGERSPELLING THE WORD 'DEAF'

first sign (EARS) uses the handshape used in the manual letter 'd'; the second sign (CLEAN-EARS) uses the components of the manual letter 'e' (index fingers); the third sign (AGREE) highlights the thumb where the letter 'a' is articulated;[2] the last sign (DEAF) uses the handshapes which are components of the BSL manual alphabet 'f' (Figure 5.3).

Fingerspelling games are an important part of American deaf culture and many other countries with one-handed manual alphabets have adopted them, including Brazil and France. However, not all countries have this tradition. Britain does not, partly because Britain uses a two-handed manual alphabet that does not lend itself so readily to finger-spelling games as the one-handed manual alphabets do. BSL ABC stories do exist, but they are not part of the British signing tradition. (Possibly the best-known one, in character with many American ABC stories, is extremely sexually explicit, and very funny.) It is not just a language difference, however, but also a cultural difference, showing the cultural reality of these different genres. For example, Ireland has a one-handed manual alphabet and Irish deaf people could play these games but histori-cally they simply have not.

Other constraint stories include number handshape stories, which follow the same rules as ABC stories but with numbers instead of letters. Single handshape stories, as their name suggests, are constrained by the need to choose signs that all use the same handshape (described in more

EARS   CLEAN-EARS   AGREE   DEAF

FIGURE 5.3 ACRONYMIC POEM USING HANDSHAPES FROM THE MANUAL LETTERS TO DESCRIBE A DEAF EXPERIENCE

detail in Chapter 13). Again, it is unclear whether some examples of these are stories or poems, or some other sort of linguistic game. Clayton Valli's poem *The Bridge* is a number constraint story that is highly poetic and his poem *Hands* uses a single-handshape. Single-handshape constraint stories seem more widespread than the ABC or number stories, and they are common in Britain and Brazil, as well as in North America. They are also popular games to teach sign language. Paul Scott's BSL poem *Bubble Measure* draws on this teaching tradition, although it goes far beyond the simple idea of creating a narrative thread with signs that have the same handshape. (We describe this poem in more depth in Chapter 14.)

Songs – defined by form and origin

Songs and song lyrics are part of a symbolic system that is 'the language of music'. The genre of signed song is somewhat controversial, as it does not originate within deaf culture (although some deaf people can hear some music or have memory of it from a time when they could). Despite this, many deaf communities have traditions that include signed translations of songs (in South Africa, for example, it is a common practice in the deaf community to 'sing' a Happy Birthday song in SASL). Cynthia Peters has observed that deaf culture and sign languages have their own visual rhythms and visual music unrelated to the music of hearing society. In fact, she notes that rhythm and music have always been associated with the body as people clap, stamp and dance, and this bodily aspect of music finds its way into some forms of sign language literature.

Within religious groups, signed hymns are acts of worship, often performed in unison by signing choirs, and for deaf members of these religious groups, the act of participating, using their own language is important. Where hymns are translated with attention to the poetic principles of sign language, they can be art forms in their own right. Dorothy Miles, for example, translated the Church of England hymn *Immortal, Invisible* into highly poetic BSL. Additionally, some countries have a tradition of signing their National Anthem. Some versions are close translations of the anthem's words and some are freer adaptations or interpretations of the ideas within the national anthem. In some countries (including France, the USA and Brazil), signed forms of the national anthem are part of deaf community life, but we have found no examples of an established BSL version of the British National Anthem. In South Africa, the National Anthem has been signed publically in SASL at various occasions, although it appears that no uniform version exists yet.

Translations of other songs, particularly of contemporary music, are increasingly common, and videos of these are often posted on the Internet. This last type of translation is sometimes done by deaf signers (particularly those with some residual hearing) but is predominantly by hearing signers, often language learners who are enjoying playing with their new language, and for whom the double-sensory experience of hearing the song with its music and seeing the signs is particularly satisfying.

Traditional deaf stories – defined by origin

Traditional stories in the canon of a deaf community's sign language heritage are defined not so much by their content or form but by their origin. Ladd (1998) called these traditional stories the 'lamppost trope', referring to often-repeated stories of deaf people standing around under lampposts to continue to sign after the deaf club had closed for the night. Deaf schools in many countries have had their own traditional stories shared among the pupils and passed down to each new generation within the school. Where the school is a national focus point (such as INES in Rio de Janeiro in Brazil, Saint Mary's and St Joseph's Schools in Dublin in Ireland or Gallaudet University in Washington DC, in the USA) the traditional stories may be known nationally, but there are plenty of well-known regional deaf stories too. The traditional deaf stories most likely to be passed on are deaf jokes and although jokes form a specific genre (that we discuss in Chapter 18), a request for a traditional deaf story in many countries often results in a traditional deaf joke.

Fictional stories for children – defined by intended audience

Sign language stories of various origin have different content and form depending on whether they are aimed at young children, older children, young adults or adults. Reading from books to deaf children in sign language is always an exercise in translation, but using signs to tell the story in a book aims to encourage deaf children to read, and teaches them about the society and culture they share with hearing people. Some story-books are written specifically for deaf children, with deaf characters, and these books can provide positive images for deaf children (especially when the authors are deaf). However, most storybooks a deaf child reads do not contain deaf characters or refer to the deaf world, even if the stories are translated into sign language.

Original fiction stories may also be created in sign language especially for younger children. These stories often contain the magical elements popular in children's stories generally, including anthropomorphism where animals and objects think, behave and use language like humans (see Chapter 7). For example, in Modiegi Moime's *The Bear Washing Day* (in South African Sign Language) specifically created for very young deaf children, the signer becomes a stuffed toy bear and expresses what it feels like to be hand-washed, hung out to dry under the sun, and become clean.

Sign language stories for young children use simple signs and have deaf characters in them so that the children can feel a sense of empathy. The settings of these stories are ones they can relate to, often with a deaf child in school or with their hearing family. There may be challenges set for the deaf character, who is able to overcome them. Richard Carter's BSL story *Owl* is one such example, in which a boy must get a good education despite his unhelpful teacher who bans sign language from the classroom. For older children and adults, magic and signing animals are no longer appropriate. Instead, action stories and realistic situations are preferred but the settings are still those that the deaf children and young adults can relate to from their experiences, and there are still the all-important deaf characters for empathy and challenges for the deaf character to overcome. These stories use increasingly complex language, presenting alternatives to the signing the young deaf person knows, such as the cinematic features used in visual storytelling. We will turn to this use of storytelling language in the next chapter.

Summary

In this chapter, we have seen that creative sign language stories can take many forms depending on their content, form, origin and audience. We have drawn on ideas and categories found by researchers on ASL and seen that they can apply in many cases to other sign languages, although we noted the importance of checking for the cultural reality of these forms in each deaf community. It is clear that stories told in sign language cross boundaries between folklore and literature and between prose and poetry. We explored the range of different forms of narrative, noting the importance of narratives of deaf experience for developing and maintaining a sense of deaf identity for signing audiences because of the messages they carry. Traditional deaf stories are especially important for their content. Cinematic stories, constraint stories and songs, on the other hand, are more important for their form as they draw on different aspects of sign languages. With the varying emphasis on form, content, origin and target audience and the resulting effects on description and action and language, we can see that models for describing stories in spoken languages only go so far in understanding the richness of sign language stories.

Notes

1. The so-called 'I-Love-You' handshape, in which the thumb, the index, and the little fingers are extended.
2. Although it may 'borrow' the manual letter 'a' from the one-handed alphabet system, which many British deaf people know.

Further reading

Bahan, Ben (2006) 'Face-to-face tradition in the American Deaf community' in H-Dirksen Bauman, Jennifer Nelson and Heidi Rose (eds) *Signing the Body Poetic* (California: University of California Press).

Lane, Harlan, Robert Hoffmeister and Ben Bahan (1996) *A Journey into the DEAF-WORLD*. (San Diego, CA: Dawn Sign Press).

Peters, Cynthia (2000) *Deaf American Literature: From Carnival to the Canon* (Washington, DC: Gallaudet University Press).

Rutherford, Susan (1993) *A Study of American Deaf Folklore* (Silver Spring, MD: Linstok Press).

Activities

1. Watch some sign language stories in a sign language you know. For BSL users, we suggest Richard Carter's *Jack in the Box* and *Owl* (posted on the YouTube channel that accompanies this book), and *Ghost Stories* by Christine Reeves and Rachell Bastikar; Jerry Hanifin's *Speed*, and Arthur Dimmock's *Wartime Memories* and *Trip Abroad* on the DVD accompanying Sutton-Spence and Woll, 1999).

    (a) Are they translations of stories in another language, adaptations of stories in another language or original creations?

    (b) Are there deaf characters in these stories?

2. Find some sign language stories aimed at deaf children (Jerry Hanifin's *Little Red Riding Hood* on the DVD accompanying Sutton-Spence and

Woll, 1999, may be a good example for BSL users). Are they translations of stories in another language, adaptations of stories in another language or original creations? Are there deaf characters in these stories?

3. (a) Look for 'stories with constraints' in a sign language that you know. What constraints do they follow?

(b) Make up your own 'stories with constraints':

- Make up your own ABC story using the manual alphabet from your country.
- Make up a number story that goes from 1 to 10 or from 10 to 1.
- Make up a single handshape story that uses only the 'B' handshape or the 'V' handshape.

Describe the difficulties and satisfactions in creating your stories.

6 Storytelling Techniques

In previous chapters, we have repeatedly noted that sign language literature is characterised by the way it foregrounds language in its text and performance. We will now focus on some of the techniques that skilled storytellers use to create performances that community members value. We will look at some techniques that have been described for good storytelling, considering especially structures within stories, and some ways in which language is foregrounded in sign language stories, particularly through the techniques that are based on cinematic features that create very powerful visual images.

Visual images – tell it, show it, become it

For sign language literature to be effective, it needs to generate emotions in its audiences, and signers frequently achieve this by manipulating elements of their signing to produce striking visual images. At the most basic level, every sign is visual because sign languages are produced in a visual medium, but the extent to which they directly represent a visual image varies according to the signer's intentions.

Sign languages allow signers a range of visual options to refer to things. They can simply *tell* what they are talking about by using vocabulary signs. For example, we can talk about a car accident by using established signs CAR and ACCIDENT, which in many sign languages are visually motivated (for example, depicting the steering wheel for CAR and a colliding gesture using two hands for ACCIDENT – see Figure 6.1a and b). Although some signs appear to be arbitrary or minimally visually motivated (such as BSL signs for SISTER, BROTHER, WORK, LIVE), many signs have some visual link, whether direct or metaphorical, to the referent (CAR, CUP, CAT, PHONE, TREE). Creative signers often exploit the visual motivation of these signs to create a visual image, and can boost their visual effect by revitalising aspects of the sign that may not seem especially visually significant when it is out of the art-sign context.

As well as telling audiences what they are referring to by naming and identifying referents, signers can *show* what they are talking about by using classifier constructions, which are highly productive signs that show the form, location and movement of the referent (see Chapter 1). Instead of referring to the car accident by the established signs CAR and ACCIDENT, we can describe what physically happened by using a flat 'B' handshape classifier (facing down) representing a car and how it crashed into a wall (also represented by a 'B' handshape facing sideways) – see Figure 6.1c and d. These classifier constructions are mostly signed with the hands, although the head, arms and torso can form classifiers too.

Finally, signers can also *become* what they are talking about by using the technique that we will call constructed action, although it has many names, including role shift, incorporation, person transfer and personation. Using the car accident example once again, the signer can take on the role of the people involved in the accident (such as the driver or passenger), and so 'become' them, to directly report what happened to them, how it happened, and what they felt about it (shock, fear, anger, and so on) as shown in Figure 6.1e and f.

In summary, then, when signers refer to something, they can tell it, show it or become it. We see all three techniques in good storytelling.

Signing in good storytelling

Steven Ryan (1993) identified some features of good signing in ASL storytelling. Many of these features are driven by the idea that the signing creates visual moving images. The most fundamental feature he identified is that a well told sign language story follows the structure and grammar of 'strong' sign language. By 'strong', he meant that it would be driven by the visual grammar of all signed languages, rather than the grammar of spoken languages, which is much less driven by the need to be visual.

Ryan noted that fingerspelling is used very little in sign language storytelling. In deaf communities that use the manual alphabet, fingerspelling is used particularly to identify things, especially for the names of people and places or for words that have a specific meaning in the spoken language but no widely available signed equivalent. Partly because there is little need to name people or places in sign language stories, and partly because sign language storytelling tries to 'show' rather than 'tell' there is often very little fingerspelling in sign language storytelling. Often, audiences report that fingerspelling interferes with their enjoyment of visual pieces, because it creates forms of written words with no visual motivation and because fingerspelling uses very different handshapes and

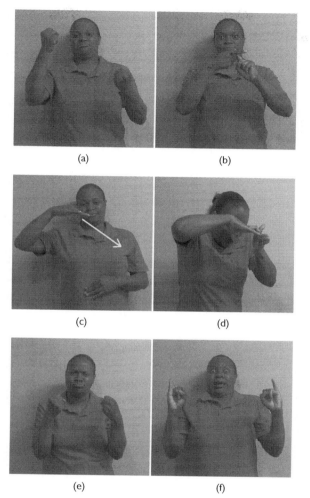

FIGURE 6.1   DESCRIPTION OF A CAR ACCIDENT BY AN SASL SIGNER, USING ESTABLISHED SIGNS CAR (A) AND ACCIDENT (B) TO 'TELL', USING CLASSIFIERS TO 'SHOW' (C AND D), AND USING CONSTRUCTED ACTION TO 'BECOME' (E AND F)

movements, being influenced by the phonology of a different language. One of Dorothy Miles' best-known BSL poems *Trio*, controversially includes the fingerspelled word 'bat' which many audiences find a jolt in the smoothness of an otherwise seamless visual poem. However, when the fingerspelling is used very creatively (as in Paul Scott's poem *No Mask Like Home*) it can contribute to the emotional effect of the work.

This type of visual story grammar includes creating characters as they are introduced in the story and it is here that we often see the pattern of 'tell it, show it, become it'. In Ben Bahan's creative ASL piece *Ball Story*, for example, each new character is named by a sign (such as DOG or OLD MAN) followed by a shift into the role of the character, and then represented by a classifier sign as the hand shows something of the form of the character as it moves.

The first time good signing storytellers introduce characters, they will make sure that the audience can identify them again later. In Richard Carter's *Owl*, for example, the teacher is carefully described when she is first introduced. Characters' names are far less important in sign language stories than they are in many written stories. Often it is enough simply to say something about the person such as 'the hearing woman' or 'the cabin attendant' or 'the man with the scowl'.

The visual image of the character is made stronger by showing audiences where the characters are within the story scene, what they look like and how they behave, especially by becoming the character through constructed action. This can be done by using nonmanual features, such as facial expression, and carefully selected gaze and eye aperture (for example, if the eyes are wide open or squinted). We will discuss more of these in Chapter 17. These nonmanual features are often exaggerated because exaggeration is one way for storytellers to emphasise a point. In her discussion of ASL literature, Cynthia Peters (2000) highlights the importance of exaggeration when she suggests that humour and 'the burlesque' are central to a lot of signed narrative. In *Owl*, Richard Carter creates the character of the horrible teacher using strong caricaturing characterisation that focuses on her physical appearance, behaviour, facial expression and body posture. The owl is also clearly presented but we are shown less of the owl's appearance. Instead, we see its behaviour, facial expression and body posture, and, most importantly, we see its special style of signing (see Chapter 7 for more details).

Once the character has been identified, the chosen facial expression and body movement used in constructed action will show the characters and events as the storyteller lets characters speak and act for themselves. Constructed action can replace signs that name and identify actions, so there is no need for the signer to 'tell' them. For example, there are signs that name actions, states or intentions such as LOOK, NOD, FRUSTRATED, ASTONISHED, WANT or LIKE, but these signs merely name the ideas. When signing storytellers become the character, they can use their own eyes, body and facial expression to show the character looking or nodding, or performing actions that show the character is frustrated or astonished, and can show their reactions to a situation that indicate they want or like it.

There are many ways of knowing who is who in the story. Sometimes, just taking the role of a character is enough – facial expression, gaze and body movement will tell us who is acting, once this information has been established. This is especially true if there is a simple interaction between two characters. When we read a dialogue between two people in a novel (for example a mother and her son), once the identity of the two characters has been established, there is no need to use 'she said' and 'he said' on every line, and similar turn-taking arises in sign language stories. In Richard Carter's *Owl*, we see the mother, looking down sternly at her son, ordering him to get out of bed. Richard then shifts character to become the boy, looking up indignantly to ask 'Why?!' The audience has no need of any other information to keep track of the characters. However, if it has been a while since the character was mentioned, they are often re-introduced, either with their name or a sign saying who they are, or with a point to the area where they were last located (Morgan, 2002).

A good visual story will also make sure that people and other objects are carefully placed in space so the audience can keep track of them and the events in the story. Classifier signs can be placed and moved in space to show more information about a person or thing, which adds to the visual image (as we saw in our example of a car crashing into a wall). The classifiers are often placed in space symmetrically (especially to the left and right of the signer) and Ryan noted that good storytelling will use plenty of symmetry. We will see in Chapter 16 how important symmetry is for a great deal of artistic signing but for now we will note that stories and poems that balance signs in opposing parts of space or balance events at different points are often considered very satisfying by their audiences.

The 'visual vernacular' and cinematic features in signed narratives

Stories that create very strong visual images use specific techniques that have been termed visual vernacular by the deaf actor Bernard Bragg. In the documentary and poetry collection *The Heart of the Hydrogen Jukebox*, he explained:

> Marcel Marceau invited me to study mime with him in Paris. I created another performance technique based on his method. I developed something that I called VV – it is a form of mime. It is not really a traditional mime structure. I changed it into a smaller frame size, and utilized film techniques. I used cuts and edits, close ups and long shots. I started that style, and I called it Visual Vernacular, for lack of a better term. (Bragg in Nathan Lerner and Feigel, 2009, 18:33)

Visual vernacular and the lexicon of film techniques can be used to analyse sign language literature. We have seen in Chapters 4 and 5 that film has influenced sign language storytelling. Many sign language stories rec-reate the images seen in films or on television, and older deaf people often report that their school experiences of sign language stories were based on recounting what the children saw at the cinema. The filming and edit-ing techniques used in filmmaking find a ready parallel in sign language stories. Bernard Bragg understood that film and ASL were closely related, and his visual vernacular style formalises the way that signers present moving visual images in a way that highlights cinematic techniques.

Stories that are not based on films can still use these filmic techniques. Martial arts films have inspired original sign language stories and the films in *The Matrix* series have been particularly influential on this style because of the action scenes. The popular *Deaf Ninja* videos published on YouTube and Richard Carter's *Children's Park* are good examples of these.

The film editor Walter Murch (1997) has noted the similarities between editing film and creating poetry. He explains that cutting between shots in a film creates an aesthetic impact as the viewer constantly compares each image with the previous ones as it is presented. The film editor presents the audience with contrasting images, such as close-up to wide, light to dark, rough to smooth and slow to fast. Murch suggests that these can be seen as the visual equivalents of poetic techniques such as rhyme, allusion, alliteration and metaphor.

Murch was comparing film techniques to written and spoken poetry but Dirksen Bauman (2006) has compared film techniques with sign lan-guage literature, because sign language art forms use whatever resources they can to create moving images, and Bauman notes that the grammars of sign languages and film are very similar.

Signed narratives and poems delivered in this visual vernacular style become like a one-person performance of a film, in which the signer is the narrator, all the characters and the scenery, as well as the camera and editor.[1] Bauman (2006) suggests that we can describe sign language storytelling using the cinematic ideas of 'camera', 'shot' and 'editing'. He has argued that any signed story or poem can be analysed using these ideas, whether or not the poets and storytellers deliberately use cinematic techniques.

To explore his ideas further we will use David Ellington's *The Story of the Flag*.

The signer acting as the camera can produce images using angles (such as high, low, left and right), movements (such as pan and track) and points of view of different characters. If we understand a 'shot' to be merely the presentation of a visual image, every sign is a shot of some kind, so the choice of shots is fundamental to the structure of stories.

The opening section of *The Story of the Flag* pans across two areas to show them to the audience – firstly in a close-up across the flag, we see a detailed image of each of its different quarters, and secondly in a distance shot across the countryside, we move from the river, up the hill to the flag.

The signer can create almost infinite combinations of shots in a story, and the shots can be of varying distance (close-up, distance, or many stages in between). In sign languages, the close-up shot uses constructed action as the signer becomes the referent, mapping the body of the signer onto the body of the character (termed 'character scale' by Smith and Cormier, 2014). The medium shots represent general areas of the body so, for example, the fist can represent the head and the forearm the body. The distance shots use the hand to represent the whole character, in a classifier construction that is sometimes called an entity classifier (and called 'observer scale' by Smith and Cormier, 2014).

Different distances of shot in *The Story of the Flag* show a horseman and his companions in different ways. Figure 6.2a shows a close-up character shot where the signer's head and body have become the horseman, mapping his body exactly on to the body of the horseman character. Each finger, however, represents a whole person to show his companions on either side, and these are shown as though by a distance, observer shot, where we cannot, for example, see their faces. Later, as we see in Figure 6.2b the horsemen come to a rapid halt and we see a medium shot, as the fist and forearm represent the heads and bodies of either the horses or the horsemen dipping when they stop. Again, the lead horseman is shown at the same time as a close-up shot, so we see his head and body as full size, also dipping as the group stops.

This poem also shows a cinematic zoom effect of things getting bigger as we see them closer, by using more fingers to make the flag appear bigger as the horsemen approach (Figure 6.3).

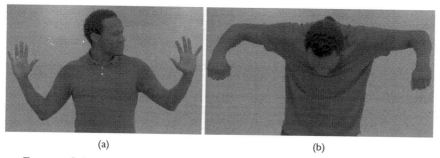

(a)   (b)

FIGURE 6.2   DIFFERENT SHOTS FROM DAVID ELLINGTON'S *THE STORY OF THE FLAG* (A) CLOSE-UP AND DISTANCE SHOTS (B) CLOSE-UP AND MEDIUM SHOTS

FIGURE 6.3   THE ZOOM-IN EFFECT FROM DAVID
ELLINGTON'S *THE STORY OF THE FLAG*

Any shot can vary in length, being short, long, very short, very long, or anything in between. As we see in films, signs and scenes may be shown from the narrator's or the character's perspective and they may be shown 'intercut' so we see the same scene from their different perspectives. Figure 6.4a shows the view of the narrator (or perhaps the horseman) observing as an arrow flies towards the flag. Figure 6.4b shows the same event from the perspective of the (personified) flag that tries to dodge the arrow. The first image presents a distance shot and the second is a close-up. The shots here are short and the cutting between the two perspectives of the horseman and the flag is rapid, creating a fast pace in the story.

Signs can be at 'normal' speed, matching the speed at which an event happened, or speeded up or signed slowly for visual effect. It takes considerable skill to sign in slow motion but the effect is very much like the slow motion technique that we see in films. (Richard Carter uses this device in *Children's Park*, *The Race* and *Looking for Diamonds*.) Slow motion signing is often very amusing to watch but can also increase dramatic impact, as emotions shown in slow motion are much stronger. In Rimar Segala's Libras piece *The Ping-Pong Ball* (*Bolinha de Ping-Pong*) signs are made increasingly quickly as the ping-pong match heats up until slow motion

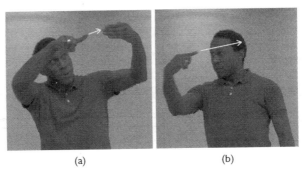

(a)   (b)

FIGURE 6.4   TWO SHOTS, CUTTING BETWEEN THE TWO PERSPECTIVES
OF (A) THE HORSEMAN WATCHING THE ARROW HEADING TOWARDS
THE FLAG, AND (B) THE FLAG SEEING THE ARROW APPROACHING

suddenly changes the atmosphere of the piece. Rimar becomes the ball being battered between the two players, and the anguished expression of the ball is presented as it moves very slowly, repeatedly struck by the bats. At this moment, the audience comes to understand the suffering of the ball – in this case a metaphor for the suffering of a powerless human caught up in the battles of more powerful people.

Visual cinematic storytelling and mime

As this storytelling is so visual, we may ask 'Why isn't this mime?' After all, mime conveys actions and emotions through gestures, and is not word-based, as it is a powerfully visual art form that is easily understood by speakers of different languages. We know sign languages aren't mime because they have large vocabularies and complex grammars, and they are used daily by communities in many social and cultural situations. Nevertheless, signers use gesture within sign language, and a lot of visual artistic signing seems to have characteristics of mime. Even visual vernacular, which is very gestural and uses very few vocabulary signs, is not the same as mime, and Bernard Bragg made it clear that he adapted mime to suit sign language. Mime uses the whole body; but signing rarely occurs below the hips. Mime artists move across the floor to show the path of movement of a character; signers stay in one place and move their hands and bodies to show a character's path of movement. Mime uses the full extent of vertical space, including the floor; signers keep within a much smaller space. Mime greatly prefers constructed action, in which the mime artist becomes the referent; signers mix this form of representation with others, so they show close-up, medium and distance shots, sometimes simultaneously, while mime mostly uses the close-up shot. Finally, mime keeps one perspective much longer than signing. We do not see the rapid 'cross-cutting' in mime that we see in sign language storytelling (Sutton-Spence and Boyes Braem, 2013).

Summary

We have seen in this chapter that signing in good storytelling uses visual grammar to create strong visual images that audiences find satisfying. Signers are able to achieve this visual art form by combining signs for referents that will 'tell it, show it or become it'. Given the importance of characters in stories, signing storytellers use vocabulary and constructed action to create ones that are clearly identifiable. Exaggeration is especially common as a way to make images even stronger, and to emphasise certain features. Signers can create a visual story by using visual vernacular techniques parallel to angle, shot and editing in another visual storytelling art form, cinema. Although the visual vernacular form has a lot in common with artistic mime, it has some fundamental differences that mark it out as being a part of a sign language art form.

Note

1. A complication is that they can be the actual editor – as in Wim Emmerik's *Growth*, in which he (or his editor) edits the filming of his poem so that they literally have close-ups and zoom-out views.

Further reading

Bauman, H-Dirksen (2006) 'Getting out of line: toward a visual and cinematic poetics of ASL' in H-Dirksen Bauman, Jennifer Nelson and Heidi Rose (eds) *Signing the Body Poetic* (California: University of California Press).

Murch, Walter (1997) 'Walter Murch in conversation with Joy Katz', http://filmsound.org/murch/parnassus/ (accessed November 2015).

Nathan Lerner, Miriam and Don Feigel (2009) *The Heart of the Hydrogen Jukebox* (DVD) (New York: Rochester Institute of Technology).

Sutton-Spence, Rachel and Penny Boyes Braem (2013) 'Comparing the products and the processes of creating sign language poetry and pantomimic improvisations', *Journal of Nonverbal Behavior*, 37(3) 245–280.

Activities

1. Consider some sign language stories in a sign language you know. In BSL, you might like to consider Richard Carter's *Prince Looking for Love* and *Looking for Diamonds*, and Donna Williams' *My Cat* (posted on the YouTube channel that accompanies this book). Ben Bahan's *Ball Story*, although in ASL, should be fairly accessible to people who do not know ASL.

Pick out examples of times when the signer:

- tells us something,
- shows us something,
- becomes something.

2. Dirksen Bauman suggests we can look at sign language storytelling by considering the cinematic ideas of 'camera', 'shot' and 'editing'. Using a sign language story or poem (you can use one of the poems/stories suggested above):

   (a) Look for examples of 'the signer as camera'. Find the angle that the signer uses to present the images, such as high and low, left and right, and show the point of view of different characters.

   (b) Look for examples of signs that could be described as 'shots':

   - with varying distance (close up, distance or in between),
   - of different length (short, long, very short, very long or in between),
   - of different speed (normal speed, fast motion or slow motion).

   (c) Look for examples of 'editing' where the shots are presented in a certain order. Find examples of 'dialogue editing' (cutting between characters) or montage (showing a sequence of images that build a visual story without any narration).

3. Find examples of sign language literature that uses the visual vernacular. How would you reply to the person who asked you 'So, isn't this just mime?'

7 Anthropomorphism

Anthropomorphism is 'an interpretation of what is not human or personal in terms of human or personal characteristics' (www.merriam-webster.com). We often think about non-human things as though they were human in some way – as though they have human emotions and personalities – and sometimes we even act as though they can use human language. Stories, especially children's stories, are filled with talking animals and inanimate objects such as trees, cars and trains that have human characteristics. We can even give imagined human forms and behaviour to abstract ideas such as 'time', 'envy' and 'beauty'. Animals or inanimate objects that behave like humans in stories or other settings (for example in advertisements) are often used to allude to human values and behaviour. For this reason, we can say that anthropomorphism is a kind of metaphor, as we talk about one thing (humans) in terms of another (non-humans). We will discuss metaphor more in Chapter 10, but in this chapter we will see that anthropomorphism is the key to a lot of creative signing. Deaf storytellers and poets around the world, in many different sign languages and from many different backgrounds, often actively show the perspective of non-humans in their stories.

Constructed action and signed anthropomorphism

Anthropomorphism in creative sign language occurs as part of constructed action where signers 'become' the character they are talking about (recall our discussion of constructed action in Chapter 6). When signers take on the role of a human character, they use their body to represent the body of that human character. When they take on the role of a non-human character, they do their best to use their human body to represent the body of the non-human. Paul Scott becomes a book in *Two Books* using his arms as the pages and body as the spine. Richard Carter becomes a mirror in his story *Mirror*, mapping the flatness of his hands on that of the mirror (Figure 7.1). Much of the delight in watching signed anthropomorphism comes from seeing how the skilled signer manages to do this.

It is considerably easier for signers to give human form to the non-human things they are talking about than it is for users of any spoken

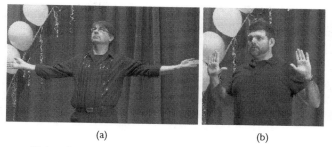

(a)   (b)

FIGURE 7.1   (A) PAUL SCOTT REPRESENTING AN OPEN BOOK IN *TWO BOOKS*, (B) RICHARD CARTER REPRESENTING A MIRROR IN *MIRROR*

language, because signers are using their human bodies rather than spoken words to talk about them. This is the fundamental difference between anthropomorphism in sign language literature and in spoken language literature. Signing storytellers and poets can represent the form of non-humans directly by turning themselves into the things they want to describe. In other words, they can 'map' the non-humans onto their body, giving them eyes, a mouth, head, hands, and so on because the signer has them. Spoken language literature can talk about the perspective of non-humans, but it cannot directly show how they are transformed into humans (unless it is accompanied by illustrations).

Anthropomorphised characters appeal to audiences because we can empathise with them. By giving human qualities to non-humans, we can identify with them and have friendly feelings toward them. A sign used for anthropomorphism by some signers can also mean 'to change places with someone'. When a deaf person feels they can truly identify with a character because they feel they can change places with them, the story is successful. (In fact, there is a BSL sign CHANGE-PLACES-WITH to explain this feeling of identification.) Children often anthropomorphise animals and objects at an early stage of their development, so many books written for younger children catch their attention through talking animals and other non-human characters.

Targets of anthropomorphism

Animals

Mammals such as dogs, cats, cows, rabbits or horses are familiar in our daily life. They are physically fairly similar to us (having eyes, a head, a face, feet and so on), so their body parts can easily be mapped onto the signer's body. This makes them a good target for anthropomorphism through constructed action in sign languages. Animal legs and feet can be represented by human legs and feet, but because signers mostly maintain their signing space in the upper body, they use their arms, hands or fingers rather than their legs (they do this to represent human legs, too). Paul Scott's hands become the paws of the dog in *Roz: Teach a Dog a New Trick* and in *Snow Globe* Richard Carter's arms and hands become a reindeer's legs and hooves. In Donna Williams' *My Cat* and John Wilson's *For Two Special People*, the cat's legs and paws are sometimes shown by the performer's arms and hands, and at other times through their creative use of body-part classifiers, such as bent index fingers to show the cat's bent leg, or two fingers to show the paws (Figure 7.2). While the arms and hands represent the legs and feet in all these examples, the signer's head, face and body are understood to represent the head, face and body of the animal.

Where humans and the animals do not share the same bodily features, signers can use their hands and arms to create substitutes, so we see even more clearly an image that is a blend of human and animal. For example, human ears are not shaped for a good match with long- or big-eared animals such as horses, rabbits and elephants, but the signer can represent the ears with their hands placed on or beside their head where the animal's ears would be on its head. Humans don't have a tail but Paul Scott uses a wagging finger to become a dog's wagging tail in *Roz: Teach a Dog a New Trick*, while his face and head show the face and head of the dog and his other hand represents one of the dog's paws (Figure 7.3). Humans don't have antlers either, but in *Snow Globe* Richard Carter's hands placed at his temples represent them (and the reindeer signs with them – see our discussion in the next section).

Non-mammals are usually more challenging to anthropomorphise through constructed action because their bodies are less like ours but signers often manage, especially by using different parts of the body, to

FIGURE 7.2   DONNA WILLIAMS AND JOHN WILSON SHOWING
DIFFERENT WAYS OF REPRESENTING A CAT'S LEGS AND PAWS

FIGURE 7.3 PAUL SCOTT REPRESENTING A DOG'S WAGGING TAIL

represent the target's body parts. Although humans lack wings, signers can use their arms or their hands as a good shape-substitute. The owl's wings in Richard Carter's *Owl* are represented by hands in the 'B' handshape. The fins of the fish in his story *Goldfish* are represented by the hands fixed firmly at the chest (and much of the amusement here comes from seeing the chest used to represent the fish's body). In *Surprise Apple*,[1] Richard's head and body represent the head and body of a caterpillar eating through a series of apples, and the caterpillar's mouth is represented twice – by the signer's mouth and by the hands copying the movements of the mouth (Figure 7.4a). However, when the physical structure of an animal is too different from a human (for example, a snail or a snake) the animal is usually represented almost entirely as though it were human – perhaps with a hint of the animal. However, signing poets love a creative challenge, so even a virus can be portrayed through constructed action (in Donna Williams' *Red and Green*) where the tiny hair-like filaments of the virus are shown by the signer's wiggling fingers (Figure 7.4b).

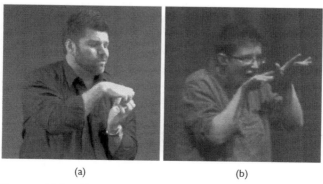

(a)   (b)

FIGURE 7.4 CONSTRUCTED ACTION CREATING NON-MAMMAL CREATURES (A) A CATERPILLAR AND (B) A VIRUS

Plants

Plants are even less like humans than mammals, birds or even insects are (for example, they don't have eyes or a face, they don't move around and they don't appear to communicate with each other), but signers will still use constructed action to represent them, and this gives signers a greater option to anthropomorphise them. The tree is a particularly popular target of constructed action and anthropomorphism. This is partly due to its familiar presence in our environment, its positive attributes (it is strong, solid, firmly rooted, and it grows and bears fruit) and the fact that it goes through similar life stages to humans (birth, growth, reproduction and death). However, its resemblance in shape to a human body also makes it easy to project human features onto the tree so that anthropomorphisation is straightforward (for example, the trunk is the body, and the top area with branches and leaves can be identified as a head, and branches and twigs can also be seen as hands and fingers). Examples in the collected anthology of BSL poetry include Richard Carter's *Deaf Trees* and Paul Scott's *Tree* among many others.

Inanimate objects, constructed action and human emotions

Compared to the popularity of 'talking' animals in spoken language literature, it is less common to anthropomorphise inanimate objects, but skilled signers do it with apparent ease. Indeed, although we have already mentioned that a shared physical structure can be the base for good anthropomorphism, skilled signers can attribute human forms and qualities to things which share little similarity with humans. In these examples, the face and body are often important for showing the emotions and desires given to the inanimate objects. In Maria Gibson's *Kettle*, her hands show the boiling water inside the kettle but she shows the kettle entirely by her face and body. The constructed action using the human face allows even the kettle to express certain feelings, such as intensity while it boils and a sort of release once it has boiled, although this is perhaps not clearly human behaviour. In Siobhan O'Donovan's *Sixty-One Steps*, the body, head and face again show the feelings and outlook of the kindly steps, and Siobhan's open flat hands skilfully blend the shape of the steps seen from the outside human's perspective with the steps' inside perspective, where those hands become the steps' hands carefully holding the people climbing them. In John Wilson's *Lift* the hands represent the lift doors throughout, but constructed action through the head, face and eyes shows the lift looking about in a human way, as it hopes to find passengers to carry.

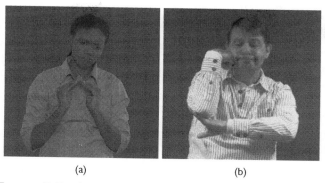

(a)   (b)

FIGURE 7.5 ANTHROPOMORPHISED PLACES FROM (A) MODIEGI MOIME'S *SOWETO* AND (B) PAUL SCOTT'S *NO MASK LIKE HOME*

Cities, places and houses can be anthropomorphised through con-structed action as well. Modiegi Moime's *Soweto* tells a story of daily life in a township in South Africa from the perspective of the township itself, and her facial expression suggests that the township is someone that will-ingly contains people and feels lonely when they go out to work (Figure 7.5a). In Paul Scott's *No Mask Like Home*, the house is mapped onto the human body as a sympathetic friend of the protagonist who patiently listens to his grumbles (Figure 7.5b).

Natural elements such as water, and very large objects such as mountains or the sun and moon can also be given human characteristics by showing human emotions and desires through their facial and body movements. Paul Scott's *Too Busy to Hug, No Time to See* describes a slow-burning love affair between a mountain and the sea. Paul's hands show the outline of the mountain and the movements of the waves but his facial expression shows their clear human emotions (and, again, audiences willingly accept that the mountain and sea have eyes to see with and faces to show emotions). Johanna Mesch's *Ocean* personifies the planet Earth and its oceans in a poem about human destruction of nature. For much of the poem the hands represent the water and the ships and fish in it, while the face and eyes show the emotions and behaviour of the ocean. Towards the end of the poem, though, Johanna's whole body takes on the role of the ocean, so we are able to see it being sick to its stomach from the pollution. Once again, the anthropomorphism helps audiences to empathise more strongly with the ocean.

In Paul Scott's *We'll Meet Again*, the molecules of water constantly change their shape and move around, creating a parallel with members of the deaf community who might take different paths but never com-pletely lose touch with each other. Although the hands clearly show the water as water, the nonmanual representation of the water shows it behaving with human intentions and feelings. The purpose behind the anthropomorphism in *We'll Meet Again* is different from that in *Ocean*. In *Ocean* the aim is to stimulate empathy with the ocean, while in *We'll Meet Again* anthropomorphism is used allegorically – the poem is about deaf people not water – showing how it can be a sophisticated and complex poetic device.[2]

Different levels of anthropomorphism

Having explored different targets of anthropomorphism, we will now discuss different degrees of anthropomorphism. We can see three levels of anthropomorphisation, depending on the extent of 'humanness' attributed to the targets:

1. Descriptive level.
2. Pre-linguistic level.
3. Linguistic level.

These three stages form a continuum, and individual examples of anthropomorphism can be scattered along it, from the simple attribution of human characteristics to more complex representations.

I. Descriptive level

At this level, relatively little humanity is imparted to the non-humans that are shown by constructed action, so anthropomorphism is minimal. The simple fact that the human body is mapped onto them to represent them, gives these non-humans a human form, but the signer simply represents the expressions and behaviour of non-humans (usually animals) using the human face and body. It shows what humans see animals doing, rather than how animals see their world from their own perspectives. The expressions of animals can be exaggerated but they remain fairly basic, and the animals are not considered to have complex emotions or independent thought. For example, in *Roz: Teach a Dog a New Trick*, Paul Scott describes the expressions of the dog. The dog clearly shows excitement and curiosity, and it is entertaining to see this shown on a human face, but it does not go beyond what we normally see in dogs (see Figure 7.3). Similarly, John Wilson's *For Two Special People* describes a cat from the perspective of the poet (see Figure 7.2b). We also see this descriptive level when inanimate entities are given a human body but not human emotions. Their vacant facial expressions show they are inanimate.

FIGURE 7.6 REPRESENTATION OF NON-HUMANS AT THE DESCRIPTIVE LEVEL: INANIMATE MANNEQUIN FROM RICHARD CARTER'S *SHOP WINDOW*

An example of this is seen in Richard Carter's *Shop Window*, in which the mannequin remains expressionless until the last moment (Figure 7.6). When she suddenly develops human emotion and independent thoughts and movements, the facial expression changes as she slaps the window-dresser who has taken liberties with her (which is an example of the pre-linguistic level of representation, where anthropomorphism is clearer).

2. Pre-linguistic level

At the pre-linguistic level of anthropomorphism, non-human characters show a certain level of personality, and performers look deeper into their possible thoughts or feelings. Although this still comes from human imagination, the perspective of the non-humans is presented more directly than at the descriptive level. A great many sign language poems and stories featuring non-humans work at this pre-linguistic level. The non-humans at this level are shown to think or feel independently, but they don't have language. Thus, there is little interaction with other characters but they can express all the complex feelings which are normally attributed to humans such as joy, pride, surprise, anger, frustration or disappointment. They react to pain, cold, heat and other sensations. The tree in Paul Scott's *Spring* does not sign but Paul's visual representation of the tree's feelings and reactions adds a great deal of emotion and a comical touch to it.

The distinction between descriptive and pre-linguistic levels can be seen clearly by comparing two characters in Richard Carter's *Prince Looking for Love* (based on the tale of *The Frog Prince*). Two frogs appear in this story: one with a dignified attitude (who turns out to be the

(a)   (b)

FIGURE 7.7 TWO FROGS FROM RICHARD CARTER'S *PRINCE LOOKING
FOR LOVE*. (A) FROG-TO-BE-PRINCE (PRE-LINGUISTIC LEVEL) AND (B) FROG
PORTRAYED AS A MERE LIVING CREATURE (DESCRIPTIVE LEVEL)

prince), and another with less respectable manners. Although they are
both shown by constructed action through the body of the poet, the first
frog (the prince-to-be) is anthropomorphised at the pre-linguistic level,
revealing a higher level of intelligence, while the second frog remains at
a descriptive level. The first frog shows human emotions such as pride
and confidence, and disgust toward the other frog. The second frog is
just shown as a frog, with only basic animal instincts and which does
things ordinary frogs would do, such as catching a fly. The difference
in the degree of anthropomorphism between the two frogs makes the
crucial distinction between the human (the frog prince) and animal (an
ordinary frog) in this story (Figure 7.7).

3. Linguistic level

At this stage, the anthropomorphised non-humans are given the same
level of intelligence as humans. In particular, they are considered to have
a language. This allows them to interact with other characters (both
humans and non-humans) and actively take part in the story world.
Anthropomorphism in spoken language literature often exclusively refers
to this linguistic level where animals talk to each other and even to humans.
In the pre-linguistic stage only human emotions as expressed through
human emotional facial expressions are attributed to non-humans, but at
the linguistic level, skilled signers can assign detailed characteristics to the
non-humans, so each character can be fully developed with a distinct personality. In a sign language context, anthropomorphised characters can
live the life of a deaf human, so deaf attributes such as communication

through sign language, emphasis on vision, collective thoughts, and using deaf-related objects becomes possible. The use of sign language is crucial. In sign language literature, linguistic animals (or plants or inanimate objects) are almost always seen as 'signing' beings. The idea of humans and non-humans communicating through sign language creates a sense of solidarity of deaf people as distinct from hearing people.

One part of the skill in giving non-humans language is finding body parts that the animal or object can use as 'hands' for signing. Some animals and objects have more ready-made options than others. For example, a tree is more likely to have signing skills than a pencil because the tree's branches and twigs can map to hands, but a pencil has nothing that can be used for hands. A snake, being long, thin and limbless may still be able to sign but can only do so mapping its body to a single finger (which is also long and thin). One of the greatest pleasures in watching sign language anthropomorphism lies in seeing how signers make non-humans sign. Richard Carter is especially skilled in this. For example, his reindeer in *Snow Globe* signs with the antlers, his goldfish in *Goldfish* signs with the fins, his owl in *Owl* signs with the wings, and his bear in *Sam's Birthday* signs with bear's paws (although we later find out that this bear is Sam's father dressed as a bear) – see Figure 7.8.

Size matters: the golden rule of Mrs. Pepperpot

Mrs. Pepperpot in Alf Prøysen's stories shrinks to the size of a pepperpot and becomes friends with small animals. In sign language literature, on the other hand, non-humans become the size of the humans as they are given a human body. In either case, humans and non-humans become equal in terms of their physical size, which allows them to interact. Physical equality between humans and anthropomorphised non-humans is metaphorically understood as mental equality. Mrs. Pepperpot can only communicate with

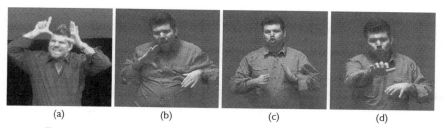

| (a) | (b) | (c) | (d) |

FIGURE 7.8 RICHARD CARTER'S EXAMPLES OF ANTHROPOMORPHISM AT LINGUISTIC LEVEL: (A) A SIGNING REINDEER, (B) A SIGNING GOLDFISH, (C) A SIGNING OWL, AND (D) A SIGNING BEAR

small animals when she is small. When she returns to human size, she can no longer talk to them. In sign language literature, non-humans can feel, think and sign when they are human size.

Apart from creating equality and a way to communicate, giving them a human size allows us to understand them better. Mrs. Pepperpot notices the detailed features of small creatures and starts to understand what it is like for them to live in a human world only when she is their size. In a similar way, anthropomorphising small creatures in sign language makes it easier to describe them by representing them in the human-size. In *Grass Hairstyle*, Richard Carter extends this creative principle to blades of grass, allowing each blade of grass to represent its hairstyle. The very idea that a blade of grass can be bothered with its hairstyle is original, and Richard's leap of imagination enlarges the grass blades to human size, so we can see their hairstyles.

Deaf people as privileged humans

According to Tess Cosslett (2006), talking animals in some children's stories in the 18th century share

> the convention by which the animals speak in human language among themselves, but cannot be understood by the humans in the story. Only the reader and the narrator, as privileged humans, can understand the animals. (p. 43)

In sign language literature, some characters cannot see the non-humans' language. However, whereas the convention mentioned by Cosslett comes from the fact that animals cannot speak to the humans even if they wish to, in sign language literature non-humans decide when to sign, and who the privileged humans are to whom they sign. Deaf people, and especially deaf children, are likely to be the privileged humans. For example, the brown tree in Richard Carter's *Deaf Trees* transforms itself into a signing tree only when it sees deaf visitors. Many of Richard Carter's non-human characters reveal their ability to sign only in front of the deaf child and pretend to be inanimate while adults are present. The spring toy in *Jack in the Box* and the owl in *Owl* both communicate with the deaf child but become inanimate (with non-directed gaze and vacant expressions) when adults are looking at them. When the adults go away, they return their gaze to the protagonist (and to the audience), and they wink and gesture 'Shhh ... (Don't tell them I can sign)' to give a sense of conspiracy to the child, and ultimately to the audience.

Blending of human and non-human features

Our last note on anthropomorphism concerns the way signers combine human and non-human features. Signed anthropomorphism is not about the complete attribution of human qualities onto non-humans. In many cases, anthropomorphised non-humans retain their original features, and skilful signers will blend human and non-human elements in the right proportion to remind us that we are seeing something anthropomorphised. It would not be so entertaining if the animal completely turned into a human and started to sign just like a normal deaf person. The fun of seeing anthropomorphism is to see the blend of human and non-human features in the character.

This blending blurs the boundary between human and non-humans, and gives talking animals an ambiguous status in stories. Cosslett (2006) has pointed out that the animals in Beatrix Potter's and Kenneth Grahame's tales exist somewhere 'between the animal and human, and also between the adult and child' (p. 174). They inherit qualities from both groups, but they belong to neither completely. Richard Carter uses this unsettled position of talking animals (or objects) in *Owl*. The identity of the owl is ambivalent in many ways. Originally brought in as a teaching prop, the owl belongs to the teacher and remains inanimate while the frightening and unlikeable hearing teacher is present, but when it is anthropomorphised, it suddenly shows lively expressions and starts to sign, and forms a close bond with the deaf children. The owl shares sign language with the children, but it understands the spoken language of the teacher as well (thus it is not deaf). It also seems to understand the hearing world, which makes it a perfect interpreter for the deaf boy in the story. The journey of the deaf boy into two worlds – both between deaf and hearing, and between adult and child – is symbolically represented by the presence of his owl, who, through anthropomorphism, occupies a space between the animal and human.

Summary

In this chapter, we have seen that anthropomorphism is an important device in creative sign language that allows performers to represent the world from non-human perspectives, often allowing the signer to show a new deaf perspective on life. Due to the embodied nature of sign languages, signers map features from non-humans onto their own body in order to represent them as directly as possible. The form of the non-human determines how easily signers can represent them, but where humans lack equivalent body structures, signers can use their hands to create something equivalent, and where the non-human lacks certain human body parts (especially eyes and a mouth) audiences readily accept them. The extent of human characterisation varies. Some non-humans appear human simply because they are directly represented by a human, others are given additional human attributes, and the most advanced are endowed with human language. By blending human and non-human characteristics, signers can present provocative and highly entertaining images of non-humans.

Notes

1. This poem has also been performed with the title *Apple Shock*.
2. We thank Gillian Rudd for this insight.

Further reading

Readers who wish to learn more about the way that skilled signers anthropomorphise may want to read the following articles:

Sutton-Spence, Rachel and Donna Jo Napoli (2010) 'Anthropomorphism in sign languages: a look at poetry and storytelling with a focus on British Sign Language', *Sign Language Studies* 10(4), 442–475.

West, Donna and Rachel Sutton-Spence (2012) 'Shared thinking processes with four Deaf poets: a window on 'The Creative' in 'Creative Sign Language', *Sign Language Studies,* 12(2), 188–210.

For anthropomorphism (or personification) in spoken language literature, we recommend the following two books:

Cosslett, Tess (2006) *Talking Animals in British Children's Fiction, 1786–1914* (Aldershot: Ashgate).

Paxson, James (1994) *The Poetics of Personification* (Cambridge: Cambridge University Press).

Activities

I. Targets of anthropomorphism

Using clips of poems and stories in any sign language you know:

(a) Find instances of animals being portrayed as humans.

(b) Find pieces that involve a tree as a central character.

(c) Find examples of inanimate objects being anthropomorphised.

Do they behave in any ways that we might call human behaviour?

2. Look at the illustrations in this chapter that show a human signer representing a non-human.

(a) What in the image makes you think it has human features?

(b) What in the image shows non-human features?

(c) What do the signer's hands represent?

3. Find five sign language poems/stories that involve non-human characters in any sign language you know. (Suggested pieces are: *The Cat* and *The Ugly Duckling* by Dorothy Miles, and from the BSL poems posted on the YouTube channel that accompanies this book: *Doll, Tree* and *Turkey* by Paul Scott, *Cochlear Implant, Grass Hairstyle, Jack in the Box* and *Goldfish* by Richard Carter, *Kettle* by Maria Gibson, *Lift* by John Wilson and *Duck and Dissertation* by Donna Williams.)

(a) List the non-human characters that appear in these clips.

(b) How are the non-human characters portrayed?

(c) Try to categorise them into descriptive, pre-linguistic and linguistic levels. They may not fit perfectly into the categories (you may feel one character is more descriptive than the other) so you could place them along the descriptive–linguistic *continuum*.

(d) How strongly do you feel they are 'deaf'? Try to place them along a deaf–hearing continuum, and explain why you feel that way.

4. Consider the following remark:

'Anthropomorphization of abstract nouns proved the most challenging [task] to the poets.' (West and Sutton-Spence, 2012, p. 202).

Why are abstract nouns not easily anthropomorphised in sign languages? What options are available for signers to anthropomorphise abstract ideas?

8 Beginnings and Endings

In previous chapters, we have touched on several aspects of the structure of signed texts. In this chapter, we will consider what makes a strong opening and a strong closure in sign language poems and stories.[1] We are often told that 'a story has a beginning, middle and end' but the way that the content of a story (or a poem) is arranged and especially the way it starts and ends influences our response to it. Stories, poems and jokes all need some sort of orientation at the beginning so audiences can follow their presentation, and the last line often creates a satisfactory ending.

Yang Ye (1996) has described the 'Ah ha!' moment that occurs when an audience experiences the full emotional impact of a poem, calling it the 'cracking whip' that gets our full attention. The point at which we understand a work opens up the sense of the whole poem. In storytelling, there is often an extra section, or coda, after the climax to resolve any points left open and gently wind down the pace of the story, and readers or audiences can feel a little shocked if it finishes suddenly. In poetry, however, the end point is often more sudden and deliberately less clearly resolved. In poetry, the full impact often occurs when the poem ends, so as we explore different aspects of closure in a selection of sign language poems, we can look for moments when 'the whip cracks'.

We should be aware that many signed performances (particularly humorous ones and ones that are performed more informally) do not have what we might call a 'punchline'. This is often because the content with a plot does not drive their structure and the form of the signing is the reason for the performance. As we saw in Chapter 4, such pieces can end because someone else wishes to take a turn or simply because the signer has run out of ideas, rather than because of any overarching structure, and audiences still find the piece very satisfying. However, where the audience has clear expectations of how things should end, if the closure is seen to be 'weak' the piece is weak.

The rules governing the opening and closing of a story vary depending on the tradition and the genre of the story. For example, Axel Olrik's (1909) laws of folklore state that stories should not start with sudden action and should not end abruptly. Instead, they should begin by moving from calm to excitement and end by moving from excitement to calm. Sudden beginnings and ends are more common in literary forms such as short stories and poems. As we have argued that the division between folklore and literary forms is blurred in sign languages, and that there is also no clear dividing line between stories and poems (see Chapter 11), we can be open to any number of different ways to open and close a piece of signed art.

It is not always easy to tell when a signed work starts and ends. The text is usually considered central to a poem, and we can focus on how that starts and ends. However, all sign language literature must be performed in some way, so the text can be framed by other performance devices such as the title and any gestures to indicate that the performance is about to begin or that it has finished (such as a nod or a bow). These performance devices may themselves be framed if the performer gives an introduction to the poem or comments on it after the performance.

Beyond this, in live performances, there are the transition moments that occur when a person takes on the role of performer and when the performer role stops, signalling that the event is over. The recording of Penny Gunn's poem *Deaf Studies* shows the impact these transition points can have on the sense of closure of a poem. After her performance, she steps out of her role as performer and her facial expression shows her personal feelings about the performance of her personal poem. Similarly, at the end of Jesus Marchan's ASL haiku *Fish*, the signer makes a brief gesture of triumph (as if to say, 'I've done it!'). The transition between the signer as a person and the signer as performer is not always seen in recordings of poems, perhaps for simple editing reasons, but it often forms a meaningful part of a live performance (captured on film) that would not have a similar equivalent in a studio setting.

Titles, introductions and other performance openers

People familiar with European-origin literary traditions are used to the idea that stories and poems begin with their title. This is particularly true with written literature but less so in oral literature. In folklore and oral situations, stories and jokes, for example, can be described as 'the one about...' rather than having a fixed title. Sign language stories, especially when they are performed informally, rarely start with a title and signing poets do not always give the title for their piece before starting the poem, perhaps in keeping with more oral traditions. When sign language poems do have titles, they usually define or describe the content of the poem, such as Paul Scott's *Tree* (which is indeed about a tree), or Dorothy Miles' *Elephants Dancing* (which describes dancing elephants). The poems' real meaning may be metaphorical (we see in Chapter 9 that *Elephants Dancing* should be understood as an attack on oralism and that *Tree* is an analogy for the resistance of the deaf community) but the titles are literal and the audiences must work to find the metaphors. In other cases, the title gives a hint or answer to the target of a metaphor. For example, Atiyah Asmal's *For My Aunt* is a poem about an anthropomorphised bee and the rose it loves. Although what they metaphorically represent is not stated in the poem itself, we know the rose represents the poet's aunt and the bee represents the poet, because of the title. Many of the titles of Paul Scott's poems are not direct or obvious representations of the content, such as *Too Busy to Hug, No Time to See,*[2] *No Mask Like Home,* and *We'll Meet Again.*

Titles sometimes describe the form of the poem, so that, for example, several sign language poems in anthologies we have seen are merely entitled *Haiku* or *Renga*. Dorothy Miles' poem *Trio* is indeed in three parts (with each stanza having its own title – *Morning, Afternoon* and *Evening*).

If a signed text has a title, the author usually chooses it, but this is not always the case. It is quite common for poems in non-literate cultures to be untitled because there is no need for titles when poet and audience are together, but when the work is recorded in some way, the compiler of a collection or anthology needs a title so it can be listed and referenced to allow other people to find it. If possible, they can consult with the author or performer, but if that is not possible, they simply have to choose one. Audiences may also choose their own title for a sign language piece, especially if there is a particular arresting sign that makes it memorable. Fernanda Machado's *Flight over Rio (Voo sobre Rio)* is often referred to by audiences as 'Kissing Birds' because of the sign she uses to express the birds' kiss, Dorothy Miles' *Trio* is frequently recognised as 'Twin-trees' because of a creative sign in the poem, and Richard Carter's *Snow Globe* as 'Signing Reindeer'.

The performer can signal the start and end of the performance with a specific body posture. Signed performances often start with the poet's hands folded low in front of their bodies and their heads lowered. They raise their head, look directly at the audience and may sign 'Title' before giving the title. This is often followed by a pause (sometimes with the hands folded again) and the performer's gaze shifts away from the audience (often looking down) before the poem begins. This prepares the audience for the start of the work and gives time to reflect on the title. Returning the hands to this position and lowering the head can also signal the end of the poem. On rare occasions, the poet walks off the stage while still performing (as in Johanna Mesch's *Earthquake*), or turns his or her back to the audience so that the performance cannot be continued (as in Paul Scott's *I Know Who (Stole My Heart)*).

Sometimes the performer gives a brief introduction to the piece, highlighting some part of it or drawing attention to a particular metaphor. This helps audiences prepare for the piece. There are introductions before the poems in the recordings we have of Nigel Howard's *Deaf* and Paul Scott's *Roz: Teach a Dog a New Trick* and there is an introduction and closing remarks in at least one version of Dorothy Miles' *Elephants Dancing*. Sometimes performers warn or advise the audience about what they are about to see. For example, John Wilson in one of his performances alerted the audience, 'It's a very short poem, so don't blink or you will miss it!' However, editors of collections don't always include these introductions as part of the collection, so it is not always easy to say how they affect the opening (or closing) of a poem.

The beginning: 'cracking the whip'

Steven Ryan, a great ASL storyteller as well as researcher (whose research we explored in previous chapters), advised novice storytellers to 'capture your audience with a well-baited hook' (1993, p. 148). This advice to hook the audience from the start is even more important in poetry where a strong poem has a strong beginning to catch the audience's attention. There will be something striking or different about the opening so that it is frequently dramatic or mysterious. Several of Richard Carter's poems begin with someone sleeping or dreaming, preparing us for something possibly surreal to happen (*Owl, Looking for Diamonds* and *Cochlear Implant* all begin this way). The poem may also start with a direct question that the audience hopes will be answered in the poem, such as Donna Williams' question 'Who am I?'

Forceful beginnings may use signs that are unusually large to capture the audience's attention. The Dutch poet Wim Emmerik's *Garden of Eden* starts with a large expansive sign EARTH and Dorothy Miles' BSL poem *The Staircase* begins with the signs FOREST DARK, both of which use both hands and forearms to make the sign and have all fingers open. Forcefulness may lead a poem to begin with a command to the audience (or imagined audience) as Paul Scott's poem *Blue Suit* begins with the command 'Blue suit, you, don't!' There may also be something unexpected about the opening of the performance. In Richard Carter and David Ellington's poem *Deaf Gay*, the two signers begin by joining hands, which is unusual and immediately catches the attention of the audience.

The ending: stopping or concluding?

All poems and stories stop eventually, but a strong piece usually ends with closure that creates a coherent, complete and stable feel to the work. Ye (1996) has pointed out that a story or poem can truly end at the last line, or it can be 'dynamic', so that is seems poised to take off again when the audience finally sees the total pattern of the piece. The sense of closure in a sign language poem can come from formal and thematic structures in the poem's text, as well as from the performance features that we considered earlier.

Poems may close gently with a sense that there is no more to be said, or sharply with something unexpected. In Richard Carter's *Identities*, the final defiant signs do not permit any further debate about the character's identity. In Nigel Howard's *Deaf*, forcing the cochlear implants into the baby is such a shocking sign after the gentle signs that preceded it, that nothing further can be added. Other pieces, however, may not close fully when they end. Richard Carter's *Shop Window* ends when the mannequin slaps the window dresser for taking liberties with her, and we are left to imagine what happens next. The ultimate conclusion of the event in the story is often not explicitly stated. This is especially effective when the ending is negative or undesirable because it leaves the audience feeling unsettled, as in Johanna Mesch's *Ocean* (which ends when the ocean has taken in the 'poison'). We also see this in Wim Emmerik's *Garden of Eden* (which ends with the eating of a forbidden apple) and Paul Scott's *Turkey* (which ends with the turkey's realisation that Christmas is approaching). Many signed haiku poems end with a surreal twist that leaves audiences with a delicious sense of chaotic poetic closure. John Wilson's *Morning* and one of Johanna Mesch's *Three Haiku* are delightfully bizarre in their closure, creating a sense of opening out as audiences try to make sense of what they see.

The poet may open the poem again just after the expected point of closure, teasing the audience with the idea that what they thought was the end is not so. Johanna Mesch's *Party* could have ended when the protagonist stabs herself and collapses, but, quite unexpectedly, she rises again. The linguistic trick here lies in the direction of the performer's hand showing how the knife is handled when the character appears to stab herself. Careful attention shows that the knife blade is pointing away from the body so the character hits her chest with the knife handle.

Like all conventions, those that create closure in a poem change and vary but there are elements that typically occur at endings and audiences recognise them as endings. We will now explore some of these conventions, drawing on the work of Herrnstein-Smith (1968).

Closure devices created by the 'voice' of the poet – showing and telling

We have briefly observed in the previous chapters that some signed pieces 'narrate' the story by addressing the audience, whereas others more directly show the action to the audience. These different ways of telling or showing are called voice (a narrative voice and a more dramatic voice), and they can create different endings. Some poems open with an image of the external world and close with an expression of thought or emotion, while others open with an expression of thought or emotion and close with an image of the external world. Ye (1996) has noted that poems in Chinese and other 'Eastern' (from a European perspective) traditions tend to end with scenic closures, while those from Western and European traditions tend to end with statements and abstractions. Many sign language poems we have seen end with presented images more like Chinese ones, especially where the poems are mainly concrete. Johanna Mesch's *Kayak* ends with an image of the setting sun glittering on the water. They may also end with a shift into a character who shows some sort of emotion, for example, as Paul Scott's turkey (in *Turkey*) that gulps in fear when it realises the implication of the falling snowflake, or the boy in John Wilson's *Icon* who punches the air with delight when he catches Marilyn Monroe's kiss.

Chinese poetry traditionally starts with concrete images, moves to more abstract ideas and ends with a more concrete image. However, we have found that most sign language poems that begin by showing ideas through concrete representation rarely shift between concrete and abstract, although they frequently end with a shift into direct representation of a character to show rather than to tell.

Sign language poems that explore ideas rather than create narratives do not have natural stopping points driven by their content and these often follow the traditional 'Western' structure of ending with abstract ideas. Donna Williams' poem *That Day* provides concrete images of a series of things she would change about the hearing world's relationship with deaf people, before making the more abstract summarising statement that on the day they have all changed she will stop claiming a Disability Living Allowance. Dorothy Miles' *Elephants Dancing* and Paul Scott's *Blue Suit* both use extended metaphor throughout the entire poem – the elephants stand for deaf people and the blue suits are a symbol of power and success – so they present concrete images, but they conclude with abstract comments, that tell rather than show, as the poetic narrator declares an opinion. For example, Paul Scott ends *Blue Suit* by appearing to step into the real world to tell the women in his audience 'No, don't do it!'

Closure devices driven by content of the text

Closure in many stories occurs when we have reached the natural end of the story and to go any further would require a major shift in plot. Because storytelling is the origin of so much sign language poetry, this influences the closure of many sign language poems. The death of the protagonist is a firm stopping point for any story and this, for example, creates the natural closure at the end of Richard Carter's *Make-up Theatre* once the diva has died. The resolution of a problem set for the protagonist is another closure point, as seen in John Wilson's *Time,* which ends when the boy has submitted his essay. If the work describes a journey, it logically ends at the destination and Paul Scott's *Train Journey* does indeed end when the train arrives. *Fashion Times* by Richard Carter and Paul Scott works through the decades from 1900 to the present day, so it ends when there are no more fashions to present.

Natural endings also occur when we can predict what will happen next so there is no need to tell us more. In *Looking for Diamonds* and *Prince Looking for Love* (both by Richard Carter), the lovers have found each other and the audience expects they will 'live happily ever after'.

It is a common folklore device for a poem or song to finish when it gets back to the beginning. Paul Scott's *Tree* and Richard Carter's *Surprise Apple* both consider the cycle of life, so that *Tree* ends when a new tree sprouts in the same way as the first tree did at the beginning, and *Surprise Apple* ends when another caterpillar emerges from another apple, like the caterpillar at the start of the poem. Audiences know that if the poem continued it would merely repeat the cycle because nothing has fundamentally changed.

Closure devices within the form of the text

While the content of a sign language text can determine its point of closure, the form of the signs often works with it. A change in the metrical regularity of a poem can indicate when the poem will close, and the concluding words in a spoken poem are often delivered with a special slowing tempo, a lowering pitch and increased force and duration, cuing the audience that the end is coming. The rhythm or speed of a sign language poem also changes, as it often slows down, with the final sign being held for an unusually long time. In many instances, the final sign is particularly arresting and often novel, as in Dorothy Miles' TWIN-TREES (which marks the end of the first stanza in *Trio*). The final sign often has a noticeably larger or sharper movement, and holding it longer than any other sign makes it appear 'louder' or more sonorous (there are many examples, of which the last sign in John Wilson's *Two Communities*

is one). However, performers have the option to break these conventions, so audiences notice when the sign is not held for the extra time
and the poem comes to an unexpectedly abrupt end. Nigel Howard's
haiku *Deaf* provides an example of this when the final sign is delivered
swiftly and Nigel appears from the poetic world unusually rapidly, to
increase the shocking effect of what he has just shown.

Other shock endings include using a taboo sign. One version of *Fashion
Times* ends with the character producing an obscene gesture and Wim
Emmerik's *Garden of Eden* ends with a sign that is frequently glossed as
'a**hole'. Paul Scott's poem *Home*, unusually for a sign language poem,
ends when it takes on the character of a hearing person, and the poem
shocks the audience when the deaf performer screams to show the hearing
person screaming. Using sound in a signed performance is highly unusual
and is an effective closure device.

Repetition creates patterns that audiences can use to know when
a poem is complete. We will see in Chapter 13 that many poems and
stories rely on patterns of three, so that when a repetition has occurred,
audiences expect that the third presentation will provide a resolution (as
in Richard Carter's *Looking for Diamonds*). This is especially common in
jokes. Sometimes poets use a pattern of 'three plus one' and the resolution
is signalled by a change in pattern when it is repeated for the fourth time
(as in Paul Scott's *Roz: Teach a Dog a New Trick*).

The structure of a sign language poem can also be determined by the structure of the signer's body. Paul Scott's *Five Senses* works through the fingers of
one hand and thus closure has to occur once he has reached the final finger.
This sense of closure is especially strong because it combines the logical
closure point of the ideas (the poet has now considered all five of the senses)
with the logical closure point of the physical possibilities of one hand.

A piece also ends when it has reached a point in its structure to give
expectations of ending, such as we see in an acrostic or in other ABC or
number stories or poems (see Chapter 5). This is sometimes called formal
parallelism. Paul Scott's acrostic *Deaf* uses signs with handshapes reflecting the letters 'd', 'e', 'a' and 'f'. The poem closes when the sign using 'f' is
complete (see Figure 5.3, p. 51).

Placing or directing signs to the centre of the poet's signing space, or
returning to a state of symmetry often signals closure. During the poem's
development, signs may be placed asymmetrically and all around signing
space – left or right, or up or down – but the final sign brings everything
together at the centre or most stable core. As we can see in Figure 8.1,
Nigel Howard's *Deaf* ends with a final, symmetrical central sign. The
moment of closure in Donna Williams' *Who am I?* occurs when she
understands her multiple identity makes her a whole person, and the signs
that have been ranged to the left and right reach the centre of the body.

FIGURE 8.1   NIGEL HOWARD AND DONNA WILLIAMS PERFORMING POEMS WHERE THE CLOSURE OCCURS WITH A CENTRALISATION OF SIGNS

Summary

In this chapter, we have examined some of the devices that signers use to increase the impact of their performances by the way they open and close them. The types of titles, introductions and other performance openers, and the extent of their use may vary, depending on whether the work is more from an oral or a literary tradition, but sign language poems, especially, often open in a way that hooks the audience in immediately. The impact on an audience's emotions is often determined by the way the piece closes, and we have seen that there are conventions of closure in sign language literature that audiences can expect. There are variations in the 'voice' the performer uses at the end of the poem, with most sign language poetry ending by showing rather than telling, as the voice of a narrator or the poetic-I is less common than the character directly appearing to the audience. The content of stories and of poems that have a narrative form can drive the point of closure, and sign language poems often follow these narrative conventions, while also playing with them for extra effect. Finally, we have seen that the signing itself will show audiences the point of closure.

Notes

1. We would like to thank students from the Sign Language Folklore class in Swarthmore College, Philadelphia, 2012, for their input and observations.

2. This poem has been performed several times, and each one has a slightly different title, such as *Too Busy to Hug, Too Blind to See.*

Further reading

The ideas in this chapter draw extensively on the ideas of Barbara Herrnstein Smith in her classic work *Poetic Closure: A Study of How Poems End* (1968, University of Chicago Press).

Yang Ye's *Chinese Poetic Closure* (1996, Peter Lang) is especially useful for suggesting how poems outside the 'Western' literary tradition might end.

If you want to read more about Olrik's laws:

Olrik, Axel (1909 [1965]) 'Epic laws of folk narrative' in Alan Dundes (ed.) *The Study of Folklore* (Englewood Cliffs, NJ: Prentice Hall).

Activities

1. Opening
   Look at the opening of five sign language stories or poems that you think are particularly effective. What is unusual or intriguing about the beginning? Are the signs or content unexpected? Does it start with a question or a statement, or does it present a strong visual image?

2. Closure
   Choose five sign language stories or poems that you think have particularly effective endings. (In BSL you might like to look at: *Duck and Dissertation* (Donna Williams), *Party* (Johanna Mesch), *Deaf* (Nigel Howard), *Make-up Theatre* (Richard Carter), *Time* (John Wilson) and *Trio* and *Elephants Dancing* (Dorothy Miles) – all available on the YouTube channel that accompanies this book.)

   - What devices do the poets use to conclude the story or poem?
   - Are they signalled by the content?
   - Are they signalled by the structure of the signs?
   - Are they signalled by the performance?

3. Find examples of sign language stories or poems that end with an unexpected twist or a swift 'punch' (signed haiku offer good examples – for instance, see the twist at the end of each of Johanna Mesch's four seasons haiku, posted on the YouTube channel that accompanies this book). How does the signer create the final impact of the sign?

9 Plots, Protagonists, Subjects and Themes

We have often referred in previous chapters to what a certain sign language story, poem or joke is 'about'. In this chapter, we will focus on what signers talk about when they produce creative signing, looking at the plots, protagonists, subjects (topics) and themes that occur in sign language literature.

The purpose of certain forms of literature affects their content. For example, the function of a text could be to offer praise (maybe to God or to an important community member), to encourage other people to change their behaviour, to express personal feelings, to change society, to teach facts, or merely to play with language, and each of these will generate different content. The importance given to these different functions of literature, varies across cultures and across literary genres. It has also varied over time. Within European literature, for example, the Romantic Movement of the first half of the 19th century, produced subjective, intimate literature, with idealistic perspectives, so Romantic stories and poems often addressed ideas of nationalism, nature and longing for things past. The Realist Movement in the second half of the 19th century, on the other hand, focused less on emotions than on matters of contemporary life. The Modernists of the early 20th century focused especially on the form of language as a way to represent an idea visually. Today, the poetic movement of slam poetry is more likely to focus on demands for social justice. Although the history of sign language literature is shorter than that of written literature, we can see all of these different approaches in sign language stories and poems.

Plot

A plot is the sequence of events that make up a story. In creative signing, the content will be determined in part by its plot. Not all fictional work or creative signing has a plot, and some poems simply describe a scene or situation. For example, the traditional haiku form expressly rejects the idea of plot and instead aims to create a single snapshot image of a moment. Nigel

Howard's signed haiku *England* is a good example of a descriptive poem with no action. (England/ Vast green fields/ An ancient brick). That said, there is action and a very brief plot development in many sign language haiku (Kaneko, 2008). Sign languages, as kinetic languages, are natural vehicles for showing action, and where action leads, plots soon follow.

Deaf communities are bilingual and bicultural, and signers are familiar with at least some of the folklore or other creative culture of surrounding hearing societies. Internationally widespread stories, especially those that have been made into popular films (making them more visually accessible to deaf people) such as *Cinderella, The Ugly Duckling* and *Little Red Ridinghood* have influenced deaf signers around the world. In addition, deaf and hearing people share their own folkloric traditions and cultural history with their national communities. Greek deaf people are especially familiar with Aesop's Fables and Greek myths because they are Greek; Brazilian deaf people know the stories of the Saci and the activities of Tiradentes and Lampião because they are Brazilian; British deaf people know about Robin Hood and Guy Fawkes because they are British. The widespread influence of these folkloric tales means that plots created by deaf artists may have similar structures. However, when signed pieces are original works rather than translations of works from outside the deaf community, the plots (in some way) also reflect a deaf person's view of the world and of how to live in it.

Booker (2004), drawing on folkloric study, has suggested that stories in all cultures draw on seven universal plots: Man against Monster, Rags to Riches, Voyage and Return, The Quest, Rebirth, Comedy and Tragedy. If he is right that they are universal, we should not be surprised to see the same fundamental plots arising in sign language stories and we can use them to see patterns in sign language literature, but we can expect them to take a specifically deaf cultural approach. Bearing in mind that one story can have several plots within it, we can see that sign language literature also draws on these plots.

Man against Monster

In sign language literature, protagonists often encounter a 'monster' (someone or something powerful that creates a problem for the protagonist). The stories that show how deaf people have survived and even thrived as deaf people, despite attempts by wider hearing society to stop them, are examples of 'overcoming the monster'. The monster may be human, animal or plant, but in whatever form, it has some human characteristics. This plot is seen in many sign language stories, where the role of the human 'monster' is played by people who try to prevent deaf characters from fulfilling their true potential. In Richard Carter's *Deaf Trees*, the man who cuts down the brown (deaf) trees is the monster who must be stopped. In *Cochlear Implant*, the monster is the implant who tries to change the protagonist's sense of being a whole deaf person.

Not all signed pieces that battle a monster have an explicitly deaf theme. Donna Williams' *Red and Green* tells of the fight of her immune system against a cold virus – a monster experienced universally. In the South African context, the monster is often the apartheid system. Deaf people ally with hearing people to fight against racial discrimination (see Brian Meyer's *District Six*). The monsters can also be more abstract problems, such as fear, guilt or ignorance. In Paul Scott's *No Mask like Home*, the protagonist is attacked by monstrous birds, books and doors, representing shame, embarrassment and bad attitudes for him to overcome.

Sometimes, although unusually, the monster wins. In Penny Beschizza's *Grass,* the strong sun (the monster) withers the gentle grass (which possibly represents deaf people). In *District Six,* the protagonist loses his house in the forced removal.

Rags to Riches

In many plots, a protagonist lacks something specific at the start and gets it by the end of the story.[1] In the terms of Vladimir Propp, the Russian folklorist, there is first a lack and then a liquidation of lack. The lack may be of money, or love, respect, knowledge or a true sense of identity. We see the transformation of lack (rags) to liquidation of lack (riches) in many sign language poems and stories, especially where the protagonist starts with no language or sense of deaf identity but learns sign language and becomes a member of the deaf community by the end. For many deaf people, these are extraordinary riches. The group of deaf people in Dorothy Miles' allegory *The Staircase* start in 'rags' of ignorance as they are lost in the forest, but as they struggle up the staircase, they are rewarded with the 'riches' of their degree (represented at one stage by a glittering golden sword). *The Ugly Duckling* is a good example of the rags to riches plot, as an ordinary, insignificant person is revealed to be exceptional. Versions of this are popular in sign language stories, as the duckling learns it is deaf and develops beautiful signing skills.

Voyage and Return

Although plots are linear, as events unroll through time, we saw in Chapter 8 that stories may end where they began. This is can be seen in plots that represent 'Voyage and Return'. The protagonist leaves home for a journey (not always willingly or planned) and returns, usually changed in some way. In Ben Bahan's *Ball Story*, the ball leaves the scientist's laboratory and travels around town, collecting companions. When it returns to the laboratory, it smiles happily. In Paul Scott's *We'll Meet Again* there is a clear voyage and return as the water droplets part and are reunited after their journey (with a sense of reassurance at the end that deaf people will be reunited after separation). In Fernanda Machado's *Flight over Rio*, the bird returns to the distant land where it came from, but now it has a (deaf) companion to love. In John Wilson's *Time*, the boy travels back to the past to learn about time and returns to his classroom in his own time with knowledge from a deaf teacher from history.

The Quest

In a quest, the protagonist deliberately sets out from home on a dangerous journey to seek something, often with companions. The quest of the Arthurian knights to find the Holy Grail is perhaps one of the best-known in English literature. Culhwch's quest for Olwen in the Welsh *Mabinogion* is another example. The film adaptation of Tolkein's *The Lord of the Rings* has made it a very well-known quest story. There are many deaf stories that involve a quest, usually at some level for the deaf protagonist to find their deaf identity or their 'true home' in the deaf community. Cynthia Peters (2000) has observed that many deaf people need to find their identity and that their quest is to find 'home'. This quest for home is common in American literature generally (Dorothy's quest for home in the *Wizard of Oz* is one example) but is widely explored in sign language literature. For example, John Wilson's *Home* can be interpreted as a deaf boy's quest (although not explicitly stated) to find where he belongs.

Dorothy Miles' *The Staircase* and Paul Scott's *Macbeth of the Lost Ark* describe quests for the protagonist to find the true and valuable knowledge of the deaf community. In *Macbeth of the Lost Ark*, it is achieved through lessons of hard work and humility, on a journey fraught with terror, blood and the threat of death. David Ellington's *The Story of the Flag* tells of a horseman and his companions who ride to capture the flag, which in this case is an allegory for their search for a good education for deaf people. Richard Carter's *Looking for Diamonds*, however is a quest that either a deaf or hearing person could go on, as the protagonist struggles through snow and bewildering dreams, temporarily even losing his home, to capture the diamond that allows him to find his true love.

On a quest, the protagonist often needs to find a path between peril-ous opposites to achieve their goal. Donna Williams' *Who am I?* rejects an impossible 'deaf identity' and an impossible 'hearing identity' to find the middle path that leads to her understanding of herself.

Rebirth or Redemption

In these stories, the protagonist redeems a bad situation, making it better. In stories such as *Sleeping Beauty*, the Prince is able to redeem the sleeping Princess and in *Beauty and the Beast*, the Princess redeems the Prince. In Paul Scott's *Guilty*, the protagonist repents his dishonest behaviour and is redeemed. In Richard Carter's *Jack in the Box*, the boy is redeemed by the personified Jack in the box who teaches him right from wrong. In Paul's *Tree* and Johanna Mesch's *Party* both involve the plot of 'rebirth' after a bad incident (cutting down the tree and breaking up with the lover, respectively). The plane in Johanna's *Aeroplane* is resurrected after the crash, leaving the audience with a sense of redemption.

Comedy

Booker's notion of comedy is very different from our general modern understanding of the word. In his explanation, comedies are not neces-sarily humorous but are plots where there is a transition from ignorance to knowledge. Stories with a 'happy ending' of liberation, fulfilment or understanding are comedies. Thus, stories of confronting monsters, quests, rags to riches and voyages can all include elements of comedy, because the end result of these is often that confusion is resolved and leads to clearer understanding. The protagonist in a comedy is essentially a 'good' person who will find fulfilment, Johanna Mesch's *Party* is not a humorous piece, but it is a comedy as it shows the protagonist come to understand she is better off out of her relationship. Richard Carter's *Cochlear Implant* is humorous at times, but is a comedy because the protagonist comes to understand that he is a whole deaf person in his own right and the coch-lear implant is not the benign technology it pretends to be.

Tragedy

Booker summarises the stages in a tragedy as: Anticipation (the hero is incomplete or unfulfilled), Dream (the hero commits to a course of action in order to find fulfilment and the action seems to be working),

Frustration (when things start to go wrong), Nightmare (as they spiral out of control) and Destruction. The protagonist in a tragedy is a 'flawed hero' who wants something that 'violates or defies some prohibition or law ... or standard of normality' (Booker, 2004, p. 173), and the tragedy ends unhappily with the protagonist's discomfort, frustration, confusion or death. Tragedy has been a very common plot in written literature – Shakespeare wrote a number of tragedies (such as *Macbeth* and *Othello*). More recently, Okonkwo, the protagonist in Chinua Achebe's *Things Fall Apart*, faithfully follows the above stages to destruction.

In sign language literature, Richard Carter's *Make-up Theatre* is an example of tragedy as the diva appears to be able to keep herself beautiful to be loved but comes to realise she is not loved, and takes her own life. Although the story is a tragedy, the earlier parts are funny, as humour is used to move the story along.

Perhaps the best-known signed tragedy is *Bird of a Different Feather* (an allegory about deaf identity, most closely associated with Ben Bahan in ASL[2] although Nelson Pimenta has recorded a Libras version), in which a songbird realises that by striving to be an eagle it has failed to be either. The little bird's 'incompletion' (in Booker's terms) is that it is not an eagle; its dream is to become most like an eagle; frustrations build up as other young eagles mock the new beak as looking like a parrot's; nightmare descends as the songbirds also reject it; destruction occurs as the bird flies into the sunset. In a tragedy, step by step, the hero becomes separated from family and friends and we see this as the songbird leaves its eagle family and then is rejected by the songbirds.

Tragedies can be light-hearted and humorously portrayed despite the name, but the hero's ultimate undoing with the realisation that his schemes have failed remains. In Richard Carter's *Shop Window*, essentially a version of *Pygmalion*, the protagonist creates and falls in love with the dummy in the shop window that he has made but when he takes his amorous advances too far, he loses all when the dummy slaps him. In *Mirror*, the mirror pushes the other mirrors aside to be chosen by the purchaser and finally comes to understand the loneliness of a mirror with no one to look at it.

Protagonists

The events that unfold in a plot usually relate to a protagonist, the character with whom audiences expect to be able to identify as they see the story unfold. This protagonist might be the real author (in a genuine narrative of personal experience), the implied author (in a story told of 'someone like me'), the narrator or a character in the story. Age, gender or physical appearance of the protagonist do not matter much in sign language literature. Unless otherwise indicated, we simply transfer the features of the poet onto the protagonist he or she is representing. What often does matter in sign language literature, however, is the question of whether the protagonist is deaf or not.

In most sign language literature, audiences identify particularly strongly with a deaf protagonist. Sometimes the storyteller explicitly says the protagonist is deaf by using the sign DEAF. Donna Williams' *Who Am I?*, John Wilson's *Home* and Richard Carter's *Deaf Trees* are just three examples from a great many. More often, however, the content of the story makes this clear, with perhaps the most obvious being that the protagonist uses sign language. Additionally, the characters may fail to hear something (for example in Donna Williams' *That Day* or Richard Carter's *Cochlear Implant*). The protagonist may use specifically deaf technology such as a hearing aid (in Richard Carter's *Snow Globe*), cochlear implants or flashing lights or vibrating alarms (as seen in *World Renga I* by Leo Loubser, Miro Civin, Deborah Van Halle, Ashni Kumar, Megan Alexander and Mark MacQueen). Characters naturally engage in behaviour that deaf people identify as deaf – tapping someone for attention (in Paul Scott's *Five Senses*), lipreading (Richard Carter's *Owl*) or standing in a circle (in Richard Carter's *Deaf Trees*).

Not all protagonists are explicitly marked as deaf, but they have other characteristics that allow audiences to identify with them. In Richard Carter's *Children's Park,* the super-hero neither signs nor speaks, but his character appeals to the deep-seated wish in many of us to have our own super-powers (in this case the ability to stop a speeding bullet and save a child's life). In some stories, the protagonist is hearing. In Richard's *Make-up Theatre*, the diva is clearly hearing (shown through the motif of music, something strongly associated with hearing people) but her grief at the loss of love is so universal that everyone can identify with her anguish.

As we have seen in Chapter 7, non-human protagonists are popular in sign language literature. Audiences can identify with them because they are portrayed as having human emotions and often go through similar life stages. In Paul Scott's *Tree*, for example, we watch a seed grow to a mature tree before it is cut down and replaced by a seed that grows to be another tree, representing the cycle of life for humans too. Non-humans also battle against surrounding forces. In many sign language stories, deaf audiences see the non-humans' struggles as metaphors for deaf people's struggles within hearing society. *Tree* can be taken as a story about the resilience of the deaf community in the face of oppression by hearing people, as the tree is cut down but another one takes its place.

Subjects and themes

The subject of a story or poem is a concrete and literal topic, being what the text is 'about'. For example, the subject of Paul Scott's *Roz: Teach a Dog a New Trick* is a dog that chases clumsily-thrown balls, and the subject of *Macbeth of the Lost Ark*, is the quest of a person who must choose a way to create light. In the story of *The Ugly Duckling*, a lonely misfit swan is the subject. The events that occur in the piece and the behaviour of the characters that form its subject will be ways to represent the theme. Themes are higher-order abstract ideas, such as life, death, eternity, justice, youth, fear, love and power. Themes are timeless, universal ideas that are relevant to everyone. There is usually a major theme in a text but there are often other, minor themes, too. The themes are rarely stated clearly and sometimes they only emerge after the reader has thought in some depth about what the text 'is trying to say'. The theme of *Roz: Teach a Dog a New Trick* is the abstract idea of the correct form of education for deaf children and the main theme of *Macbeth of the Lost Ark* is the deaf way of seeking enlightenment, while other themes might be determination, humility and courage. The theme of *The Ugly Duckling* is finding one's true sense of identity.

There has been surprisingly little work reporting surveys of larger bodies of sign language literature on themes. Most work has been done on small collections – sometimes a single poem. Sarah Taub (2006) explored sign language themes of eternity and unity in Ella Mae Lentz's ASL poem *Circle of Life*, and Alec Ormsby (1995), comparing Clayton Valli's ASL poem *Snowflake* with Coleridge's *Frost at Midnight*, found that both poems had themes of isolation and lack of shared understanding.

Christie and Wilkins (2007), however, carried out a large-scale review and analysis of 53 ASL poems by four poets. They identified themes of resistance, affirmation and liberation. These themes are also clearly visible in literature in other sign languages.

Ben Bahan (2006b) also conducted a large-scale study to analyse the themes and character categories in 500 ASL stories. He found that three main themes come up repeatedly in signed deaf narratives of personal experience:

- Communication, language and values.
- Social prejudice and ignorance.
- Sensory worlds.

Exploring these themes allows deaf storytellers and their audiences to understand their cultural heritage through their language heritage.

Although themes are universal and timeless, they relate to society, which is not universal, so it is important to understand how a deaf poet's view of society is reflected in the universal themes. Thus, which themes are chosen and what subjects express them show the importance and perspective that deaf storytellers and poets attach to the basic concepts.

Some types of literature can be expected to have certain themes precisely because they are defined by those themes. For example, elegiac poetry is poetry of mourning for the dead or a lament for lost loves, lost time, lost youth or ways of life. In many deaf communities, a poet will be called upon to perform a poem at the funeral of a community member. Barry Curtis' BSL poem *Farewell Sweet Dreamer*, for example, is an elegy to Dorothy Miles. Signed laments can be for non-deaf people too, as we can see in Alan Henry Godinho's Libras poem *Tribute to Santa Maria* (*Homenagem Santa Maria*) a lament for 233 students who died in a fire in the Brazilian city of Santa Maria in 2013. Modiegi Moime's *June 16th* is dedicated to students who died in the Soweto Uprising in 1976 (see Chapter 17).

Themes are often shown through thematic personifications – representing them through a person experiencing that particular theme. Sign language offers an ideal means for thematic personifications as poets can 'embody' an abstract notion. For example, Oppression is represented by the oppressed elephants in Dorothy Miles' *Elephants Dancing*. Liberty is seen in the dog in *Roz: Teach a Dog a New Trick* as it catches the ball and refuses to return. Resistance is shown in Paul Scott's *Tree*, Despair is seen in Richard Carter's *Make-up Theatre* and Vanity in his *Grass Hairstyle*, and Determination is seen in Donna Williams' *Duck and Dissertation*.

For the final part of this chapter, we will explore the *Life & Deaf* collection composed by deaf teenagers in London, to reveal some of the content and themes that young British deaf people consider are important. This is because we believe we can develop a much broader understanding of themes in sign language literature if we study material from signers in a broad age range, with different language, family and social backgrounds and educational experiences.

Themes in Life & Deaf

The poems in the collection *Life & Deaf*[3] were composed by deaf children and young people educated in the London borough of Greenwich. Like adults, many of the young poets make explicit reference to their deafness in their poems in a variety of ways. Unusually, they often reflect negative attitudes to their experiences. For example, Richard Achiampong says in

Look at the Front, 'I don't want to be deaf/I want to be hearing, happy, free./ Being deaf is boring/... / I hate signing, signing, signing'.[4] This is an important point to acknowledge because most adult sign language poetry celebrates deafness. Young people are finding out who they are and need to express who they feel themselves to be. Frequently, the poems express strong emotions about other people's reactions to their deafness, not their deafness itself.

They also express deep frustration to hearing people's attitudes. Tiffany Hudson says explicitly 'I hate being deaf' in *Just Like You*, but makes it clear that when her hearing friends sign 'then we are so smiley and happy, / Just like you.' This implies that it is not her deafness she hates but the fact that others will not sign to her. Hayley McWilliams' *Street Signs* objects to the way that hearing people stare at her when she signs with her friends in the street, but she makes it clear that signing with them makes her 'Laughing, giggling, chatting, all in a good mood'. Again, the problem is perceived as lying firmly with the hearing people's attitudes to her deafness and the signing that is the outward manifestation of her deafness.

The young poets may express ambivalence about their deafness or a sense of 'inbetweenness'. Sarah Teacy is uncertain how to answer the question posed in *What's it like to be deaf?* She shows an ambivalence that might be expected in a young person trying to discover their identity: 'Being deaf is cool and not cool/ It's sometimes hard to be deaf/ ... / But it's good in some ways I don't know why.' Sixteen-year-old Sean Timon's *Half Personal Poetry* shows an exceptionally mature approach to the liminal place in which he finds himself, and the way he uses language to portray this. Using signs in symmetrically opposing and yet balancing areas to the left and right, he sums up his personality traits before describing his identity as half Irish and half Caribbean, half white and half black, half deaf and half hearing and, finally, half signing and half speaking. His concluding lines 'I want to belong half in the deaf world and half in the hearing world/ I don't want to half belong in a whole world' characterise a very different world view from that portrayed by sign poets in recent years. For many deaf activists, an acceptance of a deaf identity has meant a single focus upon being a signing, deaf person, committed to the deaf world. Sean's poem rejects that identity for one more fluid, more fragmented and yet more satisfying.

Celebration of speech with the help of a cochlear implant can also be observed in this collection of young deaf people's poems. *Being Deaf* by Chi Ngo further challenges the traditional messages carried in sign language poetry, with positive remarks about a cochlear implant. This may appear surprising, as many sign language poems by deaf adults have previously rejected the cochlear implant and all that it stands for. However, the acceptance of a cochlear implant in this poem is not a rejection of either deafness or sign language. Instead, it is an acceptance of an outlook that may be described by the phrase 'Many ways to be deaf': 'Did you hear? I can hear now/ English, Vietnamese and sign language/ Always put on my cochlear implant/ Feel relaxed and have good fun.'

Summary

We saw in this chapter that sign language literature consists of the same plot types that have been described as universal in spoken and written literature, but we also saw that these plots are represented by specific language and cultural experiences of deaf people. The protagonists in these stories are frequently deaf, even when the protagonist is not human, because deaf audiences are most likely to relate to deaf protagonists, but we also saw that the hearing status is not always clear and some original signed creations include hearing protagonists. To complement descriptions of the content of sign language literature created by older signers, we looked here at the work of some younger signers and saw evidence of changes in what is expressed in sign language poetry. Despite this, the younger poets' work reflects positive deaf experiences and a sense of deaf identity, as does that of older poets.

Notes

1. As in the Japanese folktale *The Straw Millionaire,* in which a poor man who only possessed a straw at the beginning becomes a millionaire by exchanging the straw for oranges, oranges for clothes, clothes for a horse and so on.
2. Available in a DVD accompanying Supalla and Bahan (2007).
3. Life & Deaf was a speech and language therapy project aiming to develop the children's communication, confidence and self-esteem through poetry in BSL and English. The children were encouraged to use the poetry to explore their identities as teenagers, as deaf people and in other ways. Adult deaf poets guided the children but encouraged them to present their own feelings and thoughts.
4. Translations from BSL performances in this section are provided by Life & Deaf http://www.lifeanddeaf.co.uk/.

Further reading

To see more examples of different plots (in written literature):

Booker, Christopher (2004) *The Seven Basic Plots – Why We Tell Stories* (London: Continuum).

For themes in sign language literature:

Christie, Karen and Dorothy Wilkins (2007) 'Themes and symbols in ASL poetry: resistance, affirmation and liberation', *Deaf Worlds*, 22, 1–49.

Ormsby, Alec (1995) 'Poetic cohesion in American Sign Language: Valli's "Snowflake" & Coleridge's "Frost at Midnight"', *Sign Language Studies*, 88, 227–244.

Taub, Sarah (2006) 'Conceptual "rhymes" in sign language poetry' in Harvey Goodstein (ed.) *The Deaf Way II Reader* (Washington, DC: Gallaudet University Press).

Activities

1. Choose three poems or pieces of signed fiction in a sign language that you know. (David Ellington's *The Story of the Flag*, Donna Williams' *Bella's Penguins* and *Phoenix Garden*, and Johanna Mesch's *Twin Leaves* can be used as examples. They are all posted on the YouTube channel that accompanies this book.)

   What plot types of Booker's list – Man against Monster, Rags to Riches, The Quest, Voyage and Return, Rebirth, Comedy and Tragedy – do they follow? For each piece, say what appears to be the major plot type and if there are examples of other plots within it.

2. Christie and Wilkins identified the abstract themes of Oppression, Resistance and Liberation in ASL poetry. Look for examples of these themes in stories, poems or jokes in a sign language that you know. Explain how they are shown in the texts.

3. Using five poems in a sign language that you know identify the subjects of the poems and any abstract themes that they address.

10 Metaphor

In previous chapters (especially Chapter 9), we have explored various themes that appear in sign language poetry and stories. These themes are often embedded in poetic language through metaphor. The essence of metaphor is to understand and express one thing in terms of another (Lakoff and Johnson, 1980). This allows us to talk about abstract ideas that are difficult to grasp through more familiar and concrete terms. This chapter illustrates the basic mechanism of metaphor in creative sign language. We will briefly outline different views on metaphor, explore special features of poetic metaphor, and consider three major types of metaphor and some different linguistic levels in which metaphor is found.

How we apply our understanding of familiar concepts to that of less familiar ones is often governed by our bodily experience – that is, how we interact with the physical world through our body. For example, English speakers often talk about 'falling in love', based on our experience of gravity as an inevitable force and our understanding that you 'fall into' something unexpectedly and involuntarily. This understanding of a physical fall is used to describe the overpowering initial stage of being attracted to someone. The importance of bodily experience as a basis for metaphor is especially relevant in creative sign language, which uses the body as a major source of expression. As Rose puts it:

> The function of metaphor in language [can be seen] as a way to *embody* ideas, connecting thought with bodily experience…[D]eaf culture necessarily unites the body and the mind: communication and self-expression happen with the body, and thus, must be enacted or performed. (Rose, 1992, p. 8, emphasis in the original)

Creative sign language makes abstract concepts concrete by drawing on bodily experience. As sign language is embodied, creative signing can create a stronger and more direct link between thought and bodily experience than spoken languages.

Overview of metaphor

Traditional views on metaphor, represented by Aristotle and Cicero, regarded metaphor as intentional misuse of language, so that it is a deviant and decorative way to express our thought which can be rewritten with an orthodox, literal, non-metaphorical expression (for example, 'Jack is a lion.' as opposed to 'Jack is very brave.'). The Romantic poets, on the other hand, saw metaphor as insight. In their view, metaphor is not simply a decoration, but a way of shedding light on something which would otherwise remain unknown.

Since the 1980s, cognitive linguists (who study the connection between language and thought) have taken considerable interest in metaphor. Their view of metaphor differs fundamentally from earlier views in two respects. First of all, they challenge the dominant view of metaphor as something extra, unusual and deviant by claiming that metaphor is pervasive in our everyday life. In the seminal work titled *Metaphors We Live By*, George Lakoff and Mark Johnson (1980) introduced a range of examples of metaphors from our most mundane and least poetic resources – such as everyday conversations, news articles and idioms. Secondly, they believe that metaphor is not simply a matter of language but reveals how we conceptualise the world. Metaphor involves the mapping of concepts. Abstract concepts such as life, love, time and emotions are often expressed using more concrete concepts such as journeys, plants or food. A well-known example is LIFE IS A JOURNEY.[1] We tend to think, understand, and talk about life in terms of a journey. This conceptual metaphor produces a variety of expressions such as 'Look how far we've come' or 'We're at a crossroads' (Kövecses, 2002, p. 5). In general, cognitive linguists are more interested in the underlying metaphor (LIFE IS A JOURNEY) than its linguistic instantiations. Whereas linguistic metaphors may vary according to each language, the underlying conceptual metaphor is more universal because it is based on our basic cognition and bodily experience.

Three types of metaphor

Lakoff and Johnson (1980) identified three types of metaphor: orientational, ontological and structural.

Orientational metaphor is the association between abstract concepts and directions (such as GOOD IS UP, BAD IS DOWN). Orientational metaphors are particularly popular in sign languages, because they are spatial languages. The strength of signed language is that it can directly connect concepts and directions by simply moving the hands or locating referents in space. Movement is a formational feature of all signs, and the choice of direction of movement may be governed by metaphor. For instance, examples of GOOD IS UP, BAD IS DOWN can be found in the lexicon of many sign languages. Many BSL signs which have positive meaning (such as WELL, ACHIEVE, IMPROVE, INCREASE-CONFIDENCE) are signed with an upward movement; those with negative connotations (such as ILL, LOSE, NOT-CONFIDENT) move downward. We will discuss similar examples in poetic metaphor below.

Ontological metaphor allows us to talk about abstract ideas, events, states, emotions and so on as if they were concrete objects and substances. They are seen as objects that can be touched, moved, sent, kept in a certain location and so on (as in expressions like 'I can't get my ideas across to him!', 'Please send my regards', 'I put a lot of effort into this'). Ontological metaphors in sign languages are often represented through handling classifiers, which show how we manipulate objects (see Chapter 6), and can also be used metaphorically to manipulate abstract concepts. The verbs for REMEMBER and LEARN in ASL and BSL and many other sign languages use a handling classifier to express the act of putting and retaining an object in the mind (REMEMBER) and copying objects from a book and bringing them to the mind (LEARN). There is also a common expression which can be translated as KEEP-IT-AT-THE-BACK-OF-THE-MIND (to remember something for later), which can be found across different sign languages. This sign is represented literally as the act of moving an object (with a handling classifier) from the forehead to the back of the head.

Such manipulation of abstract ideas is also found in poetic metaphor. For example, in *Who Am I?* Donna Williams literally 'takes out' each of her different identities from her chest area, looks at them, and then puts them back.

Structural metaphor uses rich and systematic ways of mapping internal patterns of source and target concepts – as in the example of LIFE IS A JOURNEY. They are called 'structural' because they map a set of correspondences (not just one-to-one) between the source concept (for example, a JOURNEY) and target concept (for example, LIFE).

Such a systematic mapping between two concepts can produce a number of expressions based on each conceptual metaphor. In the case of LIFE IS A JOURNEY, English speakers may use following expressions:

- It's time to move on.
- We were side-tracked.
- I was at one of those crucial life turning points and didn't know which road to take.
- My scholarships paid my way through college.

While orientational and ontological metaphors are easily found in sign language, structural metaphors seem the least common type of metaphor in everyday signing (Wilbur, 1987). Common structural metaphors identified by Lakoff and Johnson (1980), such as LIFE IS A JOURNEY and ARGUMENT IS WAR ('can you defend your argument?'), have not been commonly observed in the lexicon of sign languages. Poetic metaphor, however, often uses common structural metaphors. The LIFE IS A JOURNEY metaphor can be found in many sign language poems, including Paul Scott's *We'll Meet Again*, Dorothy Miles' *The Staircase*, and Richard Carter's *Looking for Diamonds*.

Poetic metaphor: extending, elaborating, questioning and combining

As described above, cognitive linguists, following Lakoff and Johnson (1980), treat metaphors as everyday phenomena and use conventional metaphors to illustrate their points. However, their theories can also be applied to poetic metaphor. Poetic or literary metaphor is defined from a cognitive linguistic viewpoint as the 'non-conventional use of conventional metaphor' (Hiraga, 2005, p. 26). Although many poetic metaphors appear to be completely original and novel, they are usually based on conventional conceptual metaphor. As we observed earlier, conceptual metaphor is at the basis of how we understand the world through our body, and without the support of basic conceptual metaphor, poetic metaphor ceases to make sense. What is innovative in poetry is the way that poets revitalise existing conceptual metaphors, rather than creating completely new ones.

Lakoff and Turner (1989) identify four major ways to develop poetic metaphor out of ordinary conceptual metaphor. Poets can extend, elaborate, question or combine conventional metaphor to achieve poetic effect.

Extending turns an ordinary metaphor into a poetic one by adding new elements to the metaphor. Kövecses (2002) provides examples from Robert Frost's *The Road Not Taken* in which the poet uses a conventional metaphor of LIFE IS A JOURNEY but adds extra details such as his encounter with two roads, one of which is less travelled than the other. Similar additions of details occur in Dorothy Miles' *The Staircase* in which characters encounter a huge staircase and climb all the way to the top to achieve a certificate. The poet is using the same metaphor of LIFE IS A JOURNEY (people are travellers, the achievement of the purpose of life is reaching the destination, obstacles in life are obstacles on a journey). However, she extends its source domain by adding the details of the huge staircase and highlighting the importance of the gradual, step-by-step approach to the goal.

While extending adds a new element to the source domain, *elaboration* makes use of an existing element but uses it in an unusual way. In Lakoff and Turner's terms, the former is 'to map additional slots (in metaphorical mapping)', the latter is 'to fill in slots in unusual ways' (1989, p. 67). As we saw in Chapter 7, personification of non-humans (anthropomorphism) is a pervasive feature of sign language literature. Lakoff and Turner also identify personification as one type of conventional metaphor. Attribution of human characteristics (thoughts, behaviours, and emotions) to non-humans is neither new nor innovative, but deaf poets often map an unusual quality to a non-human entity to make it unique. For example, Richard Carter's *Deaf Trees* not only personifies trees but also gives a quality of deafness to the personified trees, and creates extra empathy when trees and humans become 'comrades'. This is an unusual way of mapping, because conventional personification does not associate lack of human language in non-humans with deafness. The poet is not simply adding a detail in the metaphor but creating a new association.

Another example of this occurs in John Wilson's *Home*, in which the destinies of Laika, the dog who was sent in to space in Sputnik, and of a deaf boy who undergoes a strict oralist education are described in parallel. The suffering of deaf children is told through the sacrifice of Laika to scientific enterprise. This is another example of 'filling in the slots' of an existing association (understanding the emotion of humans in terms of that of animals, common in many fables) in an unusual way.

The third practice of turning conventional metaphor into an original one is through *questioning*. Poets can take conventional metaphor into poetic language by pointing out its inadequacy. A commonly found example is to use the A LIFETIME IS A DAY metaphor but then indicate differences between the two concepts, such as repeatability of a day and mortality of human life. Lakoff and Turner provide the following example: 'Sun can set and return again, but when our brief light goes out, there's one perpetual night to be slept through.' (Catullus quoted in Lakoff and Turner, 1989)

In *Evening* in *Trio*, Dorothy Miles challenged the metaphor UNDERSTANDING IS SEEING. This metaphor is normally very strong in sign language poetry (seeing is crucial for signing poets and their audiences), and thus one may expect when the deaf persona is left in the darkness at the end, she is unable to do anything. However, Miles defies this metaphor by reaching out into the darkness through her sense of touch. Lack of seeing is not portrayed as the end of understanding in this particular poem (Sutton-Spence, 2005).

The last type of creating innovative metaphor is *composing* (or *combining*). According to Lakoff and Turner, composing can be the most powerful way in which poetic metaphor goes beyond conventional metaphor (1989, p. 70). It is the way to combine more than one source concept to describe a target concept. Taub (2001) observes that sign language poets also combine separate metaphors 'to form a coherent whole' (p. 196). For example, Johanna Mesch's *Ocean* combines a number of metaphors to implement the theme of pollution. It is powerfully expressed through the personified ocean becoming sick, but the same theme is also subtly expressed through orientational metaphor (BAD IS DOWN – the waste sinks deep under the ocean, the sick ocean bends down and so on) and through a break in symmetric patterns that have been built up in the poem when the boat comes to dump the waste (BAD IS ASYMMETRY).

Metaphor at the global level

While most studies in sign language metaphor focus on the lexical level, metaphor in sign language literature can be found at several levels. Sometimes an entire text is a metaphor (as in the case of *The Ugly Duckling* or Ben Bahan's *Bird of a Different Feather*). This can be called allegory, extended metaphor, or global metaphor. We will use the term global metaphor here to clarify the fact that it takes place at a global (as opposed to phonological or lexical) level across the whole poem. Lakoff and Turner (1989) suggest that although readers can develop their own understanding of the poem's global metaphor, such interpretation has to 'make sense' and be 'justified' (p. 146). They give three main constraints: the use of conventional conceptual metaphor, the use of common knowledge, and the iconic mapping between form and meaning.

For example, Dorothy Miles' *Elephants Dancing* lends itself to a global metaphor reading of deaf people's deprivation of freedom. It describes the 'dance' of an elephant which is trained to repeat the same steps with its legs chained. The elephant cannot move freely, a constraint which is associated with the oppression of deaf people. This reading is justified because, firstly, the poem uses conventional metaphors such as ANIMALS ARE HUMANS and PSYCHOLOGICAL RESTRICTION IS PHYSICAL RESTRICTION. The audience can understand this metaphor based on the common knowledge of deaf people as a minority in the society. It also makes use of iconic mapping between the signs and the meaning, such as the awkward movements of the hands to symbolise the restricted freedom of the deaf people.

As Lakoff and Turner (1989) admit, a poem often lends itself to multiple global metaphorical readings. People from different backgrounds may see the poem in a slightly different way. In the above example, although the linguistic medium of sign language can justify the identification of the elephant with deaf people, the oppressed minority could be anyone (black people, gay people, women or even particular individuals). Wilcox (2000) reports different interpretations of an ASL poem *The Dogs* by Ella Mae Lentz. This is a poem about two dogs (a snobbish Doberman and an angry mutt) who hate each other but they cannot be separated because they are tied with the same chain. They eventually accept that they are bound together, and agree to live in peace. This poem is generally understood as the conflict and reconciliation of two groups of people who are different in nature but need to coexist in society. However, when it comes to interpreting what two groups the dogs stand for, there is variation among audiences from different backgrounds. Wilcox found that deaf Americans took this as a conflict between two deaf groups, namely 'English-using educated deaf people' and 'ASL-using less educated deaf people'. Deaf people from Switzerland, where such a division among deaf people does not exist, interpreted this poem as a conflict between deaf and hearing people. Moreover, Italian deaf people took the metaphor as representing a conflict between races (Wilcox, 2000). This shows the importance of common knowledge among the audience and suggests that multiple ways to read a text is characteristic of poetic language in general.

Metaphor at the phonological level

A particular feature of sign languages is that metaphorical association can take place at the smallest language level (that is, within its phonology). In many sign languages, metaphorical mapping is involved in all the parameters that create a sign, that is, the handshape, location, movement, palm orientation, and nonmanual expressions (such as gaze and mouth patterns).

Handshape

Selection of a particular handshape in a sign language poem is sometimes governed by metaphorical principles. The target domains are 'emotional effects commonly associated with particular handshapes' (Sutton-Spence, 2005, p. 26) and physical configuration of handshapes often stands for abstract concepts. Open/closed handshapes can stand for positive and negative concepts, sharp/non-sharp handshapes can stand for unpleasant and pleasant sensations, and substantial/non-substantial handshapes can stand for weakness or strength. These are used effectively to create metaphor in sign language literature, and we will return to the symbolism of handshape in Chapter 14.

Location

Location of a sign in signing space often symbolises our understanding of abstract concepts. Firstly, certain locations are symbolically associated with abstract concepts. For example, in many sign languages (including BSL and ASL), signs whose meaning is related to mental activities (such as THINK, KNOW, UNDERSTAND) are likely to be located at the head. In contrast, signs associated with feelings tend to be produced on the chest (FEEL, LIKE, LOVE) (Brennan, 1990). Many poets treat the chest location as a place where their emotions, identities and their true self can be found (see Paul Scott's *I Know Who (Stole My Heart)*, Richard Carter's *Identities* and *Looking for Diamonds*, Donna Williams' *Who Am I?*).

Location can also be motivated by orientational metaphors. For example, signs that are placed higher up in the signing area tend to imply something good, while lower locations are often connected to signs with negative meaning (GOOD IS UP, BAD IS DOWN). This direction is also used to represent our understanding of power and suppression – HIGH STATUS IS UP, LOW STATUS IS DOWN (Lakoff and Johnson, 1980). People with power and authority are metaphorically situated higher (and therefore the act of oppression is conceptualised as downward movement). In sign language literature, hearing characters with authority (such as doctors and teachers) are often located high in the signing space, whereas deaf people are likely to be located lower than them (see, for example, Nigel Howard's *Deaf,* John Wilson's *Home*, and many of Clayton Valli's works). This highlights the theme of oppression effectively.

Signs placed at the centre of the signing space may be more important than those placed at the peripheral areas (IMPORTANT IS CENTRAL, LESS IMPORTANT IS PERIPHERAL). For example, in Donna Williams' *That Day*, the objects associated with the deaf community are located at the centre of the signing space while those related to the hearing community are pushed aside to the far right. In Clayton Valli's *Snowflake*, the deaf boy is peripheralised in the presence of his powerful hearing father. This is related to the idea that physical distance can metaphorically show emotional attachment or detachment. The conceptual metaphor underlying this is INTIMACY IS PROXIMITY (Taub, 2001). For example, in Nigel Howard's signed haiku *Deaf,* the baby is iconically and metaphorically located closer to the body while he is held by his parent. When he is given to the doctor, however, the baby is located away from the body, symbolising the emotional distance between the doctor and the baby.

Movement

Meaning in sign language can be metaphorically represented though the speed, the manner and the direction of the movement of the signs. First of all, the speed of movements can be linked to abstract notions. As Judith Jackson (2006) suggests:

> Rhythm and speed can show different emotions. Fast speed can show excited, confident, or overconfident, such as 'I can do this!' 'I'm okay!' Slow could be discouraged, tired, or old, but it could also be positive, happy, relaxed, and content, a sense of pressure is eased.

In *Five Senses*, Paul Scott signs much more quickly in the final section of his poem when he describes the sense of seeing. This increase in speed of signing highlights the importance and efficiency of sight to deaf people and the sense of freedom it brings (Sutton-Spence, 2005).

Johanna Mesch's *Party* builds up a sense of suspense through different speeds. It starts with normal speed in which the protagonist prepares supper for her lover in a self-assured manner. When the lover arrives and starts talking to her (and the nonmanual elements show it is not a pleasant talk), the speed changes from normal to very fast, with the climax of her throwing her ring at her lover and shutting the door. After this, the speed of movement becomes markedly slow, as she leads up to her apparent suicide.

Manner of movement also has metaphorical association. Repetitive and mechanical movement that is characteristic of many of Wim Emmerik's poems (*Garden of Eden* and *Desert*) is often a metaphor for undesirable or unavoidable events such as banishment or death. Circular movement often represents the passage of time, as in Paul Scott's *Tree*, Richard Carter's *Surprise Apple* and Ella Mae Lentz's ASL poem *Circle of Life*. The circularity is metaphorically linked to the theme of 'circle of life' in all these poems.

The directions of movement also play a significant role in metaphorical signing, based on orientational metaphors. For example, there is clear and strong association between upward movement and positive meaning, and conversely, between downward movement and negative meaning. We have already seen some examples of this in the established lexicon in our discussion of orientational metaphor. In poetic metaphor, this up and down direction is used coherently. For example, Dorothy Miles' *The Staircase* relies on this metaphor. The movement of climbing up the staircase is perceived as the way to achieve success, and many dangers (obstacles) are displayed with downward movement such as sinking into the ground and the head being cut off and falling down. Johanna Mesch's *Aeroplane* describes a tragic plane accident, but the upward movement representing the ascension of the plane's soul (to heaven) provides a positive tone at the end.

Moving forward is often seen more positively than moving backward. In English, a 'forward-looking' person is a positive thinker, and a 'retrograde' step makes the situation worse. This same metaphor can be observed in poetic signing. In the SASL poem *For My Aunt* by Atiyah Asmal, the protagonist (a personified bee) is in deep sorrow when she loses her beloved aunt (a personified rose), but decides to 'fly forward' (literally) at the end of the poem, meeting other people and seeing new places.

Another example of contrastive use of directions is based on the direction away from the body (outward) and toward the body (inward). There are many possible contrasts associated with these directions. Firstly, as we discussed in relation to locations above, inward movement can be associated with emotional closeness and privacy, whereas outward movement can be seen as emotional detachment or indifference. A different interpretation is that outward movement represents something open and positive, whereas inward movement leads to the sense of confinement (and thus less positive). A third possible interpretation is that inward movement represents the act of being forced to do something, or something is forced upon someone. The pressure of deadlines in Donna Williams' *Duck and Dissertation* is expressed with the sign DEADLINE-APPROACHES moving sharply toward the poet. In both John Wilson's *The Fates* and Richard Carter's *Identities,* someone (presumably a hearing person) demands unreasonably that a deaf character should use speech or be straight (instead of gay). Such pressure comes in the form of characters approaching the protagonist, expressed with an inward movement. The deaf protagonists flatly refuse by moving their hands outward or with a gesture of chasing the hearing person away (with an outward movement).

Palm orientation

Palm orientation can produce metaphorical interpretation, and Wilbur (1987) observed the metaphorical use of palm orientation in the basic structure of lexical signs. The ASL sign GOOD is made with the palm facing up and BAD is with the palm facing down. This potential semantic value is reactivated in creative signing.

The palm often represents the front or the visible (and thus salient) side of a two-sided object (for example, the printed side of a piece of paper), while the back of the hand represents the back or the invisible side of an object. This leads to the orientational metaphor GOOD IS FRONT, BAD IS BACK, which in English produces expressions like 'face your enemies', instead of 'stabbing them in the back' or 'she turned her back on me' (meaning, she refuses to talk to me). Showing the palm in many Western cultures (palm upward or outward) is often considered to be open and positive, while showing the back of the hand (palm downward or inward) can represent something slightly negative, undesirable, or private. In Richard Carter's *Mirror*, the palms of the poet face outward when the personified mirror is happy; when it is sad or lonely, the palms face inward. In the war scene in John Wilson's *For a Deaf Friend*, the army troop is represented by a collective classifier with palms facing outward when they are alive but they face downward when soldiers are killed in action (Figure 10.1).

In *Twin Leaves*, Johanna Mesch anthropomorphises a pair of leaves. They love each other and are always together until a storm separates them. At the beginning, Mesch illustrates the twin leaves mostly with her palm facing outward as in LEAVES-ON-THE-TREE, HAPPY-PAIR-OF-LEAVES. However, after the storm, the palm faces downward and inward (as in SAD-LEAF). The last sign represents the reunited, happy pair of leaves again, but this time they are facing down, poetically suggesting the fact that they will wither shortly after.

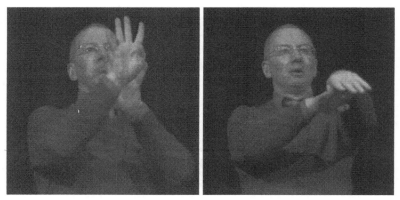

FIGURE 10.1   METAPHORICAL USE OF PALM ORIENTATION
IN JOHN WILSON'S *FOR A DEAF FRIEND*

Nonmanual features

Nonmanual features, especially gaze and mouth actions, also play a crucial role in metaphorical operation in sign language literature. For example, gaze directions convey examples of orientational metaphors. We will talk more about this in Chapter 17.

Summary

This chapter presented an overview of metaphor in sign language literature. We introduced the notion of metaphor held by cognitive linguists, and discussed how poetic metaphor develops out of conventional metaphor through extending, elaborating, questioning and combining. We have seen three different types of metaphor identified by cognitive linguists and discussed examples in sign language. Finally, we gave a detailed account of metaphor at the global level and at the phonological level in sign language literature. Metaphor in sign language literature is often 'unresolved' (a term coined by Paul Williams, 2000). It means the language may hint at possible metaphorical interpretations but does not clarify them. We saw in our examples of global metaphor that there is often more than one way of reading the metaphor in a poem/story. How an audience interprets a metaphor in poetic signing depends on who they are, where they come from and what their expectations are.

Note

1. Conceptual metaphors are conventionally written in upper case.

Further reading

For seminal works on metaphor by cognitive linguists:

Lakoff, George and Mark Johnson (1980) *Metaphors We Live By* (Chicago: University of Chicago Press).

Lakoff, George and Mark Turner (1989) *More than Cool Reason: A Field Guide to Poetic Metaphor* (Chicago: University of Chicago Press).

Phyllis Wilcox's *Metaphor in American Sign Language* (Gallaudet University Press, 2000) and Sarah Taub's *Language from the Body* (Cambridge University Press, 2001) provide detailed accounts of metaphor in ASL. Each has a chapter that explores metaphors in ASL poetry.

If you want to read more about the relationship between iconicity and metaphor:

Kaneko, Michiko and Rachel Sutton-Spence (2012) 'Iconicity and metaphor in sign language poetry', *Metaphor and Symbol*, 27(2), 107–130.

Activities

1. Using poems or particularly creative narratives in a sign language that you know (Paul Scott's *Macbeth of the Lost Ark*, on the YouTube channel accompanying this book, would be a good choice in BSL), identify examples of orientational metaphors (for example, GOOD IS UP, DOWN IS BAD), ontological metaphors (for example, KNOWLEDGE IS AN OBJECT) and structural metaphors (for example, LIFE IS A JOURNEY, UNDERSTANDING IS SEEING).

2. Compose a short sign language poem for each season (spring, summer, autumn and winter). Adjust the speed (fast or slow) and size (big or small) of signing, and/or use orientational metaphors, to symbolically illustrate the different nature of four seasons – for example, you may want to sign your poem about spring at a fast speed to suggest that it is a season of changes.

   You can make a similar quartet for different times of the day (morning, afternoon, evening and night) and for different stages of life (infancy, youth, middle age and old age).

   Watch Dorothy Miles' *Trio* and *Seasons*, and *Three Haiku Quartets* by Paul Scott, Richard Carter, Johanna Mesch and John Wilson (again, these are posted on our YouTube channel) to give you some ideas. (These are in BSL but are sufficiently visual that you should be able to understand them if you are already familiar with any sign language.)

11 Prose and Poetry

In this chapter, we ask what criteria exist for separating prose from poetry in written language literature and try to apply these to sign language literature. We have seen in previous chapters that deaf communities have a long tradition of 'prose' storytelling, but what we call 'sign language poetry' only emerged in certain countries in the 1970s or 1980s (and not all deaf communities create it, even today). Although there is no satisfactory way to separate sign language poetry from sign language 'prose' (that is, any literature which is not poetry) because the distinction is ultimately an artificial one, for the purposes of understanding and appreciating signed creativity we explore here what people consider to be prose and what makes a poem. Our aim is to find criteria to determine whether something is more like a story or a poem.

Paul Valéry said that prose is like walking or running, while poetry is like dancing (Valéry, 1958). We walk or run to get somewhere – there is a clear purpose of reaching the destination and, so long as that purpose is fulfilled, we rarely pay much attention to how we walk or run. Similarly, in prose, the language is used to communicate the content of the work, and as long as the message is successfully conveyed, how the language is used does not hugely matter (which is why we can translate prose into another language relatively easily). In contrast, when we dance, we dance for the sake of dancing. How we dance can be very important. Every step, movement and expression matters, and they are carefully planned. Poetry also exists for its own sake and every choice of language element is deliberate and has meaning. The purpose of conveying a message is secondary to aesthetic pleasure (which is why translating a poem into another language requires a very different approach).

Although this is a useful analogy, the reality of distinguishing between poetry and prose is far less clear. There are prose stories which are told in the most eloquent and thoughtful language, and there are poems whose content is as important as the language they use. Moreover, the same text can be seen as prose or poetry, depending on how it is presented. Passages in Shakespeare, for example, are sometimes presented on the page as prose, sometimes as verse (for example, the Nurse's speech in Act I of *Romeo and Juliet*). T.S. Eliot (1958), at the age of 69, declared: 'I have never yet come across a final, comprehensive, and satisfactory account of the difference between poetry and prose ... I do not believe that any distinction between prose and poetry is meaningful' (p. xvi).

While we would not presume to argue against Eliot, differences between the central idea of poems and prose stories point to the different kinds of creative effort involved. Even though we cannot separate them as two mutually exclusive categories, we can at least talk about certain qualities which are typically associated with poetry or prose. In this sense, the poetry/prose distinction can be seen as a continuum – some works have more poetry-like features and can be located towards the poetry end of the continuum, and vice versa. Here are some ideas and suggestions for what these qualities that are characteristic of poetry or prose could be.

Length

One possible distinction is that poems are usually shorter than stories. It is rare to tell a prose story in a few words, but poetry does. Haiku highlights the linguistic compression of poetry. Traditional Japanese haiku strictly consists of 17 syllables, which is usually fewer than ten words. The following haiku by Yosa Buson (1716–1784) expresses the deep loss felt by the poet in a few words:

Mini shimu-ya
Naki tsumano kushio
Neyani fumu

(A sudden chill underfoot
I stepped on my late wife's comb
In our bedroom)[1]

Dorothy Miles, talking about sign language poetry, said in an interview on the BBC television programme *See Hear!* in 1983 that poetry is 'a way of putting meaning very briefly so people will see it and feel very strongly' (cited in Sutton-Spence, 2005, p. 14). There is a strong view that poetry is a compressed form of language, and therefore requires fewer words. However, we cannot define poems and stories purely based on length. Many jokes or humorous stories are told in a very concise manner, and some works which are relatively long are still seen more as poems than stories. Epic poems, for example, can be extremely long and there are many sign language poems as long as sign language stories – such as Richard Carter's *Gondola*. In general, signed texts are shorter than written ones so, while poems do tend to be short, length alone cannot distinguish between poetry and prose.

Line segmentation

The notion of a 'line' is arguably the most common way of distinguishing poetry from prose in written literature. It is observed both in Western and non-Western literary traditions (although the techniques may be very different). In novels and other forms of prose, line breaks happen arbitrarily according to the typesetting, not as a result of any artistic intention. In poetry, on the other hand, part of the poet's artistry is to decide when to break lines and poetry can use unusual line breaks and punctuation to maintain rhythmic structure and sound patterns (rhyme, alliteration) or to emphasise certain words. Poets may even change the word order to do this.

The convention of poetic lines is so strong that we often decide whether a piece of writing is a poem or not by simply looking at how lines are presented on the page. To demonstrate this, we invite readers to take any ordinary, non-poetic sentence out of its context (a sentence from the newspaper, an instruction written on a bottle of aspirin, a definition of a word in the dictionary and so on), break it into shorter lines, and present it in the form of poetry. For example:

This cream nourishes dry and damaged skin and is particularly suitable for use against irritations, reddening and burns.

can be rewritten as:

This cream nourishes dry
And damaged skin
And is particularly suitable
For use against irritations,
Reddening and burns

Although the words remain identical, it certainly bears a poetic touch now, which also affects how we read it. Line breaks have the power to turn a perfectly mundane expression into a poem, at least on a very superficial level. However, the existence of lines in sign language poetry is questionable, especially as lines are fundamentally associated with a written form of poetry and sign language poems are not written.

Clayton Valli, an American deaf poet and linguist, pursued the notions of line divisions in ASL poetry in 1990s to see if they might help define sign language poetry (1990, 1993). Dirksen Bauman (2006), in his thoughtful discussion of lines in sign language poetry, notes that Valli began by translating English poems to see how the lines were marked in ASL. Finding that lines in English poetry were often marked by rhymes at the end, Valli suggested we could find lines in ASL poems by finding rhyming patterns. In his poem *Snowflake*, for example, LEAVES-FALL and GRASS-WITHERS share path movement, eyebrow movement and hand-shapes, so Valli suggested these are rhymes. By following the logic seen in the English poetry he had studied, Valli proposed that the location of signed rhymes reveals the end of a signed line. However, although written translations of the signs and linguistic analysis could make the signs look like line-end rhymes, when deaf signers watched the poem, they did not see line breaks there.

Additionally, as Bauman observes, there are many different kinds of poetry (for example, free verse, concrete poetry, prose poetry, performance poetry) and each one defines 'line' differently. Equally, there are many different styles of sign language poetry so, although Valli's ASL poetry was influenced by poets who used verse and line-ends to create similar structures, other signing poets create different ASL poetry with patterns that show poetry can be understood visually without the need for rhymes.

Thus we can see that division of lines in sign language poetry is often artificial, and could result in squeezing the spatial and simultaneous capability of sign languages into temporal and sequential arrangements which they do not really fit. This does not mean that a poem in sign language cannot be broken into smaller units, but they are not necessarily the equivalent of lines in written poetry,[2] and no research so far has identified a means of segmentation in artistic signing which can be used conclusively to distinguish poetry and prose.

Purpose and function

Valéry's metaphor that prose is like walking or running, while poetry is like dancing suggests that one useful way to distinguish poetry and stories is in their different purposes and functions. Stories aim to deliver a coherent narrative that describes a sequence of events. It is important that the reader (or the viewer) will understand the events told in a story. In other words, successful communication is the primary purpose of prose storytelling. Poetry, on the other hand, does not necessarily seek immediate success in delivering a message. Some poets even claim that they do not really mind whether the audience get the 'meaning' of their poems or not.[3]

Poetry is rather seen as a form of art which exists for its own sake. If there were a purpose in poetry, it would be to explore the height of artistic language – to push linguistic boundaries and discover new, bold and original expressions that can convey the poet's thoughts. In fact, this leads to another important criterion to distinguish prose and poetry: the former uses everyday ('normal') language, established vocabulary and accepted grammar to ensure the content is understood, whereas the latter often breaks the rules and uses unusual, odd and distorted language to create something new and different. As Jan Mukařovský points out, poetry is 'an aesthetically purposeful distortion of standard language' (quoted in Freeman, 1970, p. 6).

Two ideas are useful in highlighting this function of poetic language: *foregrounding* and *defamiliarisation*. *Foregrounding* is an attempt to make something (a word, an image) stand out in its context, so that it attracts the reader's attention. For example, the sign COCHLEAR-IMPLANT in Nigel Howard's *Deaf* is foregrounded as it is the only sign that uses a bent 'V' handshape and stands out against the background of the open '5' handshape which is predominant in the poem. Foregrounding the sign COCHLEAR-IMPLANT sheds light on the significance it occupies in this particular poem. The significance given to a foregrounded word or image is not inherent in the word itself, but something that is generated within the context of the poem. The same word can be foregrounded in one context and serve as a background in another.

According to Geoffrey Leech (1969), foregrounding takes place in two ways: *obtrusive regularity* (parallelism) and *obtrusive irregularity* (poetic distortion). Obtrusive regularity refers to unusually regular repetitions of forms which force the reader to take note of the pattern, such as the repetition of sounds, as in the tongue twister, 'She sells sea shells on the sea shore'. This is a feature commonly found in poetry but is far less common in prose. In sign language poetry, many elements are repeated to create regularity and make the language noticeable (see Chapter 13). Obtrusive irregularity refers to the violation of rules and conventions in language. Poets constantly search for unusual ways to say something. For example, Richard Carter's works often distort signing speed and Paul Scott's poems frequently use handshapes which are not permissible in standard BSL to create poetic effect. For example, *Tree* uses an unusual and impermissible classifier using all fingers and thumb to represent the four legs and the head of a dog. This allows the poet to 'lift up' one of the legs of the dog (the thumb) to cock his leg at the bottom of the tree (see Figure 12.2). Dorothy Miles' famous TWIN-TREES sign in *Trio* is highly unconventional (not least because the two arms make contact at the elbow), and has a strong aesthetic appeal (Figure 11.1). Obtrusive regularity and irregularity work together. Often the former is used to establish a certain pattern, which is then distorted by a sudden irregular element to awaken the audience.

Defamiliarisation is the literary practice of presenting ordinary, familiar things in an unfamiliar way to force the readers to pay attention to things

FIGURE 11.1   UNUSUAL TWIN-TREES SIGN FROM DOROTHY MILES' *TRIO*

which they have taken for granted. This does take place in storytelling to some extent. Anthropomorphism, which we discussed in Chapter 7, is an example of defamiliarisation because it presents the world from the perspective of non-humans and it can occur in prose stories. However, we could say that poetry intensifies this process of defamiliarisation. It defamiliarises not only the content but also the language. Deaf poets take a familiar sign and skilfully turn it into something unusual. For example, in Johanna Mesch's *Three Haiku*, the common signs for SUN (an open '5' handshape, with slightly bent fingers) and SUNSHINE-LESSENS (an open '5' handshape closing into a fist) are defamiliarised by the sequence in which the poet forcefully opens up her own fingers to regain the sunshine (see Figure 12.4). This is a good example of metalinguistic play with signs as the poet plays with the formational features of a sign, often resulting in a surreal and comical result. It has an intense poetic effect as it alters the way we look at these ordinary signs.

Both foregrounding and defamiliarisation aim to create a new way of perceiving language and reality – which is an important function of poetry.

Flexibility of text

We briefly discussed the difference between text and performance in Chapter 3, in relation to the notion of oral literature. It can be applied to the distinction between poetry and storytelling in sign language literature. Heidi Rose (1992) suggests that the distinction between poetry and prose is the degree to which a signed piece can be fixed and frozen. Poetry usually has a fixed text, whereas prose stories can be adapted according to audiences or situations, making them more performative, free and flexible.

This also means that poetry is almost always pre-structured to generate a text prior to the performance. That is, the poet explores different possibilities of expressions and chooses the best ones, and polishes their work before it is shown to the public (whether live or through recording). Stories can be much more spontaneous. The time for composition can be very short, and we often create a story as we tell it. However, as we saw in Chapter 3 when we considered oral poetry, poets often create work on the spot and in many cultures, a poet's ability to create a poem spontaneously is highly valued.

Additionally, some poems change over time as a poet performs the same poem repeatedly, with minor or major amendments to improve it. They also adjust their poems according to different audiences. For example, Richard Carter used the sign FIRE-STARTING-PISTOL when performing his poem *The Race* to a predominantly hearing audience but DROP-HANDKERCHIEF when he performed to a mostly-deaf audience, to refer to the culturally appropriate way to start a deaf race. Fernanda Machado modifies her 'signature poem' *Flight over Rio* in each town she performs by incorporating images of the host town into the poem. However, as we saw in Chapter 2, Ben Bahan (2006a) has noted that changing a story to match the audience is also a characteristic of any good storyteller.

While poems can be more flexible in their construction than it might initially appear, with the advance of video technology (recall our discussions in Chapter 3), more and more stories are seen in fixed forms, blurring the distinction between poetry and prose in this aspect.

Vocabulary

Stories use a wide range of vocabulary to develop the sequence of events. Stories in sign language are likely to have a higher frequency of 'established' signs (those accepted widely among the community) to ensure that everyone understands. In contrast, poetry uses more productive, creative, or even 'new' ways of signing.

Owing to the visual and iconic nature of sign language literature, deaf poets can experiment with new signs much more than hearing poets composing in written language can. Whereas English language poets cannot create a poem only using new words and make them understood by the reader, signing poets can invent new vocabulary which is intelligible to the audience. For example, Richard Carter and Paul Scott's duet poem *Fashion Times* consists almost entirely of neologistic signs (signs which have never been used before – we will discuss this more in the next chapter) but what is being described is as clear as their other stories conveyed through standard BSL lexicon.

Poetic and prosaic signing can be contrasted by the degree to which it relies on manual signs. Storytelling uses many established signs, for which manual components (hands) are indispensable. Poetry relies much less on manual signs, but instead makes full use of nonmanual elements (anything that is not produced by hands) – facial expressions, gaze, body movement, space, speed, rhythm and so on. The British deaf poet, Judith Jackson, told a seminar group:

> In poetry, expression is important, especially the use of eyes more than hands. The manual signs are made into minimum in poetry. In stories you need lots of vocabulary, whereas in poetry you need more focus [:] focus on eyegaze and facial expression, handshape and speed and pace.[4]

For example, John Wilson's haiku poem *Lift* is presented almost entirely through the eyes and facial expression. The poet's hands (in a 'B' handshape) are fixed in space to represent the doors of the lift and they do nothing else. The facial expressions and gaze of the poet convey the content of the poem – the presence of people passing by, the excitement of the personified lift and the disappointment when no one wants to use the lift.

Eyes, as Judith Jackson pointed out, are especially important in poetry. Gaze in narratives is relatively straightforward, mainly because, as we discussed above, the primary purpose of storytelling is communication. Thus, signers constantly look at the audience or use their gaze as they enact certain characters to keep the attention of the audience and make the story easy to follow. In poetry, however, the poet does not need to meet the eyes of the audience all the time, resulting in a wider variation of gaze patterns. We will discuss this more in Chapter 17.

Rhythm

Rhythm and signing speed are important in any good performance of sign language literature, regardless of whether it is a poem or a prose story, but their functions may be slightly different. While stories may use different rhythms and signing speeds to highlight actions or emotions (reflecting what is happening in the story), poetry manipulates them in a more deliberate and aesthetic manner to foreground the language itself rather than the content. A good example is Richard Carter's *The Race*, which is told in slow motion to highlight every movement of the poet's body and expression. The speed of signing does not reflect the actual speed of running, but is added 'extradiegetically' as something outside the story world (like sound effects in a film which are added at the stage of editing and do not refer to actual sounds in the film). Such aesthetic use of speed can be seen more as a feature associated with poetry.

Plot and characters

Another way of distinguishing poetry and prose is that the latter is likely to have a plot – that is, a sequence in which a story unfolds. Poems don't always have one. Quoting Judith Jackson again:

> In poetry, you need not necessarily know what's happening. It's more about self-expression. It doesn't matter if it follows a particular chronological order. It's more flexible than stories in this aspect. If you jump around in stories, the reader will get lost. So you can use more placement and role shift in stories.[5]

In stories, a series of events are gathered in meaningful ways (in chronological order, or in cause-and-effect relationship). In mysteries or detective stories, for example, all events are carefully put together to give clues to 'whodunit', leading to the climax of revelation. Because they involve a sequence of events, stories almost always develop around a set of characters – what happens to whom, when, where and how are important aspects of stories. The storytellers often become the characters (using constructed action) and tell the story from their perspective with lively facial expressions. In short, stories are eventful. We cannot simply describe a static scene and make it a story, but that is acceptable in a poem.

Many haiku poems (both in signed and spoken language), as well as the works by Imagist poets such as Ezra Pound and William Carlos Williams, simply aim to reproduce a poetic snapshot – a brief (but intense) description of a scene in nature or in daily life. Wim Emmerik's poem *Falling Leaf* provides a good example of this, as it is a straightforward description of a leaf falling from the tree. Perhaps one of the reasons Richard Carter's *Gondola* feels more like a poem than a story, despite its length, is that it simply repeats the movement of the gondolier and the kissing of the lovers, without having any clear plot. It is also characterised by a deliberate lack of facial expressions, something that is highly marked in the canon of Richard Carter's works, which are normally full of actions and expressions.

Rules

Poems often follow specific rules such as strict rhyming schemes, metric structures or mandatory choice of particular kinds of words (for example, traditional haiku must include *kigo,* a word that indicates the season in which the poem is set). Prose tends to be much more free and spontaneous, and the composition is less rule-driven.

Presence or absence of rules does not really help us distinguish prose and poetry in sign language literature because there are currently few established rules for the form of sign language poetry. Nonetheless, we often feel poems are somehow more 'disciplined' than stories, which are told more freely. Signing poets seem to be more disciplined in their choice of language and lay certain restrictions upon themselves (such as the fixed use of a particular parameter and manipulation of speed, space and facial expressions) in order to produce intense poetic effects within the restrictions of the form.

It is crucial to have rules in poetry, regardless of whether they are established in literary traditions or self-imposed by each poet. If there are no constraints at all, we cannot really compose a poem because part of the *raison d'être* of poetry is to challenge linguistic conventions and produce something new and meaningful within the limitations of existing language. The enormous impact poetry can produce by breaking the rules cannot happen if there are no rules to break. In poetry, paradoxically, rules provide potential and lack of rules becomes restrictive.

A pianist protagonist from the movie titled *Legend of 1900* puts this idea beautifully in his monologue to his friend:

> Take piano: keys begin, keys end. You know there are 88 of them. They are not infinite. You're infinite. And on those keys, the music that you can make is infinite. If the keyboard is infinite, there is no music you can play.

Similarly, if there is no limitation in what we can do with words, there is no poetry we can make. It is important to remember this when studying any poetry.

Summary

In this chapter, we have examined several potential criteria relevant to comparing prose and poetry in sign language literature: length, lines, purpose and function, flexibility, vocabulary, plot and rules. Although none of them can determine the status of prose or poetry alone, it is useful to think about these features and explore what constitutes our notion of sign language poetry. The following six chapters further explore features which are mostly associated with texts that are usually considered to be poetry.

Notes

1. Translation by the authors.
2. This leads to the question of what units of analysis we can propose for studying sign language literature.
3. Paul Scott showed a similar attitude in our interview with him in 2012.
4. Presentation given at a departmental seminar on 17 February 2006 at the Centre for Deaf Studies, University of Bristol, voiced over (translated) by Becky Atkinson.
5. Ibid.

Further reading

For differences between poetic and non-poetic languages in general:

Mukařovský, J. (1964) 'Standard language and poetic language' in P.L. Garvin (ed.) *A Prague School Reader on Esthetics, Literary Structure and Style* (Washington DC: Georgetown University Press).

For discussions of 'lines' in sign language poetry:

Bauman, H-Dirksen (2006) 'Getting out of line: toward a visual and cinematic poetics of ASL' in H-Dirksen Bauman, Jennifer Nelson and Heidi Rose (eds) *Signing the Body Poetic* (California: University of California Press).

Valli, Clayton (1990) 'The nature of a line in ASL poetry' in William H. Edmondson and Fred Karlsson (eds) *SLR87: Papers from the Fourth International Symposium on Sign Language Research* (Hamburg: Signum Verlag).

For Leech's notions of obtrusive regularity and obtrusive irregularity:

Leech, Geoffrey (1969) *A Linguistic Guide to English Poetry* (London: Longman).

Activities

1. Pick ten artistic works in any sign language you know. Place them along the prose–poetry continuum. Remember, you should not categorise them into two mutually exclusive groups – instead, discuss them in relative terms (for example, *Work A may be placed more towards the poetry end of*

the continuum than Work B, but not as far as Work C can be). Examine the features in each piece that made you think it is more of a poem or a story. You can use the features discussed in this chapter, or come up with your own criteria.

2. Compare the two performances by Vitalis Katakinas titled *Graduation* and *University Haiku* posted on the YouTube channel that accompanies this book. These should be accessible to people who know any sign language. Both have a similar topic and motifs, but the first one is told more like a story and the second one is created as a haiku poem. Discuss the differences between the two using the features discussed in this chapter.

12 Neologism and Ambiguity

In Chapter 11, we talked about two ways in which poetic language is foregrounded to stand out as something different from everyday language: through *obtrusive regularity* (an existing element of the language is used with unusual frequency – that is, repetition) and *obtrusive irregularity* (a new or deviant way to use the language). This chapter mainly concerns the latter means of creating poetic effect in sign language literature. Two poetic features will be explored: *neologism* (creating new words/signs) and *ambiguity* (creating more than one meaning using one form). Both present a new way of looking at the language and make the audience wonder what possible meanings it conveys.

Neologism

Neologism is the creation of new words. It captures the attention of the reader or viewer by using words no one has seen before. It showcases the performer's artistry and linguistic skills and also allows poets to maintain a certain rhyming scheme.

New words are constantly made in all languages. English continues to create new terms especially in technology ('cyberspace', 'Blu-ray' and 'podcast'), politics ('Chindia' and 'Afrocentrism') and popular culture ('chav' and 'tweet'). Many of these new words are combinations of two existing words, often with reduction in form ('China' + 'India' = 'Chindia'). Some keep the form of original words but assign a new meaning (as in 'tweet' which means 'to post a short message on Twitter'). Others borrow from other languages (the word 'chav' is thought by some people to have derived from the Romany word 'chavi' meaning 'child'). These new words can become part of the lexicon of English, although many of them fall into disuse when the referents are no longer current (as in 'Thatcherism' or 'MiniDisc').

In literature, poets and writers use neologism in a creative way. New words are especially popular in children's literature. Most of them appear only in that context and are never used again, but they leave a strong impression. In the poem *Jabberwocky*, Lewis Carroll used words such as 'slithey' ('lithe' + 'slimy') and 'mimsy' ('miserable' + 'flimsy'). Roald Dahl created words such as 'snozzcumber' and 'frobkottle' in his book *The BFG*. More recently, J.K. Rowling invented the word 'muggle' (a human with no skills in wizardry) which was added to the *Oxford English Dictionary* in 2003.

In sign language, neologism is visually motivated and is often entertaining. Neologistic signs arise spontaneously in day-to-day conversation when signers use productive signs to illustrate new ideas and experiences. They can also be created, often by experienced deaf and hearing translators, as part of a carefully deliberated process to devise new signs for situations where sign language has only recently started to be used, such as in academic terminology, technology or certain religious settings. However, creation of neologism is especially common and may have extra purposes in creative forms of sign language, especially poetry.

As briefly mentioned in previous chapters, the visual modality of sign languages, and the large productive lexicon that results from it, allows a much greater degree of freedom in creating new words in sign language poetry than in written or spoken language poetry. In English, for example, if the majority of a piece of writing consists of words no one has heard of, the reader will have very little idea what the writer is talking about. With very few exceptions (for example, *The Loch Ness Monster's Song* by Edwin Morgan contains no recognisable words but still carries the ghost of meaning), the Humpty-Dumpty approach to neologism made famous by Lewis Carroll's character ('When I use a word, it means just what I choose it to mean') simply does not work in English.

In contrast, sign language poetry does have the luxury of making new signs without significantly compromising the level of comprehension by the audience. This is due to the highly visual and iconic nature of sign language poetry and a shared understanding between the poet and the audience of how the new signs may be interpreted. Let us illustrate this point by using the poem *Fashion Times* by Paul Scott and Richard Carter. This duet poem describes different trends in British fashion history by representing typical clothing of women (Richard) and men (Paul) in each era – from Victorian dresses to 'chav' fashion in the 2000s. All the signs are 'new' in that Paul and Richard came up with their own ways of depicting the details of the clothes, such as a pencil skirt, a Pringle jumper, or Hippie fashion. Even though these signs were used for the first time, the audience had no problem understanding what they were referring to, due to direct visual representations and their background knowledge of British fashion. The equivalent of this is hard to find in spoken language.

Poetic neologism

Let us move on to explore how a poetic neologism is created in sign language. There are three choices poets can make:

1. Modify an existing sign.
2. Produce totally new signs.
3. Borrow from spoken language.

Modifying an existing sign

Poets can make changes to existing signs to add a novel appearance to them, which often adds meaning and contributes in some way to the poetic scheme. The most common method is to change one of the parameters of the sign to fit the patterns within the poem. Nigel Howard's *Deaf* changes the handshape of DEAF from 'H' to 'B', so that it does not disrupt the repetition of 'B' handshapes in all the other signs. Paul Scott changes the location of COLOUR in *Five Senses* to keep it in the same area of signing space as the other signs in that section. In Johanna Mesch's *Aeroplane*, a flapping movement is added to the fingers depicting the wings in the conventional sign AEROPLANE as it ascends to heaven, adding a heart-warming effect to this otherwise tragic poem about a plane crash.

Existing signs can also be modified by adding extra elements or arranging them in unique ways. Dorothy Miles' poem *Trio* shows different arrangements of existing signs. In the first stanza *Morning*, Dorothy creates a very poetic sign TWIN-TREES to represent the tree and its reflection in the water. The sign TREE is conventional but adding its reflection makes the sign unusual and poetic. The stanza *Afternoon* includes the simultaneous presentation of three characters, showing the dog's head (as a classifier), the bird's beak (as a classifier), and the poetic-I (represented by the performer's body and face). These classifiers and the use of the body to represent the self are not particularly new, but the simultaneous arrangement of all three is notable. In the final stanza *Evening*, the two signs which share the same handshape and location (DARKNESS and BAT-FLIES) motivate a metaphoric expression DARKNESS-FLIES-CLOSE-LIKE-A-BAT. DARKNESS is an existing sign and BAT-FLIES is a conventional classifier sign for a creature with wings, but the combination of these two makes a new sign.

Producing totally new signs

The second common way of making neologistic signs is to create entirely new signs. This happens when there is no suitable sign in the existing vocabulary, or when poets want to be more creative. The resulting new signs are always visually motivated, making use of classifiers.

John Wilson's *For Two Special People* is a brief poem about cats, dedicated to the two organisers of the poetry festival at which it was performed (both organisers were cat-lovers). It uses the productive lexicon to explore the potential of sign language creativity while creating something funny, and poetically elegant and satisfying in its patterning of the language. It starts with an unspecified referent made with both hands in the 'H' handshape. He seems to be saying there are two of something (possibly two cats), but we don't know for certain at this stage. Later, John takes on the role of a cat and describes the appearance of the cat using body-part classifiers. The bent 'H' handshapes become the paws of the cat (as we saw in Figure 7.2), then become the ears as the two fingers open apart (the 'V' handshape in Figure 12.1a). The hands return to 'H' handshapes briefly then the fingers spread again to 'V' to represent the opening of the cat's eyes (Figure 12.1b), which in turn become the whiskers (Figure 12.1c). After this, two hands in the 'H' handshape join together, and, again with the spreading of the two fingers, represents a big 'yawn' of the cat (Figure 12.1d). Throughout the poem, John never signs CAT but manages to describe the details of a particular cat using a range of neologistic classifiers.

Another set of neologistic signs using classifiers can be found in Paul Scott's *Tree* but the classifier handshapes are highly original in this poem. The poem has a sequence in which a cat, a dog and a blind person encounter the tree. The classifier for CAT is shown by a completely new handshape which does not exist in BSL – the middle finger stretches out to represent the head of the cat while the other fingers and the thumb are used to represent the four legs (Figure 12.2a). The fingers next to the

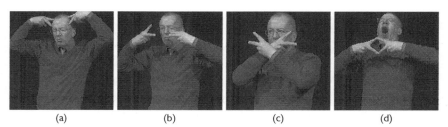

(a)   (b)   (c)   (d)

FIGURE 12.1 NEOLOGISTIC CLASSIFIERS IN JOHN WILSON'S *FOR TWO SPECIAL PEOPLE* REPRESENTING (A) THE CAT'S EARS, (B) ONE EYE OPENING (C) THE CAT'S WHISKERS (D) THE CAT YAWNING

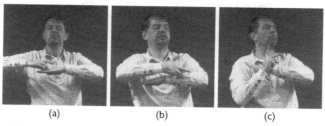

(a)   (b)   (c)

FIGURE 12.2 NOVEL HANDSHAPES (A) FOR THE CAT AND THE DOG, (B) FOR THE DOG COCKING ITS LEG, AND (C) FOR THE BLIND MAN WITH HIS WHITE STICK

middle finger (the index and ring fingers) represent the front legs, and the thumb and the little finger represent the back legs. This can represent any four-legged animal, but Paul clarifies that it is a cat by adding a 'meow' mouth pattern. He uses the same handshape, with a slightly less sinuous movement, to represent the arrival of the dog. The sign is accompanied by a 'woof' mouth pattern to clarify it is a dog. This new classifier is further elaborated when Paul creates another highly original handshape as he lifts up the thumb (the back leg) to show how the dog pees against the tree (Figure 12.2b). Finally, BLIND-PERSON also uses a new, deviant classifier. The conventional way of representing a person is to use the '1' handshape (index finger extended). However, for BLIND-PERSON, Paul also extends the middle finger and uses it to represent the white stick the blind person is carrying (Figure 12.2c).

These are completely new signs Paul made up for representations of these characters in the most visually effective, funny and economic ways. He does not need to explain whether it is a cat, or a dog or a blind person as the classifier makes it clear to most audiences with a shared culture.[1]

David Ellington's *The Story of the Flag* is the story of a group of horsemen, attacking and eventually conquering a castle or a fortress, culminating in the capture of its flag. There are many neologistic expressions in this story. For example, an open '5' handshape is used to represent a cluster of people. This is a common way of using a collective classifier to represent a mass of people but David's signing is innovative in the way he depicts how they nod in agreement by bending the fingers of each hand. Usually the finger represents a whole person and it is not expected to have body parts. Use of the finger joints to represent joints is highly neologistic. Another example is how distance and perspective are shown in this poem. As we saw in Chapter 6, David (literally) enlarges the size of the flag as the horsemen get nearer, by increasing the number of fingers opened from the fist. Although sign languages are visual, it is not easy to show distance because signers can only use restricted signing space since, unlike other performers, they do not normally walk around the stage.[2] This is a highly innovative way of showing distance without breaking the rules of sign language performance (Sutton-Spence and Napoli, 2013).

There is often overlap between the modification of existing signs and the production of entirely new signs. For example, TWIN-TREES can be seen either as a modification of the existing sign TREE (as discussed above) or as a completely new sign.

Borrowing from spoken language

Lastly, signers can borrow words from the spoken language of the community to produce neologistic expressions. As almost all deaf signers are bilingual to some extent, poets can rely on the audience's knowledge of the spoken language to extend their creative capacity. British deaf poets can play extensively with English, for example, to create an interesting fusion between the two languages. There are examples in early sign language poetry, such as the fingerspelling of 'spy' in Dorothy Miles' poem *The Cat*. In the last line of this poem in BSL ('would make a perfect spy'), Dorothy fingerspells s-p-y, and the hand configurations used for the BSL 'Y' (both hands in L handshapes) turn into the triangular shape of the ears of the cat, twitching as if to catch secret information.

Until recently, however, neologisms using English were not so common because English was not widely used in creative signing. This is related to the strong belief that sign language literature is, and should be, independent from spoken language. Paul Scott has challenged and ultimately altered this widespread belief by actively including English words into his BSL poems. He also defied the view that BSL could not incorporate English words like ASL or other sign languages could, because it requires two hands to fingerspell, which restricts the creative use of manual alphabet.[3] Paul creates 'acronyms' in which he takes an English word and develops a short BSL poem based on the manual letters used in that word. Each manual letter of a word, through its handshape, becomes a sign. For example, in *Acronym*, Paul uses two English words, 'cat' and 'deaf'. We have already discussed 'D-e-a-f' in Chapter 5. In 'C-a-t' the 'C' handshape becomes a cat's whiskers, 'A' becomes CLEVER, and the right index finger used in 'T' becomes a cat's tail, winding sinuously as the cat walks.

His poem *Home* describes a deaf home in a highly original, very different sort of ABC poem which draws on the letters spelling the English word 'home' but, unlike most poems in this genre, does not rely on signs with the handshape corresponding to each manual letter of H, O,

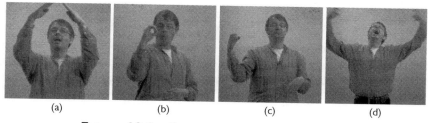

(a)   (b)   (c)   (d)

FIGURE 12.3   Fusion of forms of English into
Paul Scott's acronym poem *Home*

M and E. The first stanza, following tradition, uses signs that share the
two flat 'B' handshapes of the British manual letter -h-, describing the
structure of the house, such as its walls and roof (Figure 12.3a). The
second stanza uses the BSL sign NOTHING that has an 'O' handshape
(although this is not the British manual letter -o- but the numeral zero)
to describe what a hearing person would not find in the deaf protagonist's house (such as sound or music) (Figure 12.3b). The third stanza
draws on the 'm' mouth pattern, to express relaxation and satisfaction,
as he comments on the good things in his home such as relaxing with
a glass of wine (Figure 12.3c). The final stanza describes the noise in a
deaf person's house (including banging, shouting, teeth clattering and
doors slamming) that would make a hearing person want to scream –
and this ends with a loud, genuine scream 'Eee!' to complete the final
letter of H.O.M.E. (Figure 12.3d).

This active use of the elements of a spoken language into sign language
poetry goes beyond simple 'borrowing' – they are a fusion of signs and
words, and make the most of the bilingual creative ability of deaf people.

By definition, neologistic signs are 'new' and made specifically for one
poem. Most of them will not be used again. However, some neologistic
expressions can be recycled when they are seen to fit into other poetic
contexts. Some even become a common technique. For example, the
increase in the number of fingers in *The Story of the Flag* has been used
since then by other poets to represent distance.[4]

Ambiguity

Ambiguity allows audiences to entertain two (or more) possible interpretations of a sign at the same time. They are often very amusing.
Ambiguity is useful in poetry because it allows the poet to convey extra
meaning without the use of any extra words. It is also an effective tool
in creating very intense, complex images in a short period of time.

The two (or more) interpretations involved in an ambiguous sign can be complementary (provide additional meaning to the same scenario) or contradictory (provide different kinds of information which are incompatible and need resolving in some way). When two interpretations are in conflict this can create humour, as we will see in the examples below.

Some ambiguous signs are 'puns' – that is, one sign with two meanings that is used humorously. For example, in Dorothy Miles' *Our Dumb Friends* and Paul Scott's *Roz: Teach a Dog a New Trick*, an excited dog is described through a sign TAIL-WAGGING which has the identical form with the established BSL sign WHAT (see Figure 7.3). Within one sign, the poet can present a double illustration of an excited dog – a visual representation of its wagging tail and the inquisitive tail of a personified dog (asking 'What's up?', 'What is it?', 'What are we doing?'). The two kinds of information in this pun are complementary to each other.

In this example, the poets make the most of the underspecified nature of classifiers. A classifier provides detailed descriptions of objects (in that sense they are very specific), but it is underspecified in what it refers to. For example, a flat 'B' handshape can refer to *any* object the language treats as flat – a book, a car, a piece of paper and so on. In day-to-day conversation, such ambiguity is not a big problem because the context clarifies what the signer means. However, in poetic signing, signers may deliberately privilege the ambiguous nature of a classifier and let the audience resolve it.

A car and a book, although both can be represented by the same 'B' handshape, are very different in their size, and this aspect of classifiers allows poets to play with ambiguity of scale. John Wilson's *Morning* and Johanna Mesch's *Three Haiku* use this to provide a surrealistic turn of events. In *Morning,* the protagonist looks down on a busy morning street from his window, and the poet uses the 'B' handshape classifiers to represent cars on the street far below. Suddenly the protagonist reaches down and 'picks up' one of the cars and starts playing with it as if it were a miniature toy car. The hand which was understood to refer to a car, reduced in size (a real car is obviously much bigger than a hand), now handles an object which can be picked up and manipulated, causing us to wonder about the real size of the car and the real size of the hand. In *Three Haiku,* the poet reaches out to the sun (represented by her non-dominant hand) and forcefully re-opens the fingers in order to get more sunshine (Figure 12.4a, b). Again, the scale is completely wrong here – we cannot physically reach out to the sun and touch it – but Johanna is making use of the fact that in sign language, the sun is represented by the hand. It allows us to be unsure whether the signer's hand is the hand or the articulator representing the sun. In these examples, two

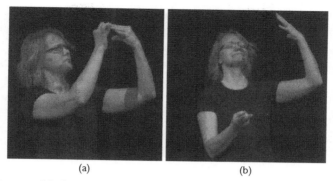

FIGURE 12.4 AMBIGUITY IN SIGNS AS THE HAND IS SEEN TO MEAN (A) A HAND AND (B) THE SUN IN JOHANNA MESCH'S *THREE HAIKU*

interpretations are conflicting because the hand and the car, and the hand and the sun, are two completely separate entities.

Johanna Mesch is a master of sign ambiguity. There is a highly entertaining ambiguous sign in her poem *Twin Leaves*. As briefly introduced in Chapter 10, this poem tells the story of a pair of (anthropomorphised) leaves. In intense summer heat, the leaves start to fan each other. As in the example of the sun and the hand, Johanna makes the most of the fact that the leaves are represented by the hands, so one hand can 'fan' the other, and take turns. Such signs often produce considerable laughter among the audience.

Another of her poems *Ocean* contains several ambiguous signs. This poem also uses anthropomorphism as the main poetic feature (Chapter 7) and most of the ambiguity comes as a result of anthropomorphism. When the personified ocean 'holds the world in her arms', the sign can also be understood as the poet tracing the outline of the planet. When a boat drops some chemicals in the water and pollutes the ocean, there is an ambiguous sign which can be glossed as POISON-SPREADS-IN-THE-WATER or OCEAN-BECOMES-SICK-IN-THE-STOMACH due to the fact that it is articulated in the poet's stomach area (which also refers to the deep sea).

It is also possible to create ambiguity at the thematic level, making an entire poem look ambiguous. For example, in Johanna Mesch's *Earthquake*, she provides a bird's-eye view of a city that is constantly destroyed by earthquakes. The poet seems to be taking on a poetic persona of a malevolent god or creator who takes pleasure in causing the earthquakes and destroying the city. After a few times, however, the buildings become much stronger, and the god or the creator can no longer destroy the city. Frustrated, the persona suddenly shows a gesture of grabbing the edge of a tablecloth, pulling it sharply from the table, and seems satisfied to see that all the glasses remain on the table, intact. While the title of the poem suggests it is about the earthquakes, the audience is left to wonder whether it was really a story of a city and its buildings or about a table and glasses on it.[5] The classifiers which were originally understood as TALL-BUILDINGS can indeed refer to TALL-GLASSES and what has been perceived as the broad flat land can also be seen as a table. These two interpretations are completely disconnected (only connected through the use of underspecified classifiers) and create a satisfying puzzle for the audience to resolve.[6]

Morphing (Blending)

Morphing creates another type of ambiguous sign where one sign merges into another with such a smooth transition that it is not clear where one ends and the other starts. Some people term it morphing (as it is to do with the transformation of the form), others term it blending (as two meanings are blended in one sign). Normally this is done through using the same handshape (thus, the device can also be called 'handshape blends'). It aims to produce a smooth transition between signs (which is important in poetry) and in fusing two apparently discrete signs, it obliges the viewer to find the connection.

We see this device in many poems. For example, Paul Scott's *Three Queens* has the sign RECOGNISED (referring to BSL being recognised as an official language in the UK) which slowly moves upward and becomes the sign FLAG (the Union Jack) – see Figure 12.5. This morphing emphasises the national recognition of BSL (indicated by the flag). The connection between these two morphed signs is used to highlight the capability of sign language. In Penny Beschizza's *Sign Language,* the sign

FIGURE 12.5   BLENDING OF TWO SIGNS (RECOGNISED AND FLAG) IN PAUL SCOTT'S *THREE QUEENS*

TWO-PEOPLE-APPROACH-AND-TOUCH-EACH-OTHER (both hands in 'B' handshape, each representing a hand of each person, moving around and touching each other) becomes SIGNING (both hands are now moving as one sign). The process of two deaf people getting to know each other is skilfully represented through a smooth transition between two morphed signs.

Summary

Both neologism and ambiguity stimulate the audience's minds by creating something unexpected, and increase the joy of watching a poem in a visual language. This is very important in artistic signing, as the poets' task is to stretch the boundary of language, always seeking new expression and ways of meaning-making, using a small number of carefully-selected words. We saw that neologism occurs when signs are modified, when new signs are created and when they are borrowed from spoken language. In all cases they can draw attention to the form of the language.

Notes

1. Further evidence of the general ambiguity of this sign without the mouth pattern and the importance of shared cultural understanding between the poet and audience, comes from the fact that Brazilian audiences frequently think the animal is an anteater.
2. Some deaf performers, for example Peter Cook, do move around the stage to perform.
3. It is true that there are many fewer examples of ABC stories in BSL than in ASL but Paul has shown that it is possible to create these signed forms.
4. This poses an interesting question in terms of the ownership of neologistic expressions and the notion of plagiarism in sign language literature.
5. Johanna uses a similar trick in another poem, *Tsunami*. What the poem is really about is quite different from what we expect from the title.
6. This unresolved feeling is perhaps the biggest effect of ambiguity as a poetic tool. Humans tend to have the urge to pin down the exact nature of something, but ambiguity leaves us with a sense that something is unresolved.

Further reading

Sutton-Spence, Rachel (2005) *Analysing Sign Language Poetry* (Basingstoke: Palgrave Macmillan) has chapters that explore neologism and ambiguity separately.

To read more about the ways that sign languages can create new signs, see:

Brennan, Mary (1990) *Word Formation in British Sign Language* (Stockholm: University of Stockholm).

Cuxac, Christian and Marie-Anne Sallandre (2008) 'Iconicity and arbitrariness in French Sign Language: highly iconic structures, degenerated iconicity and grammatical iconicity' in Elena Pizzuto, Paola Pietrandrea and Raffaele Simone (eds) *Verbal and Signed Languages: Comparing Structure, Constructs and Methodologies* (Berlin: Mouton de Gruyter).

Sutton-Spence, Rachel and Donna Jo Napoli (2013) 'How much can classifiers be analogous to their referents?' *Gesture*, 13(1), 1–27.

Activities

Watch a poem in a sign language that you know that you think uses especially creative language (BSL users could use Paul Scott's *Time* and *No Mask Like Home* posted on the YouTube channel that accompanies this book).

■ Can you identify unusual uses or modifications of established signs?
■ Can you identify new signs?
■ Can you identify any borrowings from English?
■ Can you identify any example of ambiguous signs or morphing (blending) in these poems?

13 Repetition

In Chapters 3 and 4, we introduced the idea that repetition is an important part of storytelling, particularly in oral and folkloric traditions. In Chapter 11, we mentioned that poetry foregrounds language through 'obtrusive regularity', by repeating existing elements with unusual frequency. This chapter will now focus on repetition as a topic in its own right. We will explore repetition especially in sign language poetry, where it is a key characteristic, thinking about the opportunities for repetition in sign language and the effect that it creates in sign language literature.

Repetition in language has been recognised as important for generating emotions through the art of rhetoric since the days of the Ancient Greeks. There are many effects of repetition. It creates patterns to foreground the language and produces an aesthetic effect (it can be simply beautiful to see repetitions in poetry) and it also creates a challenge for the poets, so we admire their skill in keeping strict discipline of repetitive patterns. It sometimes highlights unusual relationships between words and ideas, creating further significance in the poem. Finally, it creates regularity, which produces an extra layer of poetic effect when it is broken. This last point is especially important. We often expect regularity in poetry. Poets can 'break' such expectations by suddenly introducing an irregular, unexpected element, and successfully gain the attention of the reader/viewer.

Olrik's Law of Repetition

The folklore scholar Axel Olrik identified some 'laws' or 'principles' that govern the structure of stories in European folklore (we briefly mentioned in Chapter 8 his law about how stories should end), including the Law of Repetition. Olrik noted that common numbers of repetition in folklore are three, seven or twelve, among which three is the most usual. We have not found many examples in sign languages of seven-fold repetition, but one outstanding example occurs in Ben Bahan's ASL *Ball Story*. In this story, a scientist accidentally creates a magical coloured ball after an explosion in his laboratory. The ball bounces around town, followed by an increasing line of characters, before returning to the lab. In this story, there are seven distinct classifier handshapes, representing:

1. The ball.
2. A boy on his bike.
3. A dog.
4. A girl on rollerskates.
5. An old man.
6. A bird.
7. A large lady.

The scene is shown from seven different perspectives as the line of characters moves around town. The classifier signs representing the characters move along different paths:

1. From right to left.
2. From the rear to the front – coming straight at the audience.
3. Round the corner.
4. Up the hill.
5. Over the hill.
6. Down the hill fast.
7. At speed into the closed door, stopping and falling over.

The repetition in this story serves no real narrative purpose beyond delight, although the delight is considerable. However, Ben Bahan created the piece to teach the use of classifiers, and as a sign language teaching and learning tool it is outstanding. Repetition is an important tool in the learning process, and this is another reason we see it so often in folklore because one characteristic of folkloric language is that it should be easy to remember, especially when it carries content to be remembered.

Repetition of three

As Olrik poined out, across many cultures, 'three' is a very common number to be repeated. (See Alan Dundes' 'The number three in American culture' (1968), if you are interested in the 'magic' number three.) We somehow feel comfortable when things are repeated three times.

Repetition of three can widely be found in folk stories (for example, *The Three Little Pigs*), in rhetoric (for example, '*Veni, vidi, vici*' – I came, I saw, I conquered), in jokes (for example, 'three men' jokes), and in architecture, adverts, music, films and many other artistic genres.

The patterning of three is also very common in sign language literature and folklore and it has many functions in stories and other signed performances. Signers can show the same referent in three different ways – tell it, show it, become it – to build up the image of the character. This three-fold pattern of repetition is embedded within the pattern of seven-fold repetition in the above-mentioned *Ball Story*. Each time a new character is introduced, we see vocabulary signs that name the character (tell it), followed by the classifier sign that shows the character joining the chase (show it), followed by constructed action as the signer becomes the character acting in some way (become it), before the classifier form joins in the chase with the ball.

We also see patterning of three when signers divide space into three areas (for example, the right, middle and left, or high, middle and low areas of signing space) and place signs there to create visually pleasing images, or metaphorically meaningful ones (see Chapters 15 and 16 for more details). Additionally, the same event shown by the same sign three times, sometimes interspersed by other events, builds tension, allows contrast, and creates expectation in the audiences that something will shortly change to break this pattern of repetition. Alternatively, the same event shown by three different signs provides opportunity for creativity, while the same action carried out by three different characters extends characterisation.

Richard Carter's *Owl* provides us with examples of these. Patterns of three in this story build up aesthetically pleasing balanced visual patterns. Although we are told in the story that several children are in the classroom, only three children take part in the action, and they are placed in three places on the horizontal plane: to the centre, the left and the right. The teacher tells them three things – that they must lipread, that they must not sign and that they must not laugh. Three children try to say the word 'owl', and each child struggles more to pronounce the word. At the end of the story, there are three things in the boy's graduation photograph, and this time the signing space divides vertically rather than horizontally: he is wearing a mortarboard on his head, he has the owl on his shoulder and he is holding his degree certificate at waist height.

The same sign can refer to the same event three times, interspersed each time by a different event. The teacher writes the word 'owl' on the board, and after writing each letter slowly, she turns round suddenly and rapidly to glare at the children. As she writes and turns round three times, each event is paired as one slow and one fast. This builds up a strong, visual image of the situation. It is also very funny, so the audience can enjoy the experience three times, as their anticipation and expectation build with each repetition.

Although the *Owl* narrative has many examples of three, they are dispersed throughout the story and they are not always immediately fore-grounded. In sign language poetry, signs or sequences of signs frequently occur three times as a way of foregrounding the language. Paul Scott's *Three Queens* also includes many examples of this. As the title suggests, it is a poem about three English queens (Queen Elizabeth I, Queen Victoria and Queen Elizabeth II) and it unfolds in three parts – one stanza for each queen. Certain sequences are repeated three times, such as Queen Elizabeth I's discovery of potatoes, cigarettes and sign language, each time requiring her scribe to record the discovery, and the deaf people's demands for the recognition of BSL (which finally succeed on their third attempt).

Repetition of three plus one

Another equally important number is four, or rather, '3 + 1', in which the first three instances build up a pattern and the fourth element breaks it or offers resolution to the established pattern. Stephanie Hall argues that ASL prefers this pattern of '3 + 1' over '3' in jokes and storytell-ing. Although other sign languages do not seem to make such a clear preference, there are numerous poems or stories which adopt this 3 + 1 structure: Paul Scott's *Roz: Teach a Dog a New Trick*, *Five Senses*, and *Doll*, Atiyah Asmal's *For My Aunt*, Richard Carter's *Home*, and Dorothy Miles' *Trio*, to name just a few.

Let us take the example of Paul Scott's *Roz: Teach a Dog a New Trick*. This poem uses the 3 + 1 structure to introduce three 'balls', bounced and thrown in an awkward way, and the last one, handled with the right shape, which sets the dog free. The first three wrong balls metaphori-cally refer (through handshapes) to three unsuccessful deaf education methods in the UK (oralism, cued speech and the Paget-Gorman signed speech system). Figure 13.1 shows the handshapes associated with each method. The dog tries to chase the balls, but for each of the first three oddly thrown ones, it jerks back to its owner. The fourth ball is handled as a round shape and the handshape the poet uses makes an explicit link to natural sign language, and the dog is now free to run after it. This

BALL1 (oralism)   BALL2 (cued speech)   BALL3 (Paget-Gorman)   BALL4 (sign language)

FIGURE 13.1   HANDSHAPES ASSOCIATED WITH DIFFERENT EDUCATION METHODS IN PAUL SCOTT'S *ROZ: TEACH A DOG A NEW TRICK*, CREATING A 3 + 1 PATTERN

symbolically refers to the appropriateness of using natural sign language in the education of deaf people.

The first three wrong balls establish the pattern of the human bouncing and throwing the ball for the dog: the dog looking up enthusiastically and chasing the ball when it is thrown, and finally the dog being jerked back, unable to chase the ball any further. The fourth time, this pattern is broken because the dog runs on and does not come back. The freedom of the dog (and of deaf people when they receive the correct form of education in sign language) is effectively highlighted through the 3 + 1 structure. If it had shown only two stages of failure, the impact would have been much less; on the other hand, if it had been repeated four times or more, it would have lost focus and felt too lengthy. Three plus one is the right number of repetitions to produce maximum tension and release.

Repetition of linguistic units

Let us now have a brief look at what units (elements) are repeated in sign language poetry, ranging from sub-signs to larger sequences. We will focus particularly on John Wilson's *Time* because it makes extensive use of repetition at different levels.

In this poem, a young deaf boy at school must write a composition on the topic of 'What is time?' The struggling boy falls asleep and in his dream encounters a famous deaf intellectual in early 19th century Paris, Jean Massieu. The boy asks Massieu what 'time' means, but Massieu does not understand the question because the boy has used a modern sign TIME, pointing at an imagined wristwatch, which were not widespread in the early 19th century. The boy is forced to explain what he means by 'time', searching for various examples (the passing of days, candles burning down and an hourglass). Massieu finally understands what the boy is asking, and replies that time is the distance between the cradle and the grave. The boy manages to write a good composition and proudly hands it in at school.

Repetition of sub-signs

The smallest signed units that can be repeated are so-called 'sub-sign' elements – or more precisely speaking, the parameters that constitute a sign (its handshape, movement, location, palm orientation,[1] and nonmanual features). Although each parameter is small, it can have considerable impact on the entire poem through constant repetition.

We will talk about the effects of repeated handshape in the next chapter in more depth but one example here is useful. The poem *Time* exploits the repeated use of an open 'B'/'5' handshape. It is one of the most common handshapes in sign language vocabulary, but nonetheless its excessive use in this poem is noticeable (SLEEP, PUT-ON-CLOTHES, DOOR, SMOOTH-HAIR, SAY-HELLO, MORNING, NOTEBOOK, HOMEWORK). The poet deliberately chooses the '5' handshape when there are several variations for the same sign that could have a different handshape (such as TIME, SCHOOL, WALK and HOME).

In terms of the movement parameter, a short repeated movement, usually made three times, is exploited especially at the beginning of *Time* (SLEEP SLEEP SLEEP CLOCK-TICKS CLOCK-TICKS CLOCK-TICKS), the rhythm of which resembles the tick-tock movement of the second hand of the clock, and thus corresponds to the theme of the poem. As for location, many signs are repeated to left and right (LOOK-AT-EACH-OTHER, QUESTION-THROWN-IN), or to the left, right, and centre (SAY-HELLO, GOOD-MORNING) or to the right, left and back (DON'T-KNOW) to create a balanced use of the signing space. There are also repetitions of nonmanual features in this poem. Alternation of upward gaze and downward gaze is repeated in the classroom sequence and in the conversation between the boy and John Massieu, reflecting the height of an adult and a young child. Massieu's doubtful look is repeated four times until he finally understands what the boy is asking.

Repetition of signs

Repetition in sign language poetry also takes place at the lexical level – that is, repetition of words or signs. Word repetition can follow a range of different patterns. Firstly, words can be repeated immediately one after another. In rhetoric, this is called epizeuxis and, when used sparingly, can be very effective because forceful repetition makes a very strong impact on its listeners or readers. Examples are seen in Tennyson's poem *Break, Break, Break* and British Prime Minister Tony Blair's speech in 1997 'Education, education, education!'

In John Wilson's *Time*, there are many examples of epizeuxis, as signs are repeated in succession. It occurs especially during the classroom scene, with the teacher's repeated greetings to the deaf children (GOOD-MORNING, GOOD-MORNING, GOOD-MORNING), the books that are taken out of the desks (TAKE-OUT-ONE'S-BOOK, TAKE-OUT-ONE'S-BOOK, TAKE-OUT-ONE'S-BOOK), and the children's doubtful reactions to their homework task (DON'T-KNOW, DON'T-KNOW, DON'T-KNOW). The repetition here serves to indicate the plurality of children but instead of using the established sign EVERY or ALL, the poet repeats the sign to achieve a certain aesthetic effect created through space and time.

The same word can also be repeated at certain intervals throughout a text, which is sometimes called conduplicatio in rhetoric. Examples of signs that are repeated throughout the poem at varying intervals include the most important phrase of this poem, TIME WHAT? ('What is time?'). The sign CUCKOO-POPS-OUT-OF-THE-CLOCK is another example, but it exhibits an 'irregular' repetitive pattern that creates special interest. It refers to a cuckoo in a clock on the wall, which pops out randomly and annoys the boy with its abrupt and intrusive movement. Neither the audience, nor the boy in the poem, can predict when it will come out. It is not clear what the cuckoo clock stands for in this poem, but it is certainly depicted as a hostile element, and its random repetition disrupts the flow of signing. Symbolically, it collapses when the boy finds the answer to the question 'What is time?'

Anaphora is another pattern of repetition in which the initial words or phrases of a clause/sentence/stanza are repeated. Charles Dickens' *A Tale of Two Cities* begins with an anaphoric sentence: 'It was the best of times, it was the worst of times, it was the age of wisdom, it was the age of foolishness...' We don't see anaphora in *Time,* but Paul Scott frequently uses anaphora in his poems. In his poem *Black*, the sign BLACK is repeated at the beginning of most of the clauses. Each stanza in *Blue Suit* starts with a powerful warning phrase: BLUE SUIT YOU DON'T ('Thinking of wearing a blue suit? No, don't do it!').

In epistrophe the last words or phrases in a clause, sentence or stanza are repeated, as demonstrated in Abraham Lincoln's famous speech advocating 'government of the people, by the people, and for the people'. In Paul Scott's poem *I Know Who (Stole My Heart)*, each stanza ends with the phrase KNOW WHO ('I know who'), which can be seen as an example of epistrophe.

Repetition of sequences

Repetition does not stop at the lexical level, but can happen with a larger unit of signing. A sequence of events can be repeated, to create rhythmic or thematic patterns. In *Time*, the conversation between the deaf boy and Jean Massieu is repeated in sequences:

> *The boy asks 'What is time?'*
> *The man does not understand the signs the boy used.*
>
> *Hmm…, the boy thinks*
> *And comes up with his explanation of 'time' (passing of days and nights)*
> *And repeats the question 'What is time?'*
> *The man still doesn't understand*
>
> *Hmm…, the boy thinks*
> *And comes up with another explanation (candle burning down slowly)*
> *And repeats the question 'What is time?'*
> *The man still doesn't understand*
>
> *Hmm…, the boy thinks*
> *And comes up with another explanation (sand slipping through the hourglass)*
> *And repeats the question 'What is time?'*
> *Ah-ha! The man finally understands*
>
> *The man explains what time means (a journey between the cradle and the grave)*

The middle three 'stanzas' in the translation are structurally identical, although the exact signs showing different illustrations of time vary. In the third sequence, however, the pattern is broken as Jean Massieu finally understands the boy's question. In the final stanza, another illustration of time is provided, but this time by Jean Massieu himself.

This example also shows that the repetition of sequences usually involves a slight (or sometimes drastic) change in the last sequence, to surprise the audience who have become used to the established pattern. Often the common repetition of 3 + 1 is observed – the first three sequences establish the pattern and the fourth sequence breaks it. As we saw earlier, many sign language poems adopt this technique.

Repetition of timing (rhythm)

Apart from the linguistic units that we described above, repetition of timing imposed over a narrative or a poem creates rhythm. The simplest definition of rhythm is the 'segmentation of time into perceptible units' (Bernhard, 1999, p. 55), but in poetry, it often indicates a contrastive patterning, such as motion and pause or slow and quick speed, rather than simply repeating units with the identical timing (which can become monotonous). Attridge defines poetic rhythm as 'a series of alternations of build-up and release, movement and counter-movement, tending toward regularity but complicated by constant variations' (1995, p. 3).

Both spoken language and sign language poetry create rhythm by patterning certain units, but what constitutes such units can be very different. Spoken language poetry can repeat stressed and unstressed sounds to create rhythm (meter) or exploit the quality of sound to pattern the sequence (rhyme). Different languages achieve this in different ways in their poetry, but a simple nursery rhyme shows this in English. The words and syllables highlighted here are stressed and we can see that they occur in a simple rhythmic pattern, while the words at the end of each line have the same word ending to create rhymes:

Jack and **Jill**
Went **up** the **hill**
To **fetch** a **pail** of **wa**ter
Jack fell **down**
and **broke** his **crown**
And **Jill** came **tum**bling **af**ter

Sign language poetry repeats a variety of temporal and visual features to create contrastive timings in signing, such as movement and hold (in which the hands producing the sign do not move), oscillating body posture, fast and slow speed, and proximalisation and distalisation (that is, signs placed near to and far from the signer's torso). Johanna Mesch's *Kayak* shows rhythm by oscillating the poet's body (which is an iconic description of someone kayaking in the river but also contributes to creating the rhythmic patterns), and by alternating large and small signs which use proximalised and distalised joints, respectively (see below for a discussion of movement size). It repeats the two signs alternatively: one using the poet's full upper body to enact the paddling of the kayak, and the other using the classifier (both hands in a 'B' handshape held together to represent the shape of the kayak). Alternation of these

FIGURE 13.2   TWO SIGNS FOR KAYAKING IN JOHANNA MESCH'S *KAYAK*

two signs ('close-up' and 'distance' shots in cinematic terms) creates a solid rhythmic pattern in this poem (see Figure 13.2).

Such rhythm is especially important in stories performed for younger children (see Blondel and Miller (2001, 2000) for their research on signed nursery rhymes) and in performative signing, in group events when several people participate simultaneously.

Bahan (2006a) discusses what he calls 'percussion signing' in these group-signing events, which foregrounds rhythm over any other part of the performance. He reports three patterns common in performative signing: 'one, two, one, two', 'one, two, one-two-three' and the combination of the two. These rhythms are easy for people to learn and to sign in groups. Bahan gives the following example of a duet performance in Charles Krauel's film from 1940s USA (originally reported in Ted Supalla's 1994 profile of Krauel) in which we can see that the content is not very profound so the enjoyment comes from the two signers sharing the rhythmic performance:

BOAT	BOAT	
1	2	
BOAT	BOAT	BOAT
1	2	3
DRINK	DRINK	
1	2	
DRINK	DRINK	DRINK
1	2	3
FUN	FUN	
1	2	
FUN	FUN	FUN
1	2	3

ENJOY   ENJOY
1   2
ENJOY   ENJOY   ENJOY
1   2   3

(Bahan, 2006a, p. 35)

In this example, the onlookers at the event clap along with the rhythm of the signing, so that they all participate. Such pieces with strict regular timing remain the minority in sign language poetry, however, especially in modern sign language poetry where the content and other language forms take priority over pure rhythm. Most poems adopt a looser rhythmic patterning while maintaining the natural flow of signing.

Clayton Valli (1993) showed how ASL poetry creates rhythm by producing emphasis or stress in the movement of signs. He listed four different kinds of emphasis that contribute to the rhythm:

- Hold emphasis (long pause, subtle pause, strong stop).
- Movement emphasis (long, short, alternating, repeated movement).
- Movement size (enlarged movement path, shortened movement, reduced movement path, accelerating movement).
- Movement duration (regular, slow or fast).

Wim Emmerik's *Falling Leaf*, a poem with strong rhythmic properties, provides a good example of hold emphasis. It repeats holds and movements in order to produce a regular pattern, in which holds are as important as movement. The poem is a short haiku that describes how a leaf shrinks from the mist and falls from the tree. The first four seconds are given to the performer to set up the sign for TREE (the first movement, slow and continuous), after which the performer pauses for a second (the first hold, in which the poet holds the sign TREE). During the next five seconds, he describes how the mist drifts and approaches the tree (the second movement, repetition of small distinct movements), followed by another pause (the second hold, in which we see the signs TREE and MIST-ON-THE-TREE, which is also interpreted as LEAF-ON-THE-TREE). Next, the leaf curls gradually, second by second (the third movement, repetition of small distinct movements). This curling process stops for a brief hold (the third hold), followed by a sharp fall of the leaf (the fourth movement, fast downward), and the final sign PURPLE concludes the poem. This poem is an explicit attempt by Wim Emmerik to reflect the syllabic nature of Japanese haiku in sign language, and emphasis is given to holds, which achieve a distinct, monotonous rhythm, not unlike the one produced in traditional Japanese haiku.

Movement emphasis (long and short) and movement duration (slow and fast) are rhythmic patterns used effectively in Dorothy Miles' haiku quartet *Seasons*. In this quartet, *Spring* and *Autumn* are characterised by repeated short movements with fast speed, creating a busy and restless impression of these two seasons (for example, whirling movements of wind and leaves), while *Summer* and *Winter* are signed slowly with relatively long movements. Such contrastive patterns can also be observed within each season. Ed Klima and Ursula Bellugi, the pioneering sign language researchers who published the first academic descriptions of sign language poetry in the mid-1970s, adopted music notation to transcribe the rhythmic structure of *Summer*. The repeated hemistiches (quicker repetitions of signs) at the beginning of *Summer* reflect the transition from jostling spring, while the minims in the middle reflect the slowness and drowsiness of midsummer. The hemistich reappears toward the end of *Summer*, possibly foreseeing the arrival of autumn (Klima and Bellugi, 1979).

Movement size refers to the shift between large and small signs, which produces a certain rhythm as the shift between quick and slow movements does, but changing the size of the signing has a stronger visual appeal because it uses space to create the rhythm. The above-mentioned *Kayak* by Johanna Mesch is a good example of alternating large and small movements to create a solid rhythmic pattern in this poem.

Repetition of motifs

A slightly different unit that can be repeated is a motif. A motif is a repeated idea, theme, subject or image in a piece of literature, so by its definition it includes the notion of repetition. Motifs are the key to understanding the overall meaning of many literary works. For example, in the novel *A Grain of Wheat* by the Kenyan writer Ngugi Wa Thiong'o, the Christian motif of the grain (which must die in order for the plant to grow and bring a harvest) is effectively used to foreground the theme of sacrifice which is central to the novel. The novel repeats this motif in various forms, from explicit expressions such as 'blood to rain on and water the tree of freedom' to subtler references to seeds, the earth and the harvest.

In sign language literature, motifs can be thematic (signs that refer to the same or related concepts are repeated, regardless of the way they are formed) or visual (signs which are formationally identical are repeated, regardless of what they refer to). Thematic motifs include references to 'light' (as opposed to 'darkness'), the notions of 'home' and the 'circle of life' (see also Chapter 9). In Paul Scott's *Macbeth of the Lost Ark*, there is reference to a glimmering light, a cigarette lighter, making fire by rubbing two sticks together, and the light from a lantern. Although the signs are all different, each one contributes to the overall 'light' motif in the poem that is about a metaphorical search for the light of knowledge and understanding.

Thematic motifs are common in signed and spoken language poems but visual motifs are unique to sign language literature, and their function is to create a link between two or more signs which appear at first to be thematically unrelated. John Wilson's *The Fates* provides a very good example to illustrate the use of visual motifs in sign language poetry. The poem develops around three women (an anonymous young deaf woman in modern London, Mary Shelley and Cleopatra) whose fates are controlled by Greek mythological goddesses through their practice of 'cutting the threads of life'. The goddesses control the thread of life in a metaphorical sense, but the poem makes it a literal thread. Figure 13.3 shows how the classifier with a 'V' handshape is used as a key visual motif in this poem. It represents: the pair of scissors the goddesses use to cut the thread of life (a); the glasses of the young deaf woman (b); the eyeliner of Cleopatra (c); and the snake that Cleopatra keeps and which eventually takes her life (d). A variation of the same handshape, the bent 'V' handshape, is also used repeatedly to represent: cochlear implants rejected by the young deaf woman; the electrical surge that creates the monster in Mary Shelley's Frankenstein; and Cleopatra's snake headpiece. The poet's deliberate use of the same visual motif ('V' and bent 'V' handshapes) forces the viewer to look for the connection among these distinct characters (such as their loneliness and pressure from society) and gives coherence to the poem.

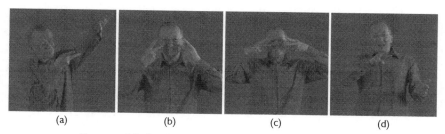

(a)	(b)	(c)	(d)

FIGURE 13.3   REPETITION OF VISUAL MOTIFS WITH THE
'V' HANDSHAPE IN JOHN WILSON'S *THE FATES*

Summary

This chapter provided an overview of the effect of repetition of various elements in sign language literature. We have seen that it can be formal or thematic, and serves to increase the poetic effect of the language used. Repetition and rhythm are arguably the most common features in a great deal of poetic language, and repetition is thus often taken for granted. However, the rich effect it can create (whether it is for aesthetic pleasure or for complex symbolism), especially when the regularity of repetition is broken, makes its study in sign language poetry worthwhile.

Note

1. There is some debate among sign language phonologists whether or not orientation is a separate parameter, but for the purposes of appreciating what the poets have done, it is enlightening to separate out orientation.

Further reading

Klima, Edward and Ursula Bellugi (1979) *Signs of Language* (Cambridge, MA: Harvard University Press). (Section IV, Chapter 14)

Sutton-Spence, Rachel (2005) *Analysing Sign Language Poetry* (Basingstoke: Palgrave Macmillan), Chapter 3.

For repetition of three:

Dundes, Alan (1968) 'The number three in American culture' in Alan Dundes (ed.) *Every Man His Way: Readings in Cultural Anthropology* (Englewood Cliffs, NJ: Prentice Hall).

Activities

1. Choose at least three pieces of sign language literature that you consider to be poetic and contain repetition. (We suggest for BSL users: Dorothy Miles' *Elephants Dancing* or *Our Dumb Friends* and Paul Scott's *Tree* or *Doll*, or Richard Carter's *Looking for Diamonds* or *Identities*, all posted on the YouTube channel that accompanies this book).

Identify repetition at the sub-sign level (repetition of handshape, location or movement) and at the lexical level (repetition of signs).

■ Identify repetition of sequences.

- Identify repetition of timing units (that is, rhythm).
- What is the poetic effect of these repetitions?

2. Using the same poems, identify the repetition of three (and of 3 + 1) and discuss its poetic effect.

3. Watch a poem where you can identify recurring motifs, both thematic and visual. (BSL users may wish to use Paul Scott's *Macbeth of the Lost Ark*, posted on the YouTube channel that accompanies this book). List these recurring motifs and explain why they are effective.

14 Handshape

Five parameters constitute a sign: handshape, location, movement, palm orientation and nonverbal elements. Any of them can be manipulated to create poetic effect in sign language literature, but of the five, manipulation of the handshape is arguably the most prominent. In this chapter, we will explore the poetic importance of handshape, focusing on its aesthetic and symbolic power. We will make occasional comparisons with English poetry, assuming that most readers are familiar with the idea of poetic repetitive patterns of sounds in spoken language poetry. As Blondel and Miller put it: 'organising the structure of a poem around the repetition of a single handshape seems to be the most usual, the most conscious and the most easily perceivable organising principle' (2000, p. 61). Deaf poets often pay great attention to the choice of handshape, because they are aware of its impact.

Within every sign language, a limited number of handshapes combine with other parameters to create a very large number of potential signs to form the vocabulary of everyday sign language. There are 57 different handshapes listed in the *Dictionary of British Sign Language*, some of which have more than 100 established signs associated with them.

The choice of handshape for a sign is often visually motivated, because a particular handshape visually represents a particular concept. For example, a 'B' handshape is used in many signs to refer to a door because it is broad and flat like a door, or an '1' handshape is used as a classifier to describe a long thin object (a pencil, a knife, or a human body) because it is long and thin like these objects. In other instances, however, the handshape of a sign has no apparent visual motivation. For example, in the BSL signs BROTHER and SISTER[1] (made with an 'Å' and 'X' handshape, respectively), the configuration of the hand has no obvious direct link with the notion of 'brother' or 'sister'.

There are two major ways in which signers can use handshape to increase poetic effect in sign language literature. One is to create visual and aesthetic pleasure, often through repetition of the same or a similar handshape. The other is to add symbolic value to a poem or story, so they are used metaphorically (recall our discussion of metaphor in Chapter 10).

Aesthetic function of handshape

Repeated use of handshape in different signs creates a visual resonance. Visual resonance creates harmony and rhythm among signs with aesthetic visual appeal. In Chapter 5, we briefly mentioned several types of stories with constraints, in which handshape can be manipulated at a very conscious and deliberate level, such as ABC stories, single handshape stories and number stories. In single handshape stories, for example, the narrator is allowed to use only one handshape to tell a story. This can be an enormous challenge, as the signer needs to produce a coherent storyline using the limited number of established signs with that particular handshape, or make use of its visual features and create new meaning. For example, an 'A' handshape can be used to refer to many established signs (such as, in BSL, MAKE, PIG, AGREE), and to represent anything that is visually solid and round (such as rocks, balls and human heads). The repetition in these stories is so inflexible (no other handshape is permitted) that there is little poetic excitement because artistic sign language requires more creativity. However, the audience's satisfaction comes from seeing how the signer meets the single-handshape challenge. We have a good example in Paul Scott's poem *Bubble Measure*, when he signs a short sequence of a story, in which all the BSL signs use only the '1' handshape (see Figure 14.1):

I see one girl walk red curls stripes walk-toward-me tell-me time what tell-her one-o'clock sniff walk-away

Translation: I saw a girl coming over to me. She had red curls and a stripy top, and she asked me the time. When I said it was 1 o'clock, she sniffed and threw her head back and walked off.

Slightly less conspicuous in its repetition, John Wilson's *Home* also follows strict handshape constraints. The poem juxtaposes the fate of a deaf schoolboy being forced to speak and that of Laika, the first dog who was sent to space in Sputnik (a Soviet space vessel) – a symbol of sacrifice in a major scientific experiment. The story alternates scenes focusing on the boy and the dog. The scenes told from the boy's perspective exclusively use handshapes 'H' and 'V' (both produced with extended index and middle fingers); the scenes in which the dog is the focus are told using only 'B' or '5' handshapes (both having all the fingers extended). Often, phonologically different variations of the same sign are used to follow this constraint – signs such as HOME, DEAF and DOG which can be produced either with 'H' (when

SEE	ONE	GIRL	CURLS
WALK-TOWARD-ME	SHE-TELLS-ME	TIME	WHAT
I-TELL-HER	ONE-O'CLOCK	SNIFF	WALK-AWAY

FIGURE 14.1   ONE-HANDSHAPE SEQUENCE IN PAUL SCOTT'S *BUBBLE MEASURE*

used in the boy sequence) or 'B' (in the dog sequence). Figure 14.2 shows these pairs of synonyms.

While these stories with constraints can be simply for linguistic challenge (and thus run the risk of becoming mechanical or superficial), aesthetic function of handshape can be achieved in a more subtle way and contributes to the poetic effect (rather than be a poetic endeavour). In John Wilson's poem *Icon*, for example, the handshape associated with the manual letter M repeatedly occurs as he describes the appearance of the beautiful woman, as a clue that the icon in question is Marilyn Monroe.

The repetition of handshapes is often considered to be an equivalent of rhyme in spoken language poetry. Rhyme is a repetition of identical sounds that come at the end of different words, and can contribute to a broad range of aesthetic patterns within a poem. Individual poets may choose where and why the rhyming words occur but they frequently occur at line ends. There are many conventional rhyme schemes, according to

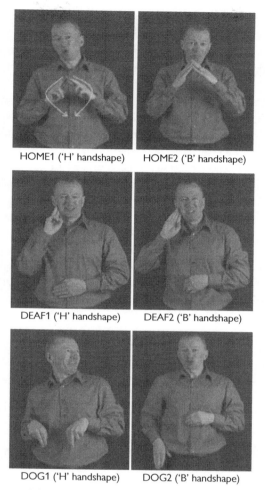

HOME1 ('H' handshape)   HOME2 ('B' handshape)

DEAF1 ('H' handshape)   DEAF2 ('B' handshape)

DOG1 ('H' handshape)   DOG2 ('B' handshape)

FIGURE 14.2   TWO VERSIONS OF SIGN SYNONYMS (WITH 'H' AND 'B' HANDSHAPES) IN JOHN WILSON'S *HOME*

where the rhyme occurs, but one example is a pattern of rhymes at the end of pairs of lines, as in the following example.

No stir in the air, no stir in the sea,
The Ship was still as she could be;
Her sails from heaven received no motion,
Her keel was steady in the ocean.
(Robert Southey, *Inchcape Rock*)

As briefly discussed in Chapter 11, Clayton Valli (1990) claimed that the repetition of handshapes in ASL poetry can serve as line-dividing rhymes (that is, the same handshape is repeated regularly to mark the end of a chunk of signs, which may be the equivalent of a line). He also claimed that the repetition of a handshape could be analogous to alliteration, the repetition of the same consonant at the beginning of successive words, such as 'whisper words of wisdom' in the Beatles' song *Let it Be*. He suggested that the repetition of the signs' movement can be compared with assonance, the repetition of word-internal vowel sounds, such as the lines from Wordsworth's *Daffodils* in which the 'o' sound is repeated: I wandered lonely as a cloud/That floats on high o'er vales and hills,/When all at once I saw a crowd,/A host, of golden daffodils.

This likening of handshape repetition to alliteration is useful for understanding sign language poetry, because handshapes have the same 'initial' effect as alliterated consonants have. Handshape is always visible at the onset of the production of a sign (just as word-initial consonants are audible at the onset of a word) whereas movement comes with time and can be seen as an in-between stage between the initial and final configuration of a sign (like a vowel that comes between two consonants). For example, the BSL sign SUN is a one-handed sign that starts with an 'A' handshape and ends with a '5' handshape, with a downward fingers-opening movement in between.

However, although such terms from spoken language poetry are useful,[2] repetition of handshape is not an equivalent of rhyme or alliteration. They both aim to create a unifying impression over the poem, but sign language does not follow a linear sequence of sounds (see Chapter 11), and thus the notion of rhyme in spoken language poetry, which is tightly linked with the notion of 'linearity', is not entirely applicable to sign language poetry. The repetition of handshapes tends to occur much more irregularly and freely. In this aspect, it is closer to the notion of 'chiming', proposed by Geoffrey Leech.

According to Leech (1969), chiming is 'a phonetic bond between words', or more specifically, the use of the same phoneme in different words that can link the words in unexpected ways. It is a simple, possibly irregular, recurrence of the same sound throughout the poem. For example, Gerard Manley Hopkins' *Spring* shows a cluster of the same consonants [w], [l], [r] and [n] in the lines:

When weeds, in wheels, shoot long and lovely and lush;
Thrush's eggs look little low heavens, and thrush
Through the echoing timber does so rinse and wring
The ear, it strikes like lightning to hear him sing;

While rhyming requires strict regularity, chiming is a more natural and subtle way of creating (and describing) resonance in a particular poem. In

FIGURE 14.3 'F' HANDSHAPE IN STILLNESS, NUT-FALLS AND MOON-RISES IN PAUL SCOTT'S *TIME*

Hopkins' poem, the repetition of [w] [l] [r] and [n] creates the feeling of steady growth and movement in spring as nature stirs.

Paul Scott's *Time* uses the marked 'F' handshape in signs that are apparently unrelated – in STILLNESS, NUT-FALLS and MOON-RISES – to create a similar chiming effect, so the audience looks for a link between the signs. In this case, it seems to us that the poem turns on the beautiful morphing of the two signs NUT-FALLS and MOON-RISES, so that the earlier sign referring to the stillness has primed us subconsciously for the exquisite poetic moment when autumn is encapsulated in the tiny falling round nut and the vast rising round harvest moon of autumn (Figure 14.3).

Symbolic function of handshape: inherent symbolism

Sometimes the aesthetic effect of visual resonance created by repeating the same or similar handshapes is enough to explain its role in the poem. In some carefully crafted poems, however, the manipulation of handshapes goes beyond simple repetition and resonance, and symbolically represents the theme of the poem in indirect ways. In other words, there is a meaningful relationship between the form (the physical configuration of a handshape) and the meaning (a concept or theme represented in the poem). Poets do not choose handshapes randomly, but can carefully select the ones whose visual appearance appeals best to the impression they intend to create in the mind of the audience.

Many scholars, studying different sign languages, have remarked that certain emotional effects can be imposed by a particular configuration of handshape, even before it is combined with other parameters to constitute a sign. Clayton Valli (1993) refers to what he calls 'soft' and 'hard' handshapes in ASL poetry; Ulrike Zeshan (2000) in her cross-linguistic research on handshapes, finds that some handshapes, such as closed and open, contribute to different impressions. Sutton-Spence (2005) points out the association of particular handshapes and the emotional effects created in the mind of the audience:

> In general, the '5' and 'B' handshapes, being open, are symbolically more 'positive' in connotation than closed handshapes, such as 'A' or 'Å'. Handshapes bent at knuckles, such as '5' and 'V' are associated with more tension and are 'harsher' than other non-claw handshapes, which are more relaxed and 'softer'. The 'G' 'V' 'I' and 'Y' handshapes are 'sharp', while 'A' and 'O' handshapes are not. 'G' and 'I' are more uni-dimensional while 'B' and '5' have more substance, and 'A', 'O', and 'C' handshapes are the most solid. (pp. 25–26)[3]

Such a symbolic view of handshapes implies that a handshape, even before it is combined with other parameters and formed into a word, has some sort of meaning by itself. In order to provide more substantial evidence, Kaneko (2011) conducted a survey of the signs listed in the *Dictionary of British Sign Language/English* and correlated their handshape and meaning in order to see if there is indeed a meaningful relationship between them.

All entries in the dictionary were categorised into three types of meaning – positive, negative and neutral. Overall, neutral signs occupy 78 per cent of the entries, negative 15 per cent, and positive 7 per cent. If we assume no handshape possesses meaning by itself, the semantic distribution for each handshape will be more or less similar to the overall (average) distribution. However, this is clearly not the case. For example, the distribution of the '5' handshape (one of the most common handshapes in BSL) was: neutral 72 per cent, negative 6 per cent, and positive 22 per cent. The number of positive signs increases and that of negative signs decreases respectively. This supports the point made above that open handshapes carry more positive meaning than closed or bent handshapes.

In contrast, the bent '5' handshape shows a very different distribution: neutral 65 per cent, negative 31 per cent, and positive 4 per cent. We can clearly see that the number of positive signs is considerably smaller than that for the open '5' handshape, while the number of negative signs has increased. Similar patterns were found in 'V' and bent 'V', another common set of open and bent handshapes.

It is clear from this study that the bent-handshapes (especially when fingers are bent with tension so that they look like a claw) often lead to negative meaning, whereas open or plain (that is, unbent) handshapes are seen more positively.

This association of hand configuration and meaning can be termed handshape symbolism, following the notion of sound symbolism in spoken language. Sound symbolism is the idea that although most speech sounds in words are arbitrary, some sounds are associated with certain concepts and thus appeal to the listener/reader's emotion. Simple, non-poetic examples are 'bursting buds' or 'sew silk'. The voiced plosive of the consonant [b] is linked to the act of buds bursting, while the voiceless fricative [s] stirs soft and delicate images of silk. Another example is that, in many languages, words that mean 'small' or 'tiny' use closed vowels (such as [i] and [e]), while those that mean 'big' or 'large' tend to use more open vowels (such as [a] and open [o]), as in the following examples:

French: 'petit' and 'grand'
German: 'klein' and 'gross'
Japanese: 'chiisai' and 'ookii'.

In these languages, the degree of opening of the mouth iconically represents the size that the sounds refer to.[4]

Some languages, such as Japanese, make extensive use of sound symbolism in the form of onomatopoeia. In onomatopoeic expressions, sounds contribute to sensory and emotional information rather than to a factual or propositional meaning. Observe the following pair:

Ame   ga shito-shito futte iru.
A gentle rain is falling.
Ame   ga jito-jito futte iru.
It's raining, damp and wet.

These sentences both convey the fact that it is raining, and only differ in one word, *shito-shito* [ʃɪtɔ ʃɪtɔ] and *jito-jito* [dʒɪtɔ dʒɪtɔ]. They are onomatopoeic terms which are used to describe how the rain is falling. Although they do not change the main proposition of the sentence ('It is raining'), they add certain information about the attitude of the speaker toward the rain. In the first example, the speaker has a positive feeling toward the rain, saying that it is raining 'gently' or 'softly', whereas in the second example, it is clear that the speaker does not like the fact it is raining. This negative feeling is conveyed through the voiced consonant [dʒ], which adds the sense of heaviness or jerkiness, and implies the fact that it is damp, wet and unpleasant.

Such representation of feeling through sounds is crucial in poetic language, and poets pay great attention to the sounds in words they choose to convey their poetry. Similarly, inherent symbolism of handshapes in sign language poetry can be used symbolically to appeal to the senses or feelings of the audience. In John Wilson's *The Fates*, signs with bent '5' handshapes are

FIGURE 14.4   THE EFFECTIVE USE OF BENT HANDSHAPES IN
JOHN WILSON'S *THE FATES*

used frequently to produce the sinister atmosphere during the sequence of the creation of Frankenstein's monster (Figure 14.4).

In what follows, we will observe how deaf poets utilise the visual configuration of handshape to express their poetic message.

Symbolic function of handshape: contextual symbolism

Although individual handshapes can be associated with certain meanings through their visual appearance (openness leads to positive feelings, 'claw at joints' produces psychological tension), such inherent symbolism of handshapes is rarely noticed in everyday signing. By this, we mean that we speak or sign in day-to-day situations without paying attention to the potential associations between the form and meaning (otherwise we would be trapped in a maze of symbolism). For example, the BSL signs APPLE and EXCITING both have a bent '5' handshape, but they do not have any negative meaning. We don't think about any creepy or unsettling associations with bent fingers when we sign APPLE because the handshape is motivated by the size, shape and tension of the grip needed to hold an apple. When placed in poetic context, however, the potential symbolic power of the handshape can be 'reactivated' and foregrounded (see Chapter 11) or creates a new way of being symbolic. Poetic context is the combination of the overall theme of the poem and linguistic environment (surrounding signs) in which a particular sign is situated. The same handshape can be seen differently depending on the context in which it is produced. We can call this 'contextual symbolism' as opposed to the 'inherent symbolism' we discussed in the previous section.

The works of the Dutch poet Wim Emmerik provide good examples to highlight the contextual symbolism in sign language poetry. His poems strongly associate bent handshapes with negative meaning. For example,

| APPLE | WORM-CRAWLS | TEMPTATION-BECKONS | HOLD-OUT-APPLE/A**HOLE |

FIGURE 14.5 THE BENT HANDSHAPES IN WIM EMMERIK'S *GARDEN OF EDEN*

the uncomfortable impression created in *Garden of Eden* (a poem with the theme of lost paradise) comes partly from the frequent use of bent fingers throughout the poem. Signs such as WORM (crawling), BECKON-ING, and A**HOLE are expressed with bent fingers. Even the sign for APPLE (more or less the same sign as in BSL, shown here held in his left hand), which we used as an example of a neutral sign above, starts to produce an eerie feeling in this poem. The dormant effect of bending the fingers tensely for APPLE (which has been suppressed in everyday use) is now awakened to contribute to the uncanny impression of the poem. Figure 14.5 illustrates these signs.

Another poem by Wim Emmerik, *Desert*, also makes use of negative handshapes. It is about a person lost in the desert, running away from a ghost, and his soul starts wandering in the desert after his death. The signs used in this poem are very simple, but highly symbolic. A careful selection of handshapes contributes to such symbolism. For example, when the poet expresses a sequence translated as 'I pass by a skeleton, and an eerie feeling occurs to me', he uses the bent '5' handshape exclusively to directly establish the eerie impressions through the configuration of the hands.

Other patterns of handshape can be used symbolically. Penny Beschizza's *Sign Language* shows the process of meeting someone and get-ting to know them, in which the number of fingers in the handshape is used symbolically.

TWO-PEOPLE-WALK-TOWARD-EACH-OTHER
TWO-PEOPLE-LOOK-AT-EACH-OTHER
TWO-PEOPLE-TOUCH-EACH-OTHER
SIGN-VIGOROUSLY

(Two strangers walk slowly toward each other
They look at each other, doubtfully
They touch each other, as if to make sure
And they sign to each other, animatedly and vigorously)

As we can see from this example, the process of getting to know each other comes in four stages: walking toward each other, looking, touching and signing. Each stage is represented with a different handshape. The walking process is represented by an upright '1' handshape classifier, the careful and doubtful scrutinising process is represented by a 'V' handshape (a classifier handshape to represent gaze), touching is done by the 'B' handshape, and signing is expressed with the '5' handshape. This involves increasing the number of extended fingers (1→2→4→5), which is symbolic as it corresponds to the increasing intimacy between two strangers.

The importance of contextual symbolism is that it often assigns a new meaning to the inherent symbolism of handshape. For example, we mentioned above that open handshapes (such as 'B' and '5') are usually considered more positive than closed ones (such as 'A' or 'O'). This is true in many poems. For example, in Paul Scott's *Guilty*, the guilt is represented by a firm 'A' handshape while open handshapes are used to represent freedom from such guilt. However, this association between an open handshape and positive meaning is not fixed, and can be rewritten in a different poetic context.

In David Ellington's *The Story of the Flag*, a group of horsemen attack and capture a flag (see Chapter 6 and 12) and the closed fist (the 'A' handshape) describes the actions and behaviour associated with the horsemen, such as drawing a bow, the hooves of a rearing horse, and the heads of the horsemen in line. It metaphorically represents the solidarity of the people and their strength, foregrounding a feature of the closed fist that is firm, rather than being closed and tense. The power and determination of the horsemen represented by the 'A' handshape is very positive in this story, whereas the weak flag is depicted to be flapping helplessly with an open '5' handshape. In this particular poem, therefore, the closed fist is seen more positively than the open handshape.

Summary

In this chapter, we have observed various ways in which handshape can be used to increase the aesthetic and symbolic power of a sign language poem or story. Manipulation of handshape is a demanding but rewarding task for the poet. It also provides an analytical tool for a critical 'reader' of sign language literature who wishes to understand hidden symbolic messages in a poem.

Notes

1. The same signs are used in SASL (South African Sign Language) which borrowed them from BSL.
2. To read more about how far we can take the analogy between repetition of parameters in sign language poetry and rhyme in spoken language poetry, see Chapter 3 of Sutton-Spence (2005).
3. This may be connected with the notion of the closed fist of logic and the open hand of rhetoric (Howell, 1961).
4. Note that sound symbolism should be seen as a *tendency*, and not applicable to all instances – for example, English adjectives 'big' and 'small' are counter examples to this (while 'tiny' and 'large' may be used to support the point).

Further reading

Kaneko, Michiko (2011) 'Alliteration in sign language poetry' in Jonathan Roper (ed.) *Alliteration in Culture* (Basingstoke: Palgrave Macmillan).

Sutton-Spence, Rachel (2005) *Analysing Sign Language Poetry* (Basingstoke: Palgrave Macmillan), Chapter 3.

Activities

1. Choose a sign language poem or story in a sign language that you know in which handshape plays a crucial role. (Paul Scott's *Train Journey*, available on DVD, is a good example for BSL users.) Observe and note the recurrence of any handshapes. Do you find any patterns in the use of these handshapes? What effects do they create?

2. Find a poem in which the poet uses signs with bent or clawed handshapes. (You can use the second half of Richard Carter's *Cochlear Implant* posted on the YouTube channel that accompanies this book, if you know BSL.) Consider the use of bent handshapes and their possible association with the theme.

3. In a group or by yourself, create a short poem in your sign language which makes a symbolic use of open and closed handshapes.

15 Use of Signing Space

Signs in good stories and poems are deliberately placed in specific areas of signing space: left or right, front or back and high or low. In this chapter, we will consider the way signers use space in creative performances, asking why storytellers and poets place signs where they do. Well-placed signs can produce clear, powerful visual images of scenes as they are laid out, but space can also be used metaphorically to represent abstract ideas such as emotions, identities, and power relations. We will consider these literal and metaphorical representations of space as they occur in sign language poems and stories.

Literal representation of space

Describing a static scene

We saw in Chapter 6 that a good narrator frequently describes the visual features of scenes and characters as they are introduced in the story before they show any action from those characters. When we look at a static image such as one in a photograph or picture, the different elements are all present at the same time, but a signer producing a version of that image often needs to produce several signs sequentially over time, and so must choose an order for them.[1] This ordering of signs that build up the image of the scene is not a random, scattered affair, but is determined by various factors.

Research on many of the world's sign languages has found that a scene or landscape is usually described by placing signs in space with the larger, less mobile objects first and the smaller, more mobile objects next (such as introducing a tree first, and then birds nesting in the tree)[2] (Napoli and Sutton-Spence, 2014). We see this pattern in the literature of all the sign languages that we have studied (such as BSL, ASL, Libras and SASL) as performers set the scene by using signs to present an essentially static image before creating moving characters.

Within this overall 'ground→ figure' order, as the signers fill in the images of the ground, the order of signs to produce the images is often motivated by the smoothness of transitions. The skilful narrator will place and move signs carefully and smoothly across the signing space to minimise distracting movements between signs. We could see this as an analogy to the way a camera moves across a scene in film (see Chapter 6) or, taking a more linguistic approach, we can note that Klima and Bellugi's pioneering work on creative ASL described how signing poets often ensure that one sign ends where the next begins. Further research by Clayton Valli (1993) and by Marion Blondel and Chris Miller (2000) have shown the importance of minimising extraneous movement in sign language poetry.

Storytellers and poets also introduce elements in the static scene in a certain order to create a sense of perspective using the signing space. David Ellington's *The Story of the Flag* places a flag high in the distance, furthest away from the signer, then places a river, low down and coming from behind the body, a flat plain higher up and just in front of the body, and a road moving forward from the body upwards to the flag. This is like the 'upward tilt' of a camera shot in a film and gives the impression of the flag being a long way away.

When storytellers describe the appearance of a person, the signs often move downwards in a way that is similar to the 'downward tilt' of a camera shot in a film. In Richard Carter's *Owl*, the teacher is described with each sign moving downwards from the bun on top of her head, to her winged glasses, her ample chest, her corseted waist and finally the skirt over her wide hips (Figure 15.1). In Paul Scott's *Three Queens*, Queen Elizabeth I is shown from the pearl above her head, to the high collar, the jewels at her neck, her puffed sleeves and her skirts (see Figure 15.2).

Movement and space in an action scene

Sign language storytellers often place signs referring to objects and people in their signing space as though they are recreating a map of real world space. Laying out signs by using a transfer of space from the real world into the signing world can be done from the external view of the narrator

BUN   GLASSES   CHEST   WAIST

FIGURE 15.1   THE 'DOWNWARD TILT' IN THE DESCRIPTION
OF THE TEACHER IN RICHARD CARTER'S *OWL*

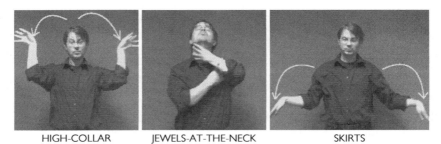

HIGH-COLLAR   JEWELS-AT-THE-NECK   SKIRTS

FIGURE 15.2   THE 'DOWNWARD TILT' IN THE DESCRIPTION OF
QUEEN ELIZABETH I IN PAUL SCOTT'S *THREE QUEENS*

or from the internal view of a character. Skilled storytellers will show both
these spatial arrangements clearly, so that audiences always know where
people and things are in relation to each other.

In Richard Carter's *Owl*, the external perspective of the narrator shows
how the children are seated in a semicircle by placing signs referring to
them in a semicircle. Richard then shows the same view from the internal perspective of a character. In Figure 15.3a, the narrator's view from
outside the story world shows the children sitting in a semicircle with the
boy (the protagonist) in the mid-point of the semicircle. In Figure 15.3b,
the audience sees the arrangement from the character's point of view as
the boy converses with the children to his left and right.

Once the essential layout of a scene is understood, we can see the
location of objects and characters from the perspectives of different
characters. Good storytelling ensures that each time we see the scene
from a different character's perspective, signs are placed correctly
to show the components of the scene in the right place. In *Owl*, the
children at their desks, the owl on the shelf and the teacher at the front
of the class all have different views of the classroom scene. In each case,
when the signer has taken on the role of the character, we see the scene

(a)   (b)

FIGURE 15.3   TWO WAYS OF REPRESENTING CHILDREN
SITTING IN SEMI-CIRCLE IN RICHARD CARTER'S *OWL*

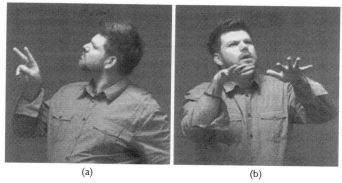

(a)   (b)

FIGURE 15.4   (A) TEACHER AND (B) CHILDREN LOOKING
AT THE OWL IN RICHARD CARTER'S *OWL*

as that character sees it. The owl is to the teacher's right, so when the signer has taken the role of the teacher, signs directed to the upper right show her look up to her right to see the owl (Figure 15.4a). However, for the children sitting in front of the teacher, the owl is to their left, so signs are directed to the upper left to show them look up left to see it (Figure 15.4b). This type of accurate placement is essential for good storytelling, and skilled signers will make many, often very swift, cross-cuts (to use the film terminology we discussed in Chapter 6) as they shift between characters, always keeping track of where things are from each character's point of view.

To achieve all the visual effects described so far, signers must make decisions on how to present the signs in space but they nevertheless place and move signs in a way that directly represents literal space to show a clear representation of a visual scene. Stories usually show literal space, but in poetry this use of space is often combined with an extra layer of symbolic or metaphorical space and it is to this that we will now turn.

Symbolic use of space

Signs representing things placed in space as we expect to see them in the real world may also carry a metaphorical meaning in their layout. Poets may place their signs in space to create extra metaphorical meaning by drawing on basic metaphors that already exist as conventions in our thinking. At other times, the signers use space based on creative metaphors that are unique to individual poems or stories and need to be established each time to reflect a particular context.[3]

Orientations (or directions) are the source of metaphorical expressions in many languages, whether they are spoken or signed. We have seen many examples in Chapter 10, such as GOOD IS UP, BAD IS DOWN, FUTURE IS AHEAD, PAST IS BEHIND, and VISIBLE IS OUTSIDE, INVISIBLE IS INSIDE. These metaphors go deeper than any particular language, or even the modality of signed or spoken languages, because they are part of the way we think, even before we put those thoughts into language. We will revisit some of these metaphors here, focusing on how space can represent them in a direct way.

GOOD IS UP

The most common example of orientational metaphor is seen in the metaphors GOOD IS UP and BAD IS DOWN. This comes from our experience of gravity, and the idea that a body is upright and higher up when it is healthy, young and conscious but curved and lower down when it is not; we get better views when we are higher up; a taller person usually has the physical advantage over a shorter person and so on. For this reason, there are many phrases in spoken languages where relative height is associated with good or bad things (for example, being at the 'top' or 'bottom' of a league table). In spoken languages, these ideas can be represented by words that talk about up and down or high and low, but in sign languages, the ideas can be shown directly in the direction of movement of the signs. The upward location or movement of manual signs and nonmanual elements (such as the head movement or gaze) can carry a positive meaning, while downward movement can be associated with something bad.

We see this in many creative pieces of sign language (recall our discussion of Johanna Mesch's *Aeroplane* in Chapter 10). John Wilson's poem *Home* also uses orientational metaphors related to good and bad, when the dog Laika is sent into space to die. Even though large movements of signs show she is physically moving upwards in the rocket (which we might consider a good thing if GOOD IS UP), each sign showing her slow death makes small downward movements, to show BAD IS DOWN. At the end of the poem, the young deaf man looks up to her statue on a pedestal to respect her sacrifice, showing here that GOOD IS UP. John's *Two Communities* is a poem about a mine explosion. Again, the up and down movement in the signs shows a literal scene, separating the underground world of the miners from the higher, aboveground world of the women. Although the deaf miners killed in the explosion were deep underground, the deaf girl's final vision of them is placed high in signing space, showing the metaphorical positive sense of her determination to keep faith with them even after their death.[4]

POWERFUL IS UP

We briefly discussed in Chapter 10 how up–down orientation also reveals power relationships between characters. In sign language stories and poems, signs for hearing characters who have power over deaf people are often located higher in space than deaf characters. In Donna Williams' *That Day* patronising hearing people lean down towards the deaf character. In Richard Carter's *Owl*, the horrible teacher towers over the deaf pupils and while sign language is banned in the classroom the children sign very low down, but the owl is able to sign from high up (even higher than the teacher), metaphorically giving more power to sign language. In Nigel Howard's *Deaf*, the parents hand their deaf baby upwards to a doctor even though there is no reason for us to suppose the doctor is taller than the parents. In Paul Scott's *Blue Suit*, as each woman finds power and success, the signs move upwards but they move downwards as disaster occurs and the women fall from grace. In this English phrase, the word 'fall' implies a downward movement. The nonmanual elements in Richard Carter's *Identities* also shift in direction as he becomes more confident in his identity. As first, he looks up at characters who 'look down on him' to tell him how to live his life. As he finds the confidence to stand up for his own identity as a signing deaf gay person his gaze changes and he looks forwards instead of up, showing he now has more power.

A higher area can be a source of pressure and we can understand from our everyday experience of gravity that something lower will feel pressure from something higher. This is not a positive experience in many cases. In Donna Williams' *Duck and Dissertation* the character is feeling the pressure of her dissertation deadline. The upper area of signing space is the source of pressure on things lower down. She sees a duck struggling against a strong river current and feels an affinity with it. The pressure of the deadline comes from the upper-right side of signing space down to the poet. The river runs in the same downward diagonal line with the baby duck located at the end. The pressure of the deadline is symbolic for the character but the pressure of the water is literal for the duck. The same use of space – one literal and one symbolic – shows that both the duck and the poet are struggling against different pressures (Figure 15.5).

As we see from these examples, we cannot predict how a poet will use space to show ideas, nor can we predict what extra meaning will be added through direction of movement. For example, not all upward movements represent metaphoric ideas related to UP (such as More, Good or Power) because the movement of signs can have a range of

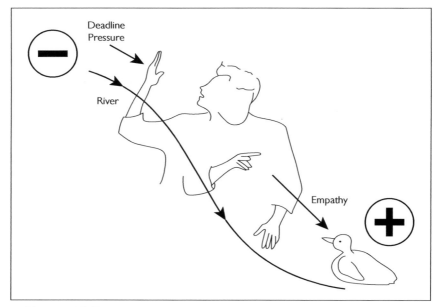

FIGURE 15.5   USE OF SPACE IN DONNA WILLIAMS' *DUCK AND DISSERTATION*

motivations depending on the content of the poem and its context. In fact, there may be no symbolic meaning attached to the space at all. A poem that is based on the structure of a human body, for example, will place things related to the head higher up than things related to the feet because that is how the two are mapped onto each other physically (recall Figures 15.1 and 15.2), not because they are better or worse.

Even when direction of movement or location is symbolic, we cannot expect that all upward-moving signs, or signs at a higher location, imply something positive (as in Figure 15.5 where negative concepts are placed high because power may be seen positively or negatively). Nor can we expect all positive signs to move upward because the poet might not choose the GOOD IS UP orientational metaphor. Positive meaning could come from downward movement (if PEACEFUL IS DOWN). In fact, upward movement may even carry negative value if the poet chooses a different orientational metaphor. For example, a poem expressing anger (which we may assume has some negative meaning) can have upward movements if it is motivated by a different metaphor ANGER IS PRESSURE and this pressure is released upwards when someone is angry.

Expressions of time through directions – FUTURE IS AHEAD, PAST IS BEHIND?

This use of space is very common in expressions relating to time in sign language. Most sign languages use the idea of 'timelines', in which signs move through space to represent the passing of time. They commonly move forward to describe time in the future and backward to describe the past, following the very widespread metaphors that FUTURE IS AHEAD and PAST IS BEHIND. However, in many Western literate cultures, signs relating to time can also move from left to right, following the metaphor that we read from left to right, so things on the left happen before things on the right. Less commonly, they can move from top to bottom, following the image on a calendar that has earlier days at the top and later days at the bottom or the way written language (in Western tradition) flows from top to bottom (thus we can say 'mentioned above' to indicate 'mentioned earlier/previously'). There are several sign language poems where signs move from top to bottom as time passes within the story (see Johanna Mesch's *Twin Leaves* and Wim Emmerik's *Garden of Eden*).

However, although these movements through space show time metaphorically in everyday signing, there are not many examples of this metaphor used creatively, probably because stories and poems in sign language are told in the 'here and now' or even, in the case of some poetry, seem to be taken out of time altogether. Plenty of signs move forwards or backwards to express when an event happened or to show the passing of the time but these are not especially creative and do not add any extra metaphorical meaning to the piece. Perhaps one exception is the cuckoo clock in John Wilson's *Time*. The cuckoo moves backwards and forwards rapidly, echoing the child's dream that takes him back to the past to find out what time is before he returns to the present with the answer.

Although signs moving forward and back refer to the future and the past, signs can also move along this axis to represent other concepts. For example, we have seen in Chapter 10 how forward movement is seen positively (showing confidence, hope, and pride).

The left and right direction – GOOD IS RIGHT?

Some cultures strongly associate left and right with symbolic meaning. Because most people are right-handed, the right is often associated with positive things and the left with negative things, so we might expect to see this in sign language too, but the reality is more complex. Paul Scott's BSL poem *Five Senses* places opposite aspects of different senses in the left and right areas of signing space, and when the poem describes 'taste' and 'smell', pleasant tastes and smells are placed on the right and unpleasant ones are on the left. However, the sensations of cold and hot in 'touch' are also signed to the right and left even though neither sensation is particularly good or bad. This, and many other instances, suggests that sign languages do not have strong metaphorical associations with the left–right contrast. In an experiment presenting two objects or concepts, and asking signers to explain which they like better (for example, the US and UK, or poetry and storytelling) they frequently placed these ideas in space to discuss them, but gave no evidence that they were using a GOOD IS RIGHT, BAD IS LEFT metaphor (Holyday, 2008). When they did show a spatial preference for which concept they chose to place where, it was more due to the order in which they placed things and their hand dominance.

Thus we can say that it is more likely that signers simply sign first to the side of their dominant hand and then to the other side, so most people sign to their right first and then to their left. It is more common to mention the good element of a contrasting pair first and then the bad thing (for example, 'right and wrong', 'rich and poor' and 'happy and sad' are more likely than 'poor and rich', 'wrong and right' and 'sad and happy'), so signing the positive aspect to the right may simply be coincidence.

Given this, it is not surprising that ideas located to the left and right in sign language poetry can be given a particular meaning in a poem, but the use of space is not metaphorical and is only maintained for that poem so that each new poem or story needs to establish the meaning of that division of space. Richard Carter's *Identities* uses signing space divided across left and right to keep elements separate: reference to being deaf is made to the right, being a signer is articulated centrally and being gay is articulated to the left. There is no suggestion that any of these three elements of his identity is better than any other, but just that they are separate elements.

Ideas of 'left' and 'right' also change depending on the perspective of the signer or the audience. For example, a duet poem in SASL by Modiegi Moime and Atiyah Asmal presents the opposing concepts of beauty and ugliness. On stage, Modiegi expresses the concept of beauty and Atiyah, standing on the left of Modiegi, expresses the concept of ugliness. However, from the audience's perspective, beauty is presented on the left and ugliness is on the right. This lack of fixed perspective makes it hard to utilise left and right direction in any symbolic way.

In and out, and close and far

Many poems carry the idea that the inside is personal, unseen and unknown, while the outside is public, seen and known. This means that the metaphor VISIBLE IS OUT (and INVISIBLE IS IN) is related to other metaphors of KNOWING IS SEEING and KNOWN IS CLOSE (so UNKNOWN IS FAR) and VALUED IS CLOSE (and UNVALUED IS FAR).[5] Signs that move inwards can suggest privacy, intimacy, security, emotion and acceptance. Paul Scott's *Guilty* contrasts signs that move and are located 'in' (that show the poet's private self) with those that are located 'out' (to show the public self) – see Figure 15.6.

Many personal explorations of identity in sign language poetry show that identities are metaphorically seen as concrete entities that are kept inside the body. The signer can 'see' or even 'talk' to their identities once they are taken out from inside the body. In both Richard Carter's *Identities* and Donna Williams' *Who Am I?* identity is located in the body, especially the chest.

The metaphor KNOWN IS CLOSE is clearly based on the real experience that things in the world need to be fairly close to us for our senses to perceive them. In Dorothy Miles' *The Staircase* and Paul Scott's *Macbeth of the Lost Ark*, the people who see the distant lights do not have knowledge, but when they get closer to the light, they understand and learn.

There is also the related idea that we will hold things close to us if we know and trust them and feel positively towards them, but we will keep them far from us if we do not. From this, we can see the idea that

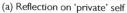

(a) Reflection on 'private' self   (b) 'public' self (talking to people)

FIGURE 15.6   THE 'IN' AND 'OUT' USE OF SPACE IN PAUL SCOTT'S *GUILTY*

psychological closeness equals physical closeness. When people who are speaking talk about something familiar or something dear to them, their gestures are made closer to their body, and signers do the same. This fact is exploited in sign language poetry too. In Richard Carter's *Looking for Diamonds*, the diamond is initially far away but the protagonist runs towards it. At first, no matter how hard he runs, the diamond gets no closer, but he perseveres and manages to catch it, holding it close to his body and finally putting it inside himself. As the diamond is a metaphor for love, we can see signing space showing the idea of unattainable love being distant, and attained love kept close to the body.

Summary

In this chapter, we have seen that good sign language stories and poems place and move signs in deliberate ways to create extra aesthetic or metaphorical effects. When skilled signers recreate visual scenes in their stories, they frequently construct literal mappings of real world space onto their signing space, but they do this in an especially aesthetic way. They minimise excess movements between signs, creating smooth movements across signing space, often choosing to work downwards if they are describing a person's appearance, although we saw that signs also move upwards and outwards to describe a scene. Poems may also use space with metaphorical meaning, even when the space also uses literal spatial mapping. We considered some orientational metaphors that can determine the symbolic use of space, including up and down, front and back, left and right, and close and far, but we also noted that different metaphors lead to different uses of space in poetry. Creative signers often also divide their signing space symmetrically, for both aesthetic and metaphorical reasons and we will consider symmetry and balance in more depth in the next chapter.

Notes

1. There is a style of signed artwork that we might call a 'tableau vivant' in which several signers take part in creating a single signed image. For example, we have seen eight Brazilian signers collaborate to construct a single image of the statue of Christ the Redeemer in Rio. In this case, the final image is presented at one moment, but the audience watches its construction over time as each signer enters the 'frame' to make their contribution.

2. This is commonly observed in written poems and novels as well. For example, the opening lines of William Blake's *Songs of Innocence* first introduce the valleys (background), then a cloud, and then a child on the cloud:

> Piping down the valleys wild,
>
> Piping songs of pleasant glee,
>
> On a cloud I saw a child,
>
> And he laughing said to me:

3. In this sense, this is similar to the distinction between inherent (existing but dormant) symbolism and contextual symbolism of handshapes we discussed in the Chapter 14.
4. Note that this poem is inspired by Philip Larkin's poem *Explosion*. In Larkin's poem, the women see the men walking 'Somehow from the sun towards them', which also suggests they are higher up, but the sign language poem shows this directly.
5. There has been a report that the gestures of politicians tend to place imminent (or important) issues closer to their body and less important issues slightly away from the body (see Cienki and Müller, 2008).

Further reading

Blondel, Marion and Christopher Miller (2001) 'Movement and rhythm in nursery rhymes in LSF', *Sign Language Studies.* 2(1), 24–61.

Lakoff, George and Mark Johnson (1980) *Metaphors We Live By* (Chicago: University of Chicago Press).

Sutton-Spence Rachel (2010) 'Spatial metaphor and expressions of identity in sign language poetry', *Metaphorik.de* (www.metaphorik.de/19/sutton-spence.pdf; accessed November 2015).

Taub, Sarah (2001) *Language from the Body: Iconicity and Metaphor in American Sign Language* (Cambridge: Cambridge University Press).

Wilbur, Ronnie (1990) 'Metaphors in American Sign Language and English' in William H. Edmondson and Fred Karlsson (eds) *SLR87: Papers from the Fourth International Symposium on Sign Language Research* (Hamburg: Signum Verlag).

Activities

1. Watch Donna Williams' poem *That Day* (posted on the YouTube channel that accompanies this book) and observe how different spaces are used metaphorically to describe hearing people (or hearing-related objects) and deaf people (or deaf-related objects).

2. Find a story or another creative signed piece in a sign language you know, in which a signer describes a static scene. (For example, BSL signers could use John Wilson's *Two Communities* and Donna Williams' *Phoenix Garden* posted on the YouTube channel that accompanies this book.) In what order does the signer describe different areas of space (for example, do the signs move top to bottom, left to right, bottom to top?)

3. Using stories or poems in a sign language you know:

   (a) Find examples of spatial layouts that are shown from an external 'narrator' perspective.

   (b) Find examples of spatial layouts that are shown from an internal 'character' perspective.

4. Using a sign language poem or poetic story (Donna Williams' *Bella's Penguins* posted on the YouTube channel that accompanies this book may be a good example for BSL users):

   (a) Find examples of signs that are placed higher up in space to carry metaphorical meaning of something being positive, or signs lower down that carry metaphorical meaning of something negative.

   (b) Find examples of signs that are placed in space some way other than higher or lower to carry metaphorical meaning of something being positive or negative.

16 Symmetry and Balance

In this chapter, we will explore symmetry in creative sign language, asking what aesthetic and symbolic effects signers create through symmetry. Symmetry means that something is well-proportioned and its parts are well-balanced (and conversely, asymmetry suggests a lack of balance or proportion). As symmetry frequently represents balance, harmony, invariance and equality, many cultures see symmetrical things as well-organised, logical and pleasing. There is evidence from psychology research that a symmetrical image is easier to process, so perhaps ease of understanding leads people to prefer it to non-symmetry. Poets can build all these understandings into their signed work creating thematic, temporal and spatial symmetry.

Because many people see beauty in symmetry (for a classic work on the topic, see Weyl, 1952) it is an important part of creating aesthetic effect in many art forms, including language art, such as poetry. We see thematic symmetry in creative sign language in the themes that are presented, especially with patterns of opposition and balance in a story's plot or in its characters. Patterns of temporal symmetry during a text are created through the order in which signs are produced. Finally, spatial symmetry is created in the way that signs are placed and moved in a visual spatial language. Although there are many forms of spatial symmetry, the best-known is reflective symmetry, in which two shapes are mirror images of each other. In this chapter, we will look at these types of symmetry created in sign language stories and poetry.

Steven Ryan (1993) proposed that good sign language storytelling would include symmetry, and we can extend this to sign language poetry, too, where symmetry is often more common than in everyday signing. A study of Italian Sign Language by Tommaso Russo, Rosario Giuranna and Elena Pizzuto (2001) found that symmetrical signs were more than twice as common in poetry than in a lecture. Symmetry in sign language art forms, as in other poetic devices we have seen, has two purposes: aesthetic and symbolic. It is pleasing to see symmetric signs (for example in Richard Carter's *Gondola*, Fernanda Machado's *Flight over Rio*, and Kabir Kapoor's *We, Not Me*) but it can also be linked metaphorically to the theme of the poem.

We saw in Chapter 11 that creative sign language draws attention to itself either by using existing features in the language in an unusual way (obtrusive regularity) or by creating new elements (obtrusive irregularity). Creative sign language can show unusually regular use of existing symmetrical patterns within the language, or can create unusual new symmetrical patterns.

Creating symmetry in language is not very easy because language is time-bound and time flows in one direction from past to future, but some symmetry is possible depending on the modality of the language used. Spoken language does not occur in space, it is linear (one sound or word follows another) and ephemeral (each sound lasts only a short time) so spoken language can only show thematic and temporal patterns of symmetry. Written language occurs in space and is not ephemeral (because the words remain on the page), so written language can create static spatial symmetry across two dimensions, as well as thematic and certain temporal patterns of symmetry. Some forms of concrete poetry create visual, spatial symmetry by placing words on the page in ingenious ways (see, for example, George Herbert's *Easter Wings*), but the symmetry is always static. Sign languages, however, can show thematic, temporal and spatial symmetry through time, using three-dimensional space. Although signs, like spoken words, are ephemeral, they can be held for much longer than speech sounds, and spatial symmetry in creative sign language is greatly helped by the fact that we have two hands to articulate signs, and these hands can be placed symmetrically. At the risk of stating the stunningly obvious, humans only have one mouth, so there is not the same option for creating symmetry with spoken languages. This all has important implications for creative sign language.

Thematic symmetry

Within the idea of symmetry, there is the concept of duality and opposition, and stories and poems are frequently balanced by opposing or contrasting ideas. Humans often organise and understand the world through contrasting pairs, such as good and evil, rich and poor, war and peace, and light and darkness. Axel Olrik's study of folklore (which we briefly mentioned in Chapters 8 and 13) emphasises the Law of Contrast as a very basic rule of composing epics by which two ideas or characters are contrasted. He suggests such pieces of folklore contrast 'young and old, large and small, man and monster, good and evil' (Olrik, 1965, p. 135). For example, in many folk stories there is a rich merchant and a poor labourer, a wise man and a fool, or a beautiful young girl and an ugly old woman. Whatever characteristics and actions the protagonist may show, other characters show opposing ones.

Thematic symmetry in sign language literature and folklore often includes these basic contrasts, especially with characters who are deaf contrasting with hearing characters (recall our discussion in Chapter 5). To name just a few texts that show this, we see Richard Carter's *Deaf Trees*, Donna Williams' *That Day* and John Wilson's *The Fates*. More symbolically, David Ellington's *The Story of the Flag* contrasts the powerful university run by hearing people (presented as the flag) and the disempowered but determined deaf students (presented as the horsemen). Sign language and speech can also be presented as thematic contrasts that are important for deaf audiences, such as in Richard Carter's *Owl*. Thematic contrasts are so fundamental to sign language literature that we may barely notice them, and they extend well beyond divisions between the deaf world of 'us' and the hearing world of 'them'. Donna Williams' *Red and Green* humorously contrasts the evil cold virus and the battered but determined human immune system. Paul Scott's *Tree* contrasts the enduring, static tree with the transient, moving animals. John Wilson's *Two Communities* contrasts the women above ground with the men below ground. All of these produce the thematic sense of balance and proportion that audiences consider satisfying.

Although thematic contrast is common in creative language in any modality, sign languages can show thematic contrasts by placing signs in contrasting parts of space. Russo, Giuranna and Pizzuto (2001) noted that symmetrical signing emphasises opposing ideas. Where the opposing concepts are balanced to create symmetry and harmony, poets and storytellers have an option to use spatial symmetry to create a pleasant visual sensation (and to use deliberate lack of symmetry if they are not balanced to create less comfortable feelings of opposition). We will explore this further below when we consider geometric symmetry.

Temporal symmetry

In spoken and signed languages, stories and poems can construct temporal patterns of symmetry and asymmetry, for example through the timing and rhythm of pieces. Blondel and Miller (2001) have shown how words spoken or signed rapidly, then slowly, and then rapidly again create a symmetrical pattern across time.

In temporal symmetry, the form of the beginning and end of the poem or story can echo each other, creating a 'sandwich' effect. At the start of Richard Carter's *Operation*, a classifier verb shows a puzzled child approaching the poet. At the end, the verb is repeated with the opposite movement as the child leaves, satisfied with what she has learned. As is clear from this example, although the beginning and end echo each other, there is often some change in a situation or a character's emotion.

We saw in Chapter 8 that a common ending in folklore is for the form of the text to come back to where it began, although the audience usually feels something has changed so now they see the same information in a different light. As T.S. Eliot wrote in his poem *Little Gidding*, 'the end of all our exploring will be to arrive where we started and know the place for the first time.' We saw in Chapter 9 that protagonists are expected to undergo some sort of change by the end of a story. Romantic poets and novelists effectively highlighted the theme of transformation (from 'innocence' to 'experience') using temporal symmetry. Mary Shelley's *Frankenstein* and Samuel Taylor Coleridge's *The Rime of the Ancient Mariner* use 'frame' stories to foreground the change in a character before and after he hears the story told by the protagonist. Although the end echoes the beginning in both stories, there is a distinct change in the mood of the character who now experiences the world very differently – a change that is also experienced by the readers. William Blake's poem *The Tyger* famously starts with the question 'What immortal hand or eye/ Could frame thy fearful symmetry?', and ends with almost exactly the same question, 'What immortal hand or eye/ Dare frame thy fearful symmetry?' The second time, the reader is better able to consider the answer to both questions.

Richard Carter's tense sign language thriller *Children's Park* begins and ends with the children playing in the park, creating a sense of symmetry through the poem, but the audience feels differently about their play at the end, having seen the foiled assassination attempt in between. Donna Williams' sign language poem *Who am I?* opens and closes with the two signs WHO and I.

In many cases, significantly, the symmetry is not perfect. Blake replaces the word 'could' with 'dare' in the last line of *The Tyger*, and in Donna Williams' poem, the first signs occur in the context of a question ('Who am I?') and the final signs occur when she knows the answer ('That's who I am'). In both cases, the small temporal asymmetry is more interesting and challenging than perfect symmetry, showing that important contrasts can be highlighted through 'asymmetry in symmetry'. In another example, Brian Meyer's *District Six* starts and ends with the protagonist walking around his neighbourhood. However, there is a distinct change in the atmosphere – the happy and friendly neighbourhood has completely disappeared due to the forced removal of the coloured people from the district. Such change is effectively foregrounded through the use of temporal symmetry.

Spatial symmetry

Sign language literature has the forte of representing symmetry visually and spatially as well as thematically and temporally. Geometric symmetry is a mathematical concept created by moving a shape (which, in our case, is a sign with a shape) so that it is in a different position, but is still the same shape and, usually, the same size. As sign languages can produce signs of varying shapes and sizes, sign language artists have the option of creating geometric symmetry. The transformations in sign language symmetry are often 'reflections', in which the hands form mirror images of each other, creating bilateral symmetry. The signer can also rotate the articulating sign through space (rotational symmetry) or slide it from one part of space to another (translation symmetry). Any of these forms of geometric symmetry can be used in creative sign language.

Richard Carter's *Mirror*, as we might guess from its title, includes many good examples of symmetry, especially reflective symmetry, where the left and right hands form 'mirror' images of each other. It also includes rotational symmetry when the two open flat hands move in a range of orientations and directions across different planes of symmetry – as the mirror poses alluringly, is wrapped up and moved, and suffers heat, scratching by a cat and loneliness when the lights go out. This story also includes good examples of translation symmetry as the two hands (already arranged with a reflective symmetry) move up and down or left and right, while staying in the same configuration.

In dilation symmetry, the sign representing an object can be made larger or smaller while keeping the same shape. Dilation symmetry in sign language may be achieved by flexing or extending the finger joints, by selecting more or fewer fingers, or by moving the hands closer or further apart. In Fernanda Machado's *Flight over Rio*, the hands move apart and the finger joints extend to show the rocks of Sugar Loaf Mountain getting larger as the birds approach it (see also Chapter 6 for our discussion of David Ellington's *The Story of the Flag* regarding how the flag appears to get bigger as the horsemen approach it). A form of dilation symmetry is also seen in film through distance and close-up shots. In *Flight over Rio*, the shape of the statue of Christ the Redeemer on Corcovado Hill is shown with crossed index fingers when the birds see it from a distance, and the same shape is then shown by the poet's body and outstretched arms as they pass over it (Figure 16.1).

Careful study of poems will show many examples of these types of symmetry but for the rest of this chapter, we will focus upon reflections, whether to the left and right, up and down or front and back.

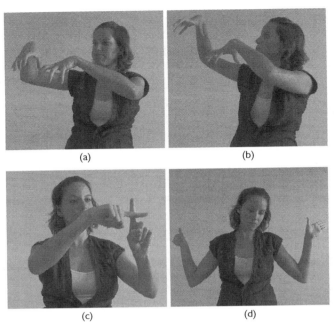

(a)   (b)

(c)   (d)

FIGURE 16.1   DILATION SYMMETRY IN FERNANDA MACHADO'S *FLIGHT OVER RIO* (A)–(B) THE ROCKS OF SUGAR LOAF MOUNTAIN APPEAR TO GET LARGER AS THE HANDS OPEN AND MOVE APART (C)–(D) THE STATUE OF CHRIST THE REDEEMER SHOWN 'SMALL' BY THE FINGERS AND 'LARGE' BY THE WHOLE BODY

Planes of symmetry

There are three important planes of reflective symmetry that signers can use to create aesthetic and symbolic effects. The vertical plane creates left–right symmetry. Our two hands are attached to our body symmetrically across this plane so this is the natural plane for sign language symmetry. Almost 90 per cent of all the symmetrical signs in BSL show left–right symmetry (based on a survey of the vocabulary in the BSL/ English dictionary of 1992, reported by Sutton-Spence and Kaneko, 2007). The horizontal plane creates up–down symmetry such as we might see in a reflection in water (hands are arranged in this sort of symmetry, for example, in the BSL signs DAMAGE, TALK and WORK and the ASL signs HARD and WORK). This is far less common and only 5 per cent of symmetrical signs in BSL are symmetrical across this plane. The vertical frontal plane creates front–back symmetry such as we see reflected in a mirror in front of us. There are fewest of these signs and only 2 per cent of symmetrical signs in BSL are symmetrical across this plane (MEET is one example). Also, many front–back symmetric signs are not strictly parallel to the frontal plane but slightly tilted to make them easier to produce. Similar figures have been found for ASL (Napoli and Wu, 2003). As ASL and BSL are historically unrelated, this similarity suggests that the difference occurs for physiological reasons.

Left–right symmetry is physiologically easiest to produce and perceptually easiest to identify. Our body is also symmetrical in this direction and, thus, left and right have equal status (which explains why some people cannot distinguish left and right instantly, whereas they have no problem in telling up and down, forward and back). This is another reason (on top of our discussion in Chapter 15) for left and right to be less likely to be a basis for orientational metaphors. Metaphorical meaning of this type often comes in pairs (good and bad, future and past) which need asymmetry in their source directions. Up and down direction is asymmetric in terms of gravity and our body structure. Front and back direction is clearly distinguished by the fact that humans naturally face forward and move forward, not back. Thus, it is easy to assign opposing concepts to these directions (hence GOOD IS UP, BAD IS DOWN, FUTURE IS AHEAD, PAST IS BEHIND). In contrast, there are no 'fixed' concepts assigned to the left and right because they are physiologically equal, and this allows sign language storytellers and poets more freedom to use this division of signing space for other things.

A continuum of symmetry

For a sign to show perfect reflectional symmetry, it must be two-handed and the handshape should be the same on both hands, the locations should be in perfect opposition across a plane of symmetry, the orientation of the palms and fingers should be the same in both hands or in complete mirror image and so must any movement. Signs in BSL vocabulary that are symmetrical in this way include RUN, AGREE and STRONG but poets can also use many classifier signs that are perfectly symmetrical. Signs that show this sort of symmetry occur in so many poems and stories that it is barely possible to choose one.

However, reflective symmetry in sign language is rarely perfect and we can see it as running along a continuum. Most signers agree that two-handed signs are more symmetric than one-handed signs; two-handed signs where the hands are at symmetric locations are more symmetric than those at non-symmetric locations; two-handed signs with the same handshapes are more symmetric than those with different handshapes, and so on.

Spatial symmetry can be achieved sequentially when one-handed or two-handed signs are placed sequentially in symmetrically opposing areas (perhaps with alternating hands in the case of one-handed signs). Even though each sign is not symmetrical, audiences construct a mental image of symmetry to experience a pleasant sense of balance. Paul Scott's *Three Queens* shows this well, as the first queen sees one new discovery in front and to her left and orders the scribe behind on her right to record it, then sees another new discovery in front to her right and orders the scribe behind to her left to record it. Other good examples can be found in Johanna Mesch's *Ocean*, where ships enter the ocean from the west and east and in Donna Williams' *Who am I?* as she holds and looks at different parts of her identity with different hands, one after the other. In Nelson Pimenta's Libras poem *Brazilian Flag*, sequential states and cities of the country are named, increasingly rapidly, by alternating hands.

Sign language poems can even create a sense of balance in signing space when one hand (usually the non-dominant hand) holds the final part of the previous sign while the other hand articulates a new sign. Holding a sign contributes to the flow of signs and is a very common feature of artistic signing, as identified by Klima and Bellugi in the 1970s. As well as looking satisfying, this linking of two signs in time and space symbolically links their meaning more closely than if the signs were just signed in sequence.

Asymmetry

If symmetry is not relevant to a piece, whether thematically, temporally or spatially, we may say it is non-symmetrical or dissymmetrical. However, if the signer has deliberately chosen to reject a symmetrical form, we can say it is asymmetrical. Wim Emmerik's poem *Garden of Eden* is a good example of deliberate use of asymmetry with symbolic meaning. Spatial symmetry and two-handed signs in this poem are connected to paradise, while asymmetry and one-handed signs are connected to the loss of paradise. At the start of the poem, when everything is perfect in the garden, the signs are symmetrical. When the snake appears, the signs are no longer symmetrical but the poet always uses both hands and keeps their location in space beautifully balanced so there is movement across the left and right hand sides of space. The final two signs show the human take a bite of the apple, causing the end of their time in paradise. These two signs are made with one hand, which is a stark contrast to all the symmetrical or balanced uses of two hands in the signs before them.

A certain amount of asymmetry in a performance may be more meaningful or effective than perfect symmetry, especially when the asymmetrical images or signs work together to create an overall feeling of harmony.

FIGURE 16.2   THE LAST SIGN FROM PAUL SCOTT'S *FIVE SENSES*

Sign language poetry that creates perfect symmetry may feel too perfect and too predictable, but asymmetry allows variety. This can lead poets to create work that uses extensive symmetry but breaks from it in small ways. Paul Scott's *Five Senses* uses many types of symmetry and towards the end there is a sequence of perfectly symmetrical two-handed signs before the last very significant sign, which is strikingly asymmetrical. It is one-handed, and the open handshape that could be a perfect symmetrical '5' handshape is 'spoiled' by keeping the ring finger and little finger together to represent his deafness (Figure 16.2). This deliberate break with symmetry at the end is more satisfying than maintaining symmetry to the end of the poem and is very symbolic as it occurs with a warm smile of contentment to show the poet has found harmony in something that is not perfect in the eyes of many people.

Breaking and remaking of symmetry

We discussed in Chapter 13 the striking effect of breaking repetition and similar effects can be observed with symmetry when it is broken. As so much of our human experience involves a tension between balance and unbalance, making, breaking and remaking symmetry creates a feeling of moving forward that echoes our path through life (Rose, 1992).

There are many poems whose highlights are made with the (sudden) loss of symmetry, such as Jesus Marchan's *Fish*, which represents the freedom of a fish through two-handed symmetrical signs but the symmetry is broken when the fish is hooked. Other poems follow the alternating pattern of making, breaking, and remaking the symmetry. For example, an

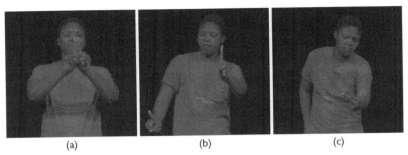

(a)   (b)   (c)

FIGURE 16.3   EFFECTIVE USE OF SYMMETRY AND
ASYMMETRY IN MODIEGI MOIME'S *LIFE'S ROAD*

SASL poem, *Life's Road* by Modiegi Moime, illustrates the relationship of a couple through a very simple, symmetric sign in which the index fingers of both hands are placed side by side to represent a couple spending their life together (Figure 16.3a). However, one of them repeatedly sneaks out and has affairs. This is represented by one of the index fingers moving aside and backward, while the other stays in the same place, thus breaking the perfect symmetry (Figure 16.3b).[1] Each affair does not last long, and the couple comes back together, remaking the symmetry. Having endured a number of affairs of the partner, the faithful lover finally falls sick, represented by the bending of the finger. The audience possibly understands that this is due to the HIV infection when the faithful lover suspiciously looks at the partner who runs away, breaking the symmetry for the last time, and this time the loss is irrecoverable. The poem ends with the death of the lover (Figure 16.3c).

Symmetry and asymmetry in duets

Signed duets also create effective symmetry, as two people are able to provide the two halves needed for balance and reflection. Charles Krauel's film from 1940s USA (Bahan, 2006a), that we mentioned in Chapter 13, shows two people signing 'against' each other in unison, to the pleasure of the audience who enjoy the spectacle of mirror images in the two signers. However, again, perfect symmetry in duets is less interesting than contrasting symmetry and asymmetry, counter-balancing contrast and unity. Giuseppe and Rosaria Giuranna's *Thanks* in LIS (Italian Sign Language) uses symmetry and deliberate counter-balance to make points about unity as the two signers create signs that either go in opposing directions (when they disagree) or reflect each other perfectly (when they agree).

In Debbie Rennie and Peter Cook's ASL performance of *Psychotic Memory* (included in the documentary collection by Nathan Lerner and Feigel, 2009), the two characters repeat the same series of signs several times to create a story. Sometimes they sign in unison and sometimes they produce the same signs but at different times. Sometimes they sign side-by-side, facing forwards, and sometimes they sign facing each other, creating different reflective images. Sometimes the two performers work together to produce a single signed image and sometimes the signs and images they create are conflicting. The disruption of the symmetry created by the timing and direction of the signing reinforces the theme of the poem about the chaos and discomfort of the psychotic memory.

As a final example, Richard Carter and David Ellington's joint piece *Deaf Gay* contains many thematic contrasts as they compare their different life experiences before concluding with what makes them similar. They perform standing side-by-side, creating left–right symmetry. With their adjacent hands, they each use one hand to form the two-handed BSL sign GAY and they hold this sign through the poem. They step forward and back (across a plane that shows front–back symmetry) to present signs that have a range of different forms that they exploit. They sign the two-handed BSL sign BORN in sequence so each person signs half of the sign at one time. They sign other one-handed signs that have opposing meanings in sequence (David signs HEARING with his right hand and then Richard signs DEAF with his left hand; David signs MENINGITIS with his right hand and then Richard signs HEALTHY with his left hand), carefully balancing the opposing ideas with the harmony of signing in symmetry. Finally, David steps forward and signs DEAF, and holds his position while Richard also steps forward and signs DEAF. They are now perfectly symmetrical, ready for the last sign GAY, which is asymmetrical in many ways but it is a two-handed sign and there is a pleasing sense of symmetry because they make it together (Figure 16.4).

FIGURE 16.4   THE JOINT REPRESENTATION OF DEAF AND GAY IN A DUET POEM BY DAVID ELLINGTON AND RICHARD CARTER

Summary

We have seen in this chapter that symmetry and balance (and asymmetry and lack of balance) play an important part in creative signing at many levels, creating aesthetic and symbolic meaning. We have observed that symmetry can be thematic, temporal or spatial. Sign language literature can exploit all of these three, whereas other modalities of poetry cannot easily represent spatial symmetry. Spatial symmetry of various geometric types is possible in creative sign language, due to its visual, spatial, kinetic properties, with reflective symmetry the most common.

Note

1. The fact that it is always the same person having an affair (represented by the right hand) also contributes to the asymmetric impression of this poem, as it prevents the poet from alternating the active hands to create a sense of balance.

Further reading

Napoli, Donna Jo and Jeff Wu (2003) 'Morpheme structure constraints on two-handed signs in American Sign Language: notions of symmetry', *Sign Language and Linguistics,* 6, 123–205.

Reber, Rolf, Norbert Schwarz and Piotr Winkielman (2004) 'Processing fluency and aesthetic pleasure: is beauty in the perceiver's processing experience?' *Personality and Social Psychology Review,* 8(4), 364–382.

Russo, Tommaso, Rosaria Giuranna and Elena Pizzuto (2001) 'Italian Sign Language (LIS) poetry: iconic properties and structural regularities', *Sign Language Studies,* 2(4), 24–61.

Sutton-Spence, Rachel and Michiko Kaneko (2007) 'Symmetry in sign language poetry', *Sign Language Studies,* 7(3), 284–318.

Weyl, Hermann (1952) *Symmetry* (Princeton, NJ: Princeton University Press).

Activities

1. Survey some sign language poems and stories. What examples can you find of thematic symmetry or contrast in the characters or their actions?
2. Try to create symmetrical patterns using signs in the different groups detailed below. For example, you could place them simultaneously or sequentially in opposing locations. What different effects can you produce?

- Strictly one-handed signs (BSL examples include KNOW, UNDERSTAND, SUN).

- Strictly two-handed signs (BSL examples include HOW, JAPAN, BROTHER, BOOK).

- Signs normally produced with one hand but can be two-handed (BSL examples include GOOD, WHAT).

- Signs normally two-handed but can be one-handed (BSL examples include MILK, CAT, CAN'T).

- Two-handed signs that have the non-dominant hand serving as a base (BSL examples include IMPORTANT, IMPROVE).

3. Using poems in a sign language you know, identify some examples of left–right symmetrical signs (you should be able to find plenty), front–back symmetrical signs and vertical (up–down) symmetrical signs. (Dorothy Miles' *Trio* in BSL and Clayton Valli's *Cave* in ASL are good examples, both available on DVD.)

4. Compare a piece of non-creative signing with a piece of sign language poetry.

- Can you find evidence that symmetry and balance are more common in sign language poetry than in non-poetic signing?

- Compare the use of both hands in each piece. How many times is only one hand in use? How many two-handed signs are used? Are they symmetrical? How many signs are made with one hand while the other hand shows a sign that is held?

5. Using a poem where the poet uses symmetry to add extra meaning, observe how symmetry is created and then broken. (Johanna Mesch's *Ocean*, posted on the YouTube channel that accompanies this book, is recommended.) What effect does it add?

17 Nonmanual Features

Sign language is presented through two distinct channels: manual and nonmanual. In sign language literature, the two channels work together to present a coherent piece of creative signing. The previous chapters have primarily dealt with the manual components of artistic signing, but this chapter focuses on nonmanual components – anything that is *not* produced by the hands, including facial expression, gaze, mouth actions, and movement and posture of the head and body. While the hands convey the essential content of a story or poem (what it is about), the nonmanual features play an important role in presenting such content. The same propositional information carried on the hands can be presented very differently depending on how poets use their face and body.

In this chapter, we will discuss different nonmanual features, focusing on their roles in performing a poem or a story. Much of what we discuss is related to the performance rather than the text although, as we saw in Chapter 3, the two are ultimately inseparable.

Facial expression

Signing storytellers and performers, like actors, can show emotions directly through facial expression. Facial expression is an important constituent of oral literature and performance (recall from our discussion in Chapter 3 that sign language literature shares many features with oral literature). *A Dictionary of Oral Literature* defines facial expressions as:

> Contortion of the face by the artist to show emotion and attitude especially in the performance of poetry and narratives. For example, the narrator may smile, grin, frown, wink, stare, pout his lips etc. A good performer employs facial expressions to dramatise his material. (Sunkuli and Miruka, 1990, p. 31)

Vibeke Børdahl, in her study on Chinese oral literature, reports that apprentices of Chinese storytellers 'rigorously' study their masters' facial expression together with the words (2004, 37–38). Such facial expression, together with the use of the eyes, is understood as 'the soul' of Chinese storytelling (Li, 2004, p. 21) and we may suggest that in a similar way the facial expression and body posture of signing storytellers create the soul of sign language storytelling.

Facial expression in sign language literature fulfils several important functions. First of all, it can show the characters' various emotions, which can generate similar emotions in the audience as they watch: happiness, sadness, excitement, boredom, anger, fear, surprise, disdain, desire and so on. Facial expression in poetic signing is sufficient to convey emotions and corresponding lexical items (such as SAD and HAPPY) are rarely used.

Although the characters expressing these human emotions are often humans, we saw in Chapter 7 that non-human characters can also express complex feelings through anthropomorphism. In *Soweto*, Modiegi Moime becomes the town of Soweto and expresses a variety of emotions – joy, annoyance, surprise, loneliness and satisfaction – through her face (Figure 17.1).

Facial expression also reveals the emotions or attitudes of the poet, and thus provides affective information about the events or characters in the story (that is, how the poet, as the narrator or the convenor of the story, feels about them). For example, in his poem *Doll*, Paul Scott comments on the misfortune of the doll with a sad expression, while signing POOR DOLL. This sad expression is not attributed to the characters (a personified doll and the child tormenting it) but to the poet-narrator himself.

Apart from showing the emotional state of characters, facial expressions are also used to differentiate various characters. Chinese storytellers do this by imitating 'special facial features, such as protuberant eyes, squinting eyes, a grinning mouth, shrunken lips, etc.' associated with each character (Li, 2004, p. 21) and the same can be observed in sign language literature. This allows poets and audience to identify different characters very easily. We saw in Chapter 6 that Richard Carter's *Owl*

SOWETO-ANNOYED   SOWETO-HAPPY

FIGURE 17.1   VARIOUS EMOTIONS EXPRESSED BY FACIAL EXPRESSIONS IN MODIEGI MOIME'S *SOWETO*

GANGSTERS   LADIES-OF-THE-NIGHT

FIGURE 17.2   FACIAL EXPRESSIONS ASSOCIATED WITH
DIFFERENT CHARACTERS IN BRIAN MEYER'S *DISTRICT SIX*

uses facial expression and body posture to identify the mother and her son. In another example, in the SASL poem *District Six* by Brian Meyer, the protagonist encounters various colourful characters in his neighbourhood. They are represented through idiosyncratic facial features, such as local gangsters with intimidating big eyes, slanted gaze and pursed lips, and ladies of the night with a flirtatious sidelong glance (Figure 17.2). This helps clarify which character role the performer is taking on.

The storyteller can identify different characters by attributing to each one a psychological state, level of intelligence or personality, such as shyness, stupidity, indifference or curiosity. Some characters may exhibit a mixture of these attributes. (Paul Scott's protagonists are often very complex – pride, a sense of inferiority, ignorance and intelligence can be found in one character.) However, there are also many characters in sign language literature who have a more fixed, simplified personality, accompanied by facial expressions that are associated with it.

For example, the two main characters in Paul Scott's *Too Busy to Hug; No Time to See* are clearly distinguished by their distinct facial expressions which reveal their personalities: the Mountain mostly puts on superior, indifferent or annoyed expressions, while the Sea often has a mischievous look with twinkling eyes and a naughty smile (Figure 17.3a and b). Such differences in facial expressions, together with their manual components and gaze directions, help the audience identify which character the poet is representing, while also telling us with great economy much more about their psychological states, motivations and characteristics. Similarly, the two frogs in Richard Carter's *Prince Looking for Love* are clearly differentiated by an intelligent, proud, and superior look on one frog, and a dull, stupid look on the other (Figure 17.3c and d).

In some cases, an important turn of events can be indicated by facial expression alone, instead of manual signs (which normally convey the

(a) MOUNTAIN   (b) SEA   (c) PROUD-FROG   (d) STUPID-LOOKING-FROG

FIGURE 17.3 FACIAL EXPRESSIONS OF DIFFERENT CHARACTERS FROM (A)–(B) PAUL SCOTT'S *TOO BUSY TO HUG, NO TIME TO SEE*, AND (C)–(D) RICHARD CARTER'S *PRINCE LOOKING FOR LOVE*

plot). In Atiyah Asmal's *For My Aunt*, the most significant event in the story – the death of the rose – is first suggested by a sharp change in the poet's facial expression while manual signs continue with the routine movement of the bee flying to and back from the rose. The audience is informed that something bad has happened purely by the expression on the poet's face.

While words are not understood by those who don't know the language, most facial expressions associated with common human emotions are said to be universal (Ekman, 1999). Thus, performers can make use of facial expression to build immediate connections with the audience and create empathy.

Gaze

The eyes provide a lot of information through their aperture and gaze. Eye aperture involves the degree of opening of the eyes and we saw in the discussion above that it is usually considered part of facial expression. Gaze is the direction and length of the look, and will be discussed in detail here. For signers, gaze conveys both linguistic and non-linguistic information. It is an intrinsic part of the grammar of sign languages in general, and in artistic signing in particular.

Kaneko and Mesch (2013) propose six different types of gaze in creative sign language, based on a variety of criteria including gaze directions, functions, relationship with manual signs and the role of the poet.

1. Gaze to the audience (Narrator's gaze).
2. Characters' gaze.
3. Spotlight gaze.
4. Reactive gaze.

5. Panoptic gaze.
6. Prescient gaze.

First of all, gaze can be directed at the audience (or to the camera). This gaze is usually understood as the narrator's gaze as the performer looks straight at the audience to narrate, comment or explain what happens in the story. The performer here exists in the same time and space as the audience (in other words, *outside* of the story) and invites us into the story world as him or herself, instead of putting on any poetic persona.

For example, at the beginning of Atiyah Asmal's *For My Aunt*, the poet addresses the audience by looking at them. This sequence serves as an introduction in which Atiyah establishes what her poem is about – that is, the 'rose' (which stands for her aunt). She takes on the role of a narrator and explains about the rose, such as her colour, intelligence and the fact that she was also deaf, while looking forwards. This introductory part of *For My Aunt* is in contrast to the rest of the poem, in which Atiyah becomes the character of the personified bee who loves the rose and visits her frequently. She is now completely immersed in the story world, and no longer acknowledges audience members by making eye contact with them. This gaze behaviour is called character's gaze. The performer here becomes a character, and tells the story through his or her eyes. Whereas the-performer-as-a-narrator 'narrates' the story and thus knows what happens next, the-performer-as-a-character is inside the story world, and may not be fully aware of what is happening beyond the immediate situation.

In spotlight gaze, the gaze simply follows the sign. The function of this gaze is to foreground, reinforce and 'shed light on' what the hands are doing (hence the term 'spotlight'). By tracing the movement of their own hands, poets are inviting us to pay attention to them as well. This allows performers to focus on certain signs without altering the signs themselves.[1]

The opening sequence of Richard Carter's *Surprise Apple* is characterised by the use of spotlight gaze. The poet looks at his hands, which represent the land and a tree. They use a plain 'B' handshape and do not look particularly unusual, except that the fingers of the dominant hand are not spread, as we would normally expect in the BSL sign TREE (Figure 17.4a, b). The hands remain static during this part. However, when his gaze reaches the top of the tree, the fingers suddenly open up and what we perceived as the land floats away (Figure 17.4c, d). This second part is unusual as the sign TREE does not usually involve a sudden spread of the fingers, nor does the sign LAND include a movement. The spotlight gaze at the beginning (while hands are still static) alerts the audience to keep an eye on the hands as something strange is about to take place.

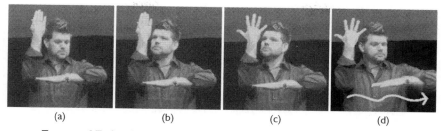

FIGURE 17.4   Spotlight gaze in Richard Carter's *Surprise Apple*

Reactive gaze also looks at the manual sign, but instead of highlighting and supporting the sign as in the case of spotlight gaze, it reacts to, reflects upon and sometimes even questions what hands are doing. Performers look at their own hands as if they do not know what is going on. In *For My Aunt*, when the rose becomes sick and dies, the poet looks at her left hand (representing the rose) in shock and surprise, questioning what has happened, and trying to do something about it.[2]

Another good example of reactive gaze is in Donna Williams' *Who Am I?*. When the poet explains that she is labelled as 'hearing impaired', she repeats the sign IMPAIRED (which could also be glossed as DAMAGED) by looking at her hands, as if to question, 'What do you mean I'm impaired (damaged)?'

Panoptic gaze aims to provide a holistic (and substantial) description of a poetic scene through the eyes and hands highlighting different parts of it. In this sense, panoptic gaze is complementary to manual signs. This is especially useful when poets want to describe the idea of 'a lot of something'. They only have two hands, but their eyes can point to a third location to add depth in their description. Examples can be found in Johanna Mesch's *Two Leaves* and Donna Williams' *My Home is My Castle* in which the presence of many objects (leaves, and books and DVDs, respectively) are indicated jointly by the hands and gaze.

Finally, prescient gaze foretells what will happen next by looking at a location where the next sign will occur. Unlike spotlight or reactive gaze in which the eyes follow the hands, prescient gaze precedes manual signs. For example, in Johanna Mesch's *Spring*, the poet sees and takes pictures of tall, grown trees (Figure 17.5a), and then notices small shoots coming out of the ground. The shoots are first indicated by the gaze (b). Johanna first looks at a lower location while her hands maintain the previous sign HOLDING-IPAD and then produces a manual sign there (c). The gaze precedes the manual sign, and foretells the location of the next sign.

Performers adopt different gaze behaviours depending on their own style (each performer may favour a different gaze pattern), on the type of

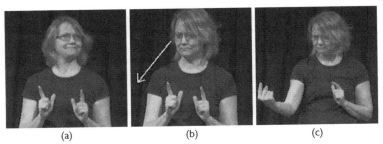

(a)   (b)   (c)

FIGURE 17.5   PRESCIENT GAZE IN JOHANNA MESCH'S *SPRING*

story or poem (stories with a lot of action and many characters are likely to use character's gaze much more than signed haiku, for example), or on the situation (the poet may engage more with a live audience than with an audience imagined through the camera).

Apart from these patterns, gaze also produces various metaphorical interpretations, making use of orientational metaphors. For example, we discussed in Chapters 10 and 15 that up and down direction can reveal power relationships among different characters. This is often expressed by the direction of gaze. Characters with authority may 'look down upon' characters with lower status in both literal and metaphorical senses. This can be observed in many poems, including Clayton Valli's *Lone Sturdy Tree* and *Snowflake*, Donna Williams' *That Day*, Richard Carter's *Identities* and *Owl*, John Wilson's *For a Deaf Friend* and *The Fates*.

Gaze can also give information about time. Sutton-Spence and Woll (1999) point out that looking sideways can indicate the past, looking straight ahead or down can indicate the present, and upward gaze can indicate the future. This can be used effectively in sign language literature where economy of signing can still produce a great deal of information. Donna Williams casts a faraway, upward gaze in *That Day*, when she talks about her ideal deaf world in the far future, and Richard Carter in *Time* looks sideways so that he literally looks back to his past.

Mouth actions

Like the eyes, the mouth can add several types of information to manual signs. Sometimes the information shown on the mouth is independent of that shown on the hands, producing a message that is the sum of the information on the mouth and on the hands. For example, in Paul Scott's *I Know Who (Stole My Heart)*, the poet explains how he went through an oral education throughout his childhood. He signs THROUGHOUT on his hands while his mouth enacts the forced speech. The meaning of 'being forced to speak throughout childhood' is created by combining these two components.

Researchers have identified two basic types of mouth action: mouthings and mouth gestures (Boyes Braem and Sutton-Spence, 2001). *Mouthings* have their origin in spoken language and may appear as if the signer is articulating the corresponding English word (such as the mouthing of the English word 'cat' while signing the BSL sign CAT).[3] *Mouth gestures* are not related to spoken languages in any way and occur spontaneously in sign languages, often as part of constructed action (for example, a tense mouth pattern describes something is done intensely or with effort). Although mouthings play a part in creative sign language, we will focus on mouth gestures here as they frequently create extra poetic effect.

Mouth gestures often evoke a vivid sensory image through their different visual appearances, such as open or closed mouth, tense or relaxed muscles, puffed or sucked-in cheeks, and round or pursed lips. The different ways of releasing the air from the mouth, such as a smooth, continuous release of air, as opposed to rough and abrupt bursts of air can also create different images. Some of these mouth actions can be understood as representing deaf performers' re-interpretation of 'sounds' and other sensory images associated with the action or object. Fowler and Heaton (2006) call them 'onomatopoeia' in BSL. These mouth actions can be based upon physical sensation, for example when the lips vibrate as part of the BSL sign DRILL, reflecting the vibration of the drill. Visual perception can also motivate the mouth action, such as when the release of air from the mouth represents air coming out of a tyre in the sign TYRE-GOING-FLAT. Fowler and Heaton also suggest the mouth action can be based on the expectation of changes of state during an action. For example, the sign GOAL-SCORE in football may involve the rapid closure of the mouth because the net is closed and catches the ball, while the mouth in the sign GOAL-SCORE in basketball does not close because the net is open to let the ball slip through. Such onomatopoeic expressions can be applied to objects that do not make real sounds, and are better understood as creative ways of representing deaf people's sensory experiences rather than as incomplete representations of the sound. Their creative nature makes them highly relevant to poetic signing.

To illustrate this, we use examples from a duet poem in SASL entitled *Ugly, Beautiful,* performed by Atiyah Asmal and Modiegi Moime. In this duet, Modiegi represents the concept of beauty, while Atiyah embodies the concept of ugliness. They describe natural forces, such as soft clouds in the sky, still water, and plants growing after the rain for Modiegi (representing beauty), and the eruption of volcanos, thunderstorms and plants destroyed by the storms for Atiyah (representing ugliness). Modiegi uses

VOLCANO   LIGHTNING   FAST-CURRENT

FIGURE 17.6 VARIOUS MOUTH ACTIONS PERFORMED
BY ATIYAH ASMAL IN *UGLY, BEAUTIFUL*

very few mouth gestures apart from a few smooth ones, where air comes through her mouth without obstruction. On the other hand, roughness associated with eruptions, thunderstorms and the destruction of lives, are expressed by Atiyah through a variety of mouth gestures. A single puffed cheek is used to describe the pressure within volcano which is about to erupt, the lightning is expressed by the sharp release of air from the mouth (we can almost hear the crack of the lightning), and a very tense 'ee' mouth action is used to represent the fierce current of water and plants being destroyed (Figure 17.6). Although the basic information is carried by the hands, these mouth gestures provide rich sensory images of the intensity of the scenes, and are essential part of this poem. They also provide a thematic contrast between ugliness and beauty – the former is seen through rough, restless and intense natural forces, while the latter is associated with smoothness. This can be analogous to sound effects in movies. Filmmakers often add gentle music to peaceful scenes, and disruptive sounds or noise to illustrate rough actions.

Body postures and movements

The use of the poet's upper body and head is also an important part of sign language literature. Unlike performers of arts, such as mime, theatre or dance, sign language poets and storytellers usually stand in one place, face the audience, and primarily present their work using only the upper half of the body. It is unusual for them to move around the stage and/or shift the angle of their body drastically.[4]

Performers use the movement of the head, shoulder, and torso (that is, above the waist) to produce aesthetic effects. For example, an oscillating movement of the upper body often creates rhythm (see Chapter 13) and also indicates that the character is 'on the move'. This is found in Richard

Carter's *Jam*, which alternates 'active' scenes (the poet walks into different supermarkets in an attempt to find the best-tasting jam) with more 'reflective' scenes (the poet reflects on the jam he has tasted). While the body remains static during a reflective, mental scene, Richard starts moving his upper body in an oscillating manner once it is over, suggesting that he is now actively involved with the physical world.

The body and head posture involves direction of movement and this, again, can be used as the source for orientational metaphors. For example, when the rose dies in *For My Aunt*, the bee hangs her head in sadness. When she comes to terms with what has happened, however, her body posture significantly changes and now she is upright, her chin position is up and forward, and she is ready to fly forward (GOOD IS UP, BAD IS DOWN and FORWARD IS GOOD, BACK IS BAD).

In Modiegi Moime's *June 16th*, a poem about the Soweto Uprising,[5] the position of the chin adds symbolic value. First of all, the poem uses up and down positioning of the chin (and the body) to represent negative and positive sequences, respectively. The chin is lowered significantly during the scene in which a student is shot dead by the police and his coffin is carried by his friends in grief. In contrast, the poem ends with an upward chin position, symbolising the improved situation of township education after the uprising. It also uses back and forward positioning of the chin to represent the attitude of students at school. As Ichida (2004) points out,[6] the 'forward' chin position tends to indicate the signer's interest or interference, and the 'back' position shows indifference or lack of engagement.[7] In the first school sequence, in which students are taught in a language they don't understand, the poet's chin position is held back, visually illustrating that they cannot engage with their study. After the uprising, students gain access to education in their own language. They start to engage more with their study, which is clearly shown with the forward chin position together with a change in facial expression.

For extra impact, however, performers can move the head and body in more unconventional ways. For example, at the end of Paul Scott's *I Know Who (Stole My Heart)*, the poet's entire body sharply turns 90 degrees to the left while his right arm is extended to the audience with an open palm (a 'stop' gesture). Until this moment, Paul has maintained the conventional practice of facing the audience, so this last sign becomes highly noticeable and successfully conveys the poet's determination that he will not let anyone take away his heart (Figure 17.7).

Another example of the dynamic use of the body can be found in Kabir Kapoor's *Evolution*. This poem starts and ends with the poet turning his

FIGURE 17.7 THE USE OF BODY MOVEMENT IN PAUL SCOTT'S *I KNOW WHO (STOLE MY HEART)*

back to the audience. Throughout the performance, Kabir uses his entire body dramatically to 'enact' the concept of evolution by becoming different creatures. Most of his signs are outside the regular signing space, showing how more 'theatrical' elements are readily incorporated into sign language poems (Figure 17.8).

Summary

This chapter has discussed various nonmanual components that contribute to the presentation of a poem or a story. Exhibiting multiple components simultaneously and adding depth to the description of a poetic scene is important in sign language literature. Audiences of artistic sign language need to pay attention not only to the manual components but also to the face, eyes, mouth, head and body of the performer.

FIGURE 17.8 THE DYNAMIC USE OF BODY MOVEMENT IN KABIR KAPOOR'S *EVOLUTION*

Notes

1. Spotlight gaze may overlap with other kinds of gaze behaviour. For example, when Atiyah takes on the character of the bee in *For My Aunt*, her gaze also traces the movement of her hands to highlight the happy and cheerful movement of the bee flying to and back from the rose. This can be understood as both character's gaze and spotlight gaze.

2. Again, this overlaps with character's gaze.

3. Mouthings occur systematically in many European sign languages (including BSL, Dutch Sign Language and Swedish Sign Language), whereas it is less common in other sign languages (including ASL, SASL and Libras). It also depends on an individual signer's educational background (their level of education, familiarity with spoken language, and if they had a predominantly oral or bilingual education), and also on sociolinguistic factors (formal signing may use more mouthings than informal signing).

4. Some performers do – see Peter Cook and Kenny Lerner, for their work in the Flying Words Project.

5. On 16 June 1976, an estimated 20,000 schoolchildren in Soweto (a township in the city of Johannesburg in South Africa) went on protests against the introduction of Afrikaans as a language of teaching and learning in local schools. Hundreds of children died. The boy who is shot dead in Modiegi's poem refers to 13-year-old Hector Pieterson, who was among the first students killed during the protests and became the symbol of the Soweto Uprising.

6. In Japanese Sign Language.

7. In another example, the hearing father in Clayton Valli's *Snowflake* leans forward to his deaf son when he wants him to 'speak' but as soon as this is over, he quickly moves backward, suggesting that his interest in his son is very superficial.

Further reading

Boyes Braem, Penny and Rachel Sutton-Spence (eds) (2001) *The Hands are the Head of the Mouth: The Mouth as Articulator in Sign Languages* (Hamburg: Signum Press).

Fowler, David and Mark Heaton (2006) 'Onomatopoeia in British Sign Language? The visuality/sensation of sound' in Harvey Goodstein (ed.) *The Deaf Way II Reader: Perspectives from the Second International Conference on Deaf Culture* (Washington, DC: Gallaudet University Press).

Kaneko, Michiko and Johanna Mesch (2013) 'Eye gaze in creative sign language', *Sign Language Studies*, 13(3), 372–400.

Activities

1. Choose a sign language poem or a story which involves a number of characters, and observe whether these characters are differentiated by idiosyncratic facial features. Suggestions are Jerry Hanifin's *Little Red Ridinghood* (in Chapter 14 of the DVD accompanying Sutton-Spence and Woll, 1999), Richard Carter's *Sam's Birthday* (posted on the YouTube channel that accompanies this book) and *Bird of a Different Feather* (by Ben Bahan in ASL or by Nelson Pimenta in Libras, both available on DVD).

2. Choose a sign language poem or a story, and look for examples of the six gaze patterns identified by Kaneko and Mesch (2013).

3. Choose a sign language poem or a story and identify different mouth actions. (Richard Carter's *Cochlear Implant* and Paul Scott's *Black*, again available on the YouTube channel accompanying this book, are good examples for BSL users.) What effects do they have on the presentation of the poem/story?

18 Deaf Humour and Sign Language Humour

In this chapter, we will consider what makes deaf people laugh and see how sign language can be a medium for deaf humour. Humour and jokes are a key part of deaf folklore and many members of the deaf community expect that sign language stories or other forms of language entertainment will make them laugh. We will consider the humour carried in sign language stories and jokes – short stories with unexpected or absurd endings – as well as other ways that deaf people can use language for laughter.

We will consider two main types of humour here, conceptual and linguistic. Conceptual humour can be conveyed just as well in any form of language – spoken, written or signed – because the language only carries the content and it is the content that is funny (although a well-told joke is funnier, of course). Linguistic humour comes from playing with the form of the language and we identify two sub-categories here. Sign language humour relies on the form of the sign language, and audiences who don't know sign language will not understand it even when it is translated because its source is lost. Bilingual humour uses puns or riddles that need people to know both sign language and the spoken language to appreciate it (Sutton-Spence and Napoli, 2009).

What is humour for?

Humour provides pleasure, fun and laughter. In many instances, that is all the purpose it needs. However, it also creates a bond between the jokester and audience that is socially and intellectually satisfying for everyone. It can help people relax and make light of difficult situations but is also useful for social control, ridiculing behaviour that is socially disapproved of, in the hope that the offenders will change their behaviour.

Conceptual humour often draws on the idea of 'the in-group' and 'the out-group' because when the humourist and audience both laugh at the humour, they can claim to belong to the in-group as 'us', especially because they understand the language and cultural references. In deaf and sign language humour, 'us' often means deaf people. The late Hal Draper, a much-loved deaf comedian in Britain, explained that deaf audiences enjoyed deaf humour by feeling part of the group:

> [They] identified with the experiences and so they laughed. They could sit and watch and laugh and think, 'Yes, I remember the same thing happening to me before.' Also, for some Deaf people who were new to the Deaf community it brought out lots of things from deep inside about themselves. They watched things being performed that they felt embarrassed about and realised, 'I am not the only one who's had this problem – all Deaf have this problem.' So in some ways the show was about humour and laughter but in other ways it was a little bit of therapy for some Deaf people who found their identity. (quoted in Sutton-Spence and Napoli, 2010)

Humour can support the in-group by insulting the out-group, so that the jokester and audience can claim to be 'us' if they both laugh at a joke that insults people who are 'them'. In a great deal of traditional deaf humour, 'them' has meant hearing people, although this may be changing now. Hal Draper also said (ibid.), 'I think most humour that deaf people like is based on hearing people making idiots of themselves.'

International deaf humour

Jokes generally spread around the world rapidly, but perhaps the specific nature of deaf humour allows it to spread especially rapidly around deaf communities because it draws on the shared experiences of deaf people anywhere. Deaf humour spreads internationally through personal contact (there is a lot of humour at international deaf social occasions where it is important to create easy social relations) or the Internet. Humour often has specific national characteristics but a joke told in one sign language can be adapted and naturalised for each country and represented in each national sign language so that the origins of the joke are hard to determine. For example, there is a joke about a lost cochlear implant:

> A man rushed home from work, walked the dog, ate a quick meal, put on a load of laundry and rushed out to the social night at the deaf club. On the way, he realised he had lost his cochlear implant but wasn't worried because he knew he would be signing with his deaf friends. As he sat chatting, his head suddenly started spinning round and round. The moment passed so he carried on chatting. Then, his head started spinning again, and stopped. His friends were concerned but he insisted he was fine. After a third attack of this uncontrollable spinning, he decided to go home and rest. When he got home, he found his cochlear implant in the washing machine.

We have been told a form of this joke in three different countries and the signer in each case believed the joke came from their own country. The exact form of the joke certainly did, but the source of the original joke is lost.

Other jokes are known to be 'international deaf jokes', such as the deaf lion. There are many versions and many embellishments, but the essential plot is the same.

> A violinist out on the African plains sees a lion running towards him, ready to eat him. The violinist plays such sweet music that the lion falls asleep. Before the violinist can escape, he sees another lion. He plays another tune and that lion falls asleep. A third lion approaches but no matter how sweetly the violinist plays, the lion keeps coming, and finally eats him. The lion was deaf.

Liina Paales (2004) describes a version of this joke in Estonian sign language and it is wellknown in many countries (sometimes the violinist is in a bull-fighting arena and the attacking animal is a bull), including Brazil, where several versions have been collected for analysis by Carolina Hessel (2015).

What makes deaf people laugh?

Deaf humour is driven by the dominant visual experience of deaf people (although other senses such as touch and even smell can be part of the amusement) and the form is usually expressed visually. However, although we can talk about deaf humour, we should note that deaf people draw upon humour traditions in the wider society, too, because there is plenty of visual humour that makes deaf and hearing people laugh together.

There are many examples of non-linguistic humour that is part of deaf folklore (Chapter 4), such as slapstick, party-games and humour in cartoon drawings. However, when we think of humour, we often think of jokes or funny stories, which have humorous content carried through the medium of language. Conceptual jokes are told in sign language, either from the wider hearing society or from the deaf community, where they have their own deaf-related content and sometimes culturally traditional formulas. We saw one example of a culturally deaf joke in Chapter 5 about the deaf honeymoon couple, there are the two in the section above, and there are more at the end of this chapter in the Activities section.

Deaf and hearing people often find the same concepts funny, and many jokes translate well from a signed to a spoken language, and vice versa. However, conceptual jokes often draw on cultural references that may not be easily accessible to people from different cultures. There are plenty of traditional deaf jokes, well-known among members of the deaf community, that hearing people understand but do not find as funny as deaf people do, because they do not have the cultural background of experiences such as using sign language, suffering oppression by hearing society, or having difficulties communicating with hearing people. For example, deaf jokes may refer to disliking speech, hearing aids or cochlear implants, or to distrusting interpreters. They may refer to behaviour seen in the deaf community that members value differently from hearing people. Despite the cultural differences, however, non-members of the deaf community can still think themselves into the scenario so that once the joke is explained they can find it amusing.

Taboo

Not all humour is friendly, polite or kind. Humour often allows a space for discussion of otherwise taboo topics and there are plenty of examples in deaf humour of dirty jokes (sexual or toilet-related), racist, sexist and homophobic jokes, or those mocking disabled people or other deaf people who are different from the deaf person signing the humour (for example, from another school or with a different language experience or attitude to living in the hearing world). Some of these jokes are signed translations of jokes told by hearing people, although others are traditional 'deaf jokes' and they have deaf characters in them and address the concerns of the deaf community. As we discussed in Chapter 4, some folklore should only be shared outside the community after careful consideration. We will not explore taboo signed humour further here, but readers who wish to do so can make their own enquiries, always being mindful of the needs and wishes of the community.

There are many jokes in which hearing people as a group are the butt of the humour and these can be controversial. Some hearing people who witness these jokes find the humour hurtful, unfair, childish or simply unfunny. They may have good personal reasons for these reactions, but people who have been invited to share in the culture of another community should consider carefully whether they should criticise the humour. If they understand that 'anti-hearing people' jokes are of stereotypes, not of individuals, they may appreciate them more. If the joke touches a nerve because it reflects their own behaviour in a negative light, they can consider learning from the humour and changing their ways. People who really do not like the humour, however, may simply choose not to participate in it.

Sign language humour

Although conceptual humour can show considerable linguistic creativity, in sign language humour, the impact comes especially from the linguistic form so that if it is phrased in any other way, the humour is lost. There are several ways in which sign language humour can be delivered, including changing the internal sign structure (and revitalising dormant aspects of parameters), metalinguistic play on signs, exaggerated facial expressions (caricature), manipulation of speed and size of signing, and anthropo-morphism (Sutton-Spence and Napoli 2012, Klima and Bellugi 1979).

Changing internal sign structure

Sign language humour often brings attention to aspects of signs that are 'hidden in plain view'. One way to do this is to change the handshape, movement, location or orientation of a sign to create a new meaning that is unexpected but seems obvious when it is introduced.

The handshape of the sign is perhaps the most common parameter to change in this form of humour. In this language play, the selected fingers or the internal movement of the sign can change, while the location of the sign and the path-movement remain unchanged, to allow people to identify the basic sign that is being modified. For example, in normal usage the index finger extends from a closed fist held at the forehead to produce the sign UNDERSTAND in BSL (and ASL, SASL and some other sign languages). The expected '1' handshape can be changed to the little finger opening instead (that is, the 'I' handshape), to mean UNDERSTAND-A-LITTLE-BIT, playing on the understanding that if the selected finger is smaller, the amount of understanding must be smaller. Alternatively, the extended index finger can close into the fist, to mean UNDERSTAND-LESS-NOW-THAN-BEFORE, playing on the idea that if opening the finger implies an increase in understanding, closing it will imply a decrease. Finally, each finger can extend sharply in turn to form an open handshape to mean OK!-UNDERSTAND-EVERYTHING! playing with the idea that the more fingers in the sign, the greater the amount of understanding (Figure 18.1).

The sign APPLAUD in many sign languages (Figure 18.2a) is a straightforward representation of hands clapping using 'B' handshapes. In language play, this 'B' handshape can be altered to an 'I' handshape (which is much less substantial than the 'B' handshape) to show that the signer is giving very small applause (Figure 18.2b). In BSL, it could also mean applauding something that is bad, because the 'I' handshape carries the meaning 'bad' in many BSL signs (such as ILL, SWEARWORD, BITTER, WORSE and POISON).

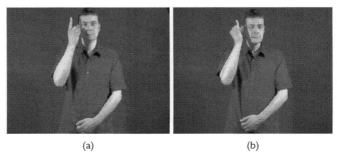

(a)   (b)

FIGURE 18.1 (A) UNDERSTAND AND
(B) UNDERSTAND-A-LITTLE-BIT

The idea of giving small applause can be taken further by pretending to pull two hairs from the head and tapping these together with the same movement used to clap two hands together.

The 'I' handshape occurs in several playfully insulting signs to under-value something as 'small' (and so not valued) or bad. The BSL signs HEARING-PERSON or INTERPRETER, which are supposed to be made with a 'I' and a 'V' handshape respectively, can be made with an 'I' handshape to make light (or fun) of them (see Figure 18.3 for the examples for INTERPRETER and BAD-INTERPRETER).

Changing a sign's location, while keeping the other parameters steady, can also be humorous. The BSL sign CONFIDENT, made at the chest using the 'C' handshape, has variant forms INCREASE-CONFIDENCE and DECREASE-CONFIDENCE, made by moving the sign up or down from that location (using the orientational metaphor that moving upwards shows an improve-ment and moving downwards shows a deterioration). This metaphor has led to playful signs such as OVER-CONFIDENT (where the sign is raised to well above head height), and UNDER-CONFIDENT (where it is lowered well below waist-height). When the over-confident person needs to be brought back to reality, the signer's non-dominant hand can push the hand making the sign OVER-CONFIDENT down to its correct location for CONFIDENT or it can push the sign UNDER-CONFIDENT up (Figure 18.4a and b).

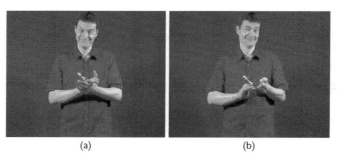

(a)   (b)

FIGURE 18.2 (A) APPLAUSE AND (B) VERY-SMALL-APPLAUSE

FIGURE 18.3   (A) INTERPRETER, (B) BAD-INTERPRETER

In signs where the handshape appears to be arbitrary, it can be given a new visually-motivated meaning. The curved 'C' handshape in CONFI-DENCE (which is arbitrarily selected based on the manual letter 'C') can be playfully reinterpreted as a small hunched creature, which slinks sadly and shyly away in the expression LOSE-ALL-CONFIDENCE (Figure 18.4c).

Another example of changing the interpretation of the meaning of handshapes is seen in the BSL sign TEACH. The flat-B handshape is seen in many signs that refer to grasping and handling objects and the two-handed BSL sign TEACH uses this handshape, motivated by a metaphor of holding and giving information to another person. In normal use, this metaphor has faded so that signers do not think about the visual properties of the handshape. In language play, however, the hands that sign TEACH can become animated as two hands that have their own will, knocking each other aside, picking each other up or tapping each other to get attention. Alternatively, they can be reinterpreted as two animals because the flat-B handshape can be used as a classifier for an animal's head. The joke allows the signs, or the hands making the signs, to behave

FIGURE 18.4   (A) PUSHING THE HAND MAKING THE SIGN OVER-CONFIDENT DOWN TO ITS CORRECT LOCATION; (B) PUSHING THE SIGN UNDER-CONFIDENT UP TO THE CORRECT LOCATION; (C) 'C' HANDSHAPE REINTERPRETED AS A CLASSIFIER HANDSHAPE IN LOSE-ALL-CONFIDENCE

(a)   (b)   (c)

FIGURE 18.5   (A) TEACH, (B) HAND-FALLS-OVER-WHILE-TEACHING AND
(C) HAND-RESCUES-OTHER-HAND-TO-TEACH

and even converse as though they are animals by opening and closing the hand to look like a mouth moving (Figure 18.5).

Metalinguistic play

Metalinguistic play means that signers are aware of how signs are formulated, and make use of the fact that signs are made with human hands, blurring the distinction between hands as articulators, and hands as hands. In the examples of OVER-CONFIDENT and UNDER-CONFIDENT being moved to the 'correct' location, the dominant hand is seen as a real hand, rather than the articulator for CONFIDENT, that can be touched and moved by another hand.

In Chapter 12, we discussed examples from Johanna Mesch's *Three Haiku* (in which the poet reaches up to the fading sun and forces the closing fingers representing the sun to re-open) and John Wilson's *Morning* (in which the poet 'picks up' a car from the street and treats it as a toy car). They blur the distinction between the two aspects of sign language: representational (signs are used to represent something, such as the sun or a car) and formational (signs are physically made with human hands). In other words, poets remind us of the obvious fact that signers do have control over what they are signing, and this realisation results in humour.

Caricature

Within this visual humour, sign language and gesture work together, so that witty and original uses of classifiers and exaggerated facial expression or body movement contribute to the humour. Caricature, where a signer over-emphasises someone's visual features or mimics the way a person behaves in an exaggerated way, is particularly valued in deaf humour for its likeness to the target. It can be directed at stereotypes of outsiders who are traditionally unpopular in the deaf community (such as doctors, teachers and social workers unsympathetic to deaf culture) although it can be directed against other deaf people. Sometimes, however, it is simply used to show the signer's skills, and there is no ill feeling towards the target.

Speed and size of signing

Humorous signs are often larger and made with stronger movements than normal and they may also be held for longer so that the audience has time to appreciate the humorous signing. Slow motion signing allows the teller to show exaggerated facial expression or movement, and takes considerable skill to achieve convincingly.[1] Richard Carter is very skilled in this. The humorous effect of one of his poems, *The Race,* comes primarily from this extremely slow signing.

Anthropomorphism

Signers value the skill of being able to show how animals and objects (such as an aeroplane, tree or lift) might have human characteristics. The facial expression showing the behaviour and reactions of these non-human objects is part of sign language wit. As we saw in Chapter 7, skilled signers can change the handshape, location and movement of their signs to accommodate the form of the non-human, which also contributes to the humour. Richard Carter is well-known for his skill in achieving this: his owl signs with all handshapes in the shape of a wing, his fish signs with the hands clamped tightly to his chest like fins, and the reindeer signs with the hands on top of the head like antlers (see Figure 7.11).

Bilingual humour

Most signers have bilingual skills and they can draw on spoken languages for bilingual humour. Cynthia Peters (2000) has argued that signed humour that uses fingerspelling is a way for signers to challenge the power of the spoken language over sign languages, as sign language appropriates it for its own use. It is also fun and satisfying to play with two languages at the same time.

Fingerspelling (as we saw in Chapter 5) is used to represent written words, so signers who use it are, by definition, referring to another language. The manual alphabet can be a source of bilingual humour in several ways. Several manual alphabets around the world, including the British one, are two-handed, so signers can have fun playing with the

216 INTRODUCING SIGN LANGUAGE LITERATURE

location of the active spelling hand. In physical games played with two people, each person provides one hand for the fingerspelling and both people must time the movement of the hand to create the letters correctly. In another game, the signer replaces the active fingerspelling hand with locations on the body to create a double, punning meaning, often on the last letter. Paul Scott's *Acronym* (see Chapter 5) provides good examples of this type of fingerspelling game.

We have already seen in Chapter 5 that languages that use one-handed fingerspelling can use the manual letters as a source for poems and stories because the forms of the letters are reanalysed as classifier handshapes and this wit can also be a source of humour. In examples from signers who know ASL and English, the letters d-r-i-l-l can be moved forwards as though a drill is going into something and, as the final 'l' handshape looks like the classifier handshape for a drill-bit, this creates an enjoyable pun. The word 'honeymoon' can be spelled with both hands, getting closer with each letter until the two hands with the 'n' handshape are next to each other, making a pun of two people in bed together because the 'n' handshape looks like the classifier handshape for humans lying down.

As well as playing with the form of written words, signers can make bilingual puns using loan translation. These can be riddles, requiring the audience to guess the spoken language word from the sign, but can also be made openly so everyone can share the humour. An example of one riddle is to ask the meaning of signing the BSL sign WHO (normally made at the chin) at the nose. It can be understood as WHO^NOSE, which can be translated back as 'Who knows'. Signing WHERE under the non-dominant hand can be understood as UNDER^WHERE, which can be translated back as 'underwear'. Other loan translations of several words as riddles include 'All my tea God' (Almighty God), 'Bee write back' (Be right back) and making the BSL sign RULE with the thumb of the active hand instead of usual the index finger that is normally used (Rule of thumb). There are many such examples in signed humour, some of them rather rude, in many signed and spoken languages, showing how signers can enjoy using their bilingual knowledge while they play with sign language.

Funny in sign language, but not in spoken language

Linguistic humour in sign language only makes sense in its visual modality, so it is lost in translation into spoken language. For example, humour based on a change in parameters is not translatable into a spoken language. We may think of Johanna Mesch's sunbathing attempt, John Wilson's real car turning into a toy car and Paul Scott's creative classifiers,

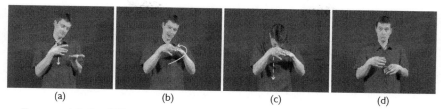

(a)   (b)   (c)   (d)

FIGURE 18.6   BSL VERSION OF THE KING KONG JOKE: (A) WANT, ADDRESSED
TO THE HUMAN GIRL ON HIS HAND; (B) MARRY; (C) DROPS THE GIRL; (D) OOPS

none of which make any sense if told in English words. Often the linguistic humour is driven by the vocabulary of a particular sign language.
A famous sign language joke, about King Kong (or a giant in some versions) is funny in ASL but the punchline in English 'I love you and want
to marry you. Oops. Sorry' is unintelligible as a punchline and not funny.
The humour occurs because he has been holding the human girl he loves
on his palm and accidentally squashes her by signing 'I want to marry
you' because the ASL sign MARRY involves clasping the hands together. In
BSL, the joke works because the BSL sign MARRY depicts putting a wedding ring on a hand with the palm facing down. As King Kong tells the
girl on the palm of his hand that he wants to marry her, he accidentally
drops her (Figure 18.6). Again, the punchline translates as 'I love you and
want to marry you. Oops. Sorry', even though the way BSL creates the
punchline is different from the way ASL does.[2]

Summary

In this chapter, we have highlighted some of the things that make deaf
people laugh, distinguishing between what they tell (the content of the
humour) and the way they tell it (the language that carries the humour).
We saw that humour in deaf communities has functions beyond the
purpose of making people laugh. Where humour is based on exploiting
divisions between the in-group and the out-group, however, it can touch
on many taboo topics. Like so much in signed and deaf folklore, humour
is influenced by surrounding hearing society, and deaf and hearing people
can share many forms of visually-based humour, but there are also specific
forms of deaf humour. The content of many deaf jokes is culturally specific to deaf communities, and based on the experiences of deaf people.
The signing in humour can be visually and gesturally amusing but signers
can also exploit changes in the form of signs for sophisticated puns that
revitalise – and revise – the motivation behind signs. Bilingual humour
can play with the form and meaning of signs, looking for dual meanings
in one language that produce unexpected meanings in the other language.

Notes

1. It requires considerable skills to coordinate all body parts to move in a unified slow manner. In poetry workshops, participants manipulating the speed tend to slow down only their manual components, and forget to slow down facial actions, eyes and mouth movement.
2. SASL and BSL use the same sign to mean marry and Libras and ASL use the same sign for marry, so this joke also works in SASL and Libras.

Further reading

Attardo, Salvatore (2007) 'A primer for the linguistics of humor' in Victor Raskin (ed.) *Primer of Humor Research* (Berlin: Mouton de Gruyter).

Bienvenu, M.J. (1994) 'Reflections of Deaf culture in Deaf humor' in Carol Erting, Robert Johnson, Dorothy Smith and Bruce Snider (eds) *The Deaf Way: Perspectives from the International Conference on Deaf Culture* (Washington, DC: Gallaudet University Press), 16–23.

Bouchauveau, Guy (1994) 'Deaf humor and culture' in Carol Erting, Robert Johnson, Dorothy Smith and Bruce Snider (eds) *The Deaf Way: Perspectives from the International Conference on Deaf Culture* (Washington, DC: Gallaudet University Press), 24–30.

Rutherford, Susan (1989) 'Funny in Deaf – not in hearing' in Sherman Wilcox (ed.) *American Deaf Culture: An Anthology* (Silver Spring, MD: Linstok Press), 310–322.

Sutton-Spence, Rachel and Donna Jo Napoli (2012) 'Deaf jokes and sign language humor', *International Journal of Humor Research*, 25(3), 311–338.

Activities

1. Here are some jokes that have been told in sign language. They are all translated here into English.

   (a) What is the source of the humour?

   (b) Is there an in-group and out-group? If so, who? Does the joke support or insult the in-group? Does it support or insult the out-group? In what ways?

   (c) Which of these jokes could be called a 'deaf joke'? Why?

   (d) Which of these jokes would rely on sign language or gesture for the full effect?

   (e) Find some other signed jokes for yourself and decide if they translate just as well into written English or if they must be seen for their humour.

The three men on a train

A deaf man, a Russian and a Cuban were on a train. The Russian opened a bottle of vodka, took a swig and threw it out of the window, shrugging and saying, 'In my country we have plenty of vodka'. The Cuban man lit a cigar, took a single puff and threw it out of the window, shrugging and saying, 'In my country we have plenty of cigars'. The ticket collector came by and the deaf man threw him out of the window, shrugging and saying, 'In my country we have plenty of hearing people.'

The man who ran over the cat

In a most unfortunate accident, a man runs over a cat in his car. He goes to the house nearby and knocks on the door. An elderly lady answers it and he says, 'I am very sorry but I have just run over your cat'. 'Maybe it wasn't mine,' said the old lady, 'What does it look like?' 'Like this,' said the man — and he makes the impression of a cat that has been run over.

The gamekeeper (A joke told by Clark Denmark, a British deaf man)

A gamekeeper kept a dog that became deaf. He taught it sign language so he could still command it to fetch birds. The first day they went hunting together, he signed for the dog to fetch the bird and the dog ran off but it did not return with the bird. The gamekeeper tracked it down and found it in the local deaf club signing with other deaf people.

The lumberjack and the deaf tree

A lumberjack who cuts through a tree, shouts 'Timber!' and the tree falls. He does this to another tree and it falls. He cuts a third tree and shouts 'Timber!' but the tree does not fall. Puzzled, he calls the tree surgeon, who examines it, and explains the tree is deaf and tells him to learn the manual alphabet. So the lumberjack does and when he is ready he fingerspells 't-i-m-b-e-r' to it and the tree falls.

2. Find examples of signing that make you laugh (or at least smile) because of the way they are signed. Try to avoid using pieces that are obviously jokes. You could choose stories and poems posted on the YouTube channel that accompanies this book (such as Kabir Kapoor's *Pixar*, Richard Carter's *Grass Hairstyle* and Rimar Segala's *Ping Pong Ball*) or from the video material that accompanies Sutton-Spence and Woll (1999) (for example the *Road Signs* sketch by Hal Draper in Chapter 14). What role do sign language or gesture play to make them funny? Could you make them funny if you translated them into a spoken language?

3. We could call the 'Deaf King Kong' joke (or the 'Deaf Giant' joke) the 'perfect' signing deaf joke. It contains a signing deaf animal, strong visual gestures, facial expression and body movement and focuses on the structure of the signs making it. Find a signed version of this joke in a language you know (or, better still, ask a deaf person to sign it to you) and explain why it is funny.

19 Style in Signed Art Forms

In this chapter, we will outline features of narrative styles, figurative styles, signing styles and performance styles in an attempt to understand the foundations of the rich variation in sign language literature. As we come to the end of this book, it should be clear that signed art forms vary greatly and that each poet and sign language artist has their own preferred style. Studying even one creative signed text will reveal a great deal about its structure, but when we review a larger amount of work, as we have in this book, we can begin to appreciate the range and diversity of creative signing. Although there is no single set of characteristics or 'rules' to define a specific signed genre, it is possible to identify different styles of poems or other creative signed pieces. Drawing predominantly upon the work of the five BSL poets whose work we have repeatedly described in the preceding chapters (Dorothy Miles, Paul Scott, Richard Carter, John Wilson and Donna Williams), and referring to some other poets as well, we will explore the different aspects of their literary styles.

There are traditions of literary analysis that focus entirely on the text, and do not consider the life experience of the poet (or their audiences). However, the life and language experiences of signing poets can help us to understand the choices behind some styles of sign language poetry. For example, the age at which the poet became deaf will influence their language style, because poets who became deaf after acquiring a spoken language have a very different relationship with written language from those who were born deaf, or became deaf at a young age. Poets with deaf parents who were brought up in a signing deaf environment have very different relationships with sign language and deaf culture from those brought up by hearing families who did not sign with them. This is often reflected in their choice of themes. Poets who grew up in deaf families and those who came later to the deaf community may all be radical and confrontational in the deaf politics of their work. However, we have seen a trend that the poets who comment more on wider politics (such as social inequality, the environment and war) often grew up in hearing families.

Deaf poets are also influenced by a variety of other poets depending on their age, national heritage and education, and this will create different styles in their signed work. Many signing poets have acknowledged the influence of written poems by hearing poets. For example, in America, Clayton Valli was influenced by Robert Frost, and his signed work is characterised by similar rhymes and rhythms to those we see in Frost's poems, while Peter Cook was influenced by Allen Ginsberg and his work, like Ginsberg's, focuses on creating strong visual images. In Britain, Dorothy Miles was influenced by Dylan Thomas, leading her to play with signs as he did with words, and Paul Scott has been inspired by Seamus Heaney, creating images that lead to complex metaphor. Other deaf poets also influence signers' work. For example, Dorothy Miles was an important influence on Paul Scott and John Wilson in Britain, and Ella Mae Lentz in the USA acknowledges the importance of Eric Malzkuhn and Bernard Bragg (Nathan Lerner and Feigel, 2009). Each of the influencing poets has a profound effect on the styles of an artist's work.

Narrative style

The narrative style of any piece concerns the 'story' of the piece ('what' it is about), and the way it is told. The same basic story can be told in many forms, such as in a poem, a piece of dramatic theatre, a short story, a novel and so on. Whatever the choice of genre, the narrative style of signing poets includes their choice of theme for the story. Trends of themes in sign language poetry change over time as they do in written work (see Chapter 1), so that the themes in sign language poems we describe from the late 20th century and early 21st century have changed and developed. A great many poets, as we have seen repeatedly throughout this book, address the theme of deaf identity, which may include the deaf community, deaf people's communication and education experiences and the celebration of sign language. This theme is so common that it is almost impossible to list the poems and poets who use them. Dorothy Miles in the UK and Ella Mae Lentz in the USA are just two examples of poets who frequently focused on these themes and all the poets whose work we have presented in this book do so, at times. Libras work by Brazilian poets such as Fernanda Machado (*D not E*), Nelson Pimenta (*Nature*) and Rimar Segala (*Ping Pong Ball*) do likewise.

Other poets may address wider, more abstract themes, such as love, national pride or a sense of home, sometimes as they relate to deaf people and sign language. The Brazilian poet Mauricio Barreto (*The Lighthouse at Barra*) blends the sense of belonging in his home city and the love of God with his love of sign language and his sorrow when it is not accepted by others. But other times, deafness is simply irrelevant in terms of content, as in Modiegi Moime's *June 16th,* which is a story of black students (none of them is deaf) protesting against the use of Afrikaans as the medium of instruction in South African schools (see Chapter 17). Many poets and storytellers use general, less deaf-focused themes, influenced by popular culture and current affairs in the wider community, especially as they are shown in film and television. Some openly gay poets, such as Richard Carter, use this part of their life experience to determine the themes of some poems.

We will now consider the ways in which poets present these themes. The first useful notion is the idea of frame, originally developed by the linguist Charles Fillmore (1982). The way that poets and storytellers create their frame of meaning creates different styles. Many stories, and some poems, operate in a single, coherent frame of meaning, using linear development of plots, often with one central character and a single event or episode. Richard Carter, for example, favours this framing style. The styles of Donna Williams and John Wilson, however, often offer contrasting frames, so that two parallel, but very different narratives are told in the same poem. John's poem *Home* interweaves the stories of the deaf boy educated in an oral environment and Laika the dog sent into space. Donna's poem *That Day* contrasts her personal experiences of an 'audio-centric' world with her dreams for a world where deaf people have easy access to visual information. Paul Scott's style is more of a 'collage', blending and interweaving several different narrative frames within a single poem, creating images across the frames for viewers to link together. His poems *No Mask like Home* and *Macbeth of the Lost Ark,* as their complex, mixed titles suggest, are examples of these mixed frames.

Styles also vary according to the 'voice' in the poem (as the poet and scholar T.S. Eliot called it) and the 'point of view' of the poem. In written literature, this often refers to the distinction between the first-person narrative and third-person narrative (and possibly second-person narrative, as in Italo Calvino's *If on a Winter's Night a Traveller*), and also the degree to which the author (or character) is involved in telling the story, which can be subjective (personal) or objective (detached, impersonal). Many people, especially those familiar with English Romantic poetry, will recognise some sign language poems as containing stories that appear to be of the poet's personal experiences, told through the 'Poetic-I'. We can see this in Donna Williams' and Dorothy Miles' work. Donna's *Who am I?* and *My Cat,* and Dorothy's *Elephants Dancing* and *Defiance* are examples of this type of lyric poetry that puts the poet at the centre of the poem. There are also styles that place the poet as the narrator of the poem even though the poem is not about them. Sometimes the narrator is clearly present, as we see in Paul Scott's *Blue Suit*, where the poet addresses the audience directly, telling the stories of the two women and adding, 'Don't!' These poems are more likely to use signed vocabulary and entity classifiers, as events and episodes are described as well as shown.

In other poems, the narrator is far less obvious and may not even be present at all, so that characters speak and act as themselves. These poems use many more handling classifiers and constructed action. Paul Scott's *Turkey* and Richard Carter's *Mirror* are examples of the many sign language poems that use this style. Paul creates an image of the turkey and then shows us everything from the turkey's perspective, while Richard presents the world from the perspective of the mirror. Brief descriptions of the mirror's surroundings (such as referring to the radiator below as it sweats, or the door that opens to let in the breeze) are kept to the minimum we need to follow the story.

Some poems do not have any active narrative voice (of the poet, of narrator, or of a character), and are told through a series of images. They also use classifiers to describe the scene visually, but usually involve many fewer actions and facial expressions. This is the case in some haiku poems, such as Wim Emmerik's *Falling Leaf*.

Figurative style

Another difference in literary style is the extent to which we see devices such as metaphor, simile, allegory and allusion in a piece. Some poets and storytellers are very literal in their work, while others prefer to use figurative language. Again, fashions for this change over time, and there have been periods in history when different figurative styles have been more or less favoured. Different genres of literature, too, use figurative language differently. For example, extensive metaphor is sometimes seen as a characteristic that defines a piece as poetry rather than prose. Even within poetry, however, different forms have different figurative styles. The traditional Japanese haiku form, for example, has a very literal style, as it attempts to create strong sensory images without metaphor.

Many signing poets enjoy using figurative language and their styles vary according to their preferred tropes. Dorothy Miles, for example, favoured overt metaphors, creating simile, and drawing on allegory, and Donna Williams' poems also show these overt contrasts. John Wilson, who acknowledges being influenced by Dorothy's poetry, often presents these comparisons where figurative links are made between two concepts, stories or characters. His piece *Home*, as we have seen above, is one such story where comparing the fate of the child in oral education and the dog in space allows him to use them both as metonyms to explore the larger theme of scientific arrogance and the suffering it causes. His poem *The Fates* draws on the experiences of three women, comparing the way they take control of their destinies.

The modality of sign language offers a visual means of juxtaposing two distinct concepts, often motivating links which are only possible in sign language. Many of Dorothy Miles' poems deliberately compare one thing to another, and her recognised figurative style was to link concepts that were similar in meaning with signs that were similar in form. Perhaps the most famous example of simile from her work is in *Trio*, where she likens darkness to a flying bat (see also Chapter 12). In English, the ideas of darkness and a bat could be metaphorically linked in various ways (most simply, bats come out at dark) but there is nothing about the form of the English words 'darkness' and 'bat' to suggest any links. In BSL, though, the signs DARKNESS and FLYING-BAT are very similar in their form. For this reason, darkness in the poem is like a flying bat, partly because the sign DARKNESS is like the sign FLYING-BAT. Similarly, the sense of shared experience of the poet and a baby duck that forms the key to Donna Williams' *Duck and Dissertation* is partly motivated by the visual similarity between the poet's hands typing frantically on the computer and the duck's feet paddling frantically against the current.

Richard Carter's poem *Operation* uses a similar figurative device by openly comparing having an operation to fixing a television. The signs showing the crazy lines of a broken television screen, the light going out on the screen and the jumble of wires inside the television that the repairman will fix have forms that are almost identical to the signs for the pain in the child's abdomen, falling asleep under anaesthetic and the jumble of intestines that the surgeon will fix.

Richard Carter is also a recognised master of anthropomorphism, which is another figurative device. We saw many examples of his work that anthropomorphise non-human characters in Chapter 7, and we can see now that choosing to create poems like this is another example of a particular figurative style.

Paul Scott's favoured style is to create many intertwined metaphors, each with complex, unresolved or even unresolvable interpretations. His figurative style carefully mixes powerful visual images with metaphorical meanings. In his densely metaphorical poem *Macbeth of the Lost Ark*, two children grow up together (they might be Macbeth and Duncan, or possibly one deaf child raised in one educational experiment and another child raised in a different experiment), growing apart, being different and yet the same. Suddenly one grabs a dagger and stabs the other. At this moment in the piece, the audience may ask, 'Where did that dagger

FIGURE 19.1   A 'HIDDEN' DAGGER IN PAUL SCOTT'S *MACBETH OF THE LOST ARK* IN THE SIGNS MEANING 'GROW UP APART', 'DIFFERENT' AND 'SAME', THEN 'STAB'

come from?' but an observant student of the poem will see that the signs describing the process of growing up sketch out the form of a dagger (see Figure 19.1). Again, there is a link between the form of the signs and metaphorical meaning in comparisons, even though Paul's style is not to make open comparisons.

Signing and performance style

All poets have their unique signing style. If we look at the five main poets chosen here, we can see that Dorothy Miles' signing style was to manipulate lexical signs. John Wilson's style is often to select lexical signs with shared parameters to create patterns of repetition. Paul Scott's work is more characterised by manipulating the sublexical features of signs, playing with the figurative implications of handshapes or locations of the signs. Richard Carter's creative signing style is especially characterised by constructed action (taking on the role of different characters) and other cinematographic effects such as varying speed or zoom-in and out. Donna Williams, with her emphasis on comparison and contrast in her work, often uses the poetically significant placement of referents in a style that is marked as hers.

Vocabulary choices mark styles clearly. In sign language poetry and storytelling, one major style division is seen between using signs from the established lexicon, whose purpose is to 'tell', and using signs from the productive lexicon, whose purpose is to 'show'. The former style is less transparent and creates less powerful visual images, although it often allows poets to create a wide variety of metaphor, and is more associated with lyric poetry; the latter style is more transparent and closer to the more dramatic visual vernacular style described in Chapter 6. Signers who have a stronger relationship with written languages often use more lexical styles even in sign language poetry (Dorothy Miles, Donna Williams and John Wilson are examples of BSL poets who use this style) and signers who relate less to written language often use more visually productive styles (such as Paul Scott and Richard Carter).

Styles can also run along a continuum of formality, ranging from scholarly (the most formal) through formal and educated, and casual slang, to colloquial (the least formal). Dorothy Miles, perhaps because of the period in which she was composing (mostly from the 1970s to 1993), used a more formal and scholarly style, choosing signs and sentence structures that may seem rather lofty to us today. Paul Scott, however, could be said to use a less formal style, one that is relaxed but educated. Scholars and poets of written languages acquire and develop this educated style by studying written texts, and many of the concepts in Paul's poetry reflect his study of written texts, such as Shakespeare's work. However, perhaps more significantly for this discussion, his style of sign language is educated in the sense that his knowledge of the language and its potential is profound and wide. In the deaf community, this type of education is not gained by reading, but by the experience of growing up within a deaf family and participating in the deaf community where such an education is possible. Richard Carter's style is characterised by slang, although not in the negative sense that some people use the term, but in the sense that his poetry and stories use newly coined words and other forms of expression that are not part of formal use. Donna Williams often uses a colloquial style, meaning that she uses the sort of vocabulary we might see in everyday signing. In such a style, each word may not be especially unusual but the words are chosen and arranged in a creative and poetic way.

Once the type of vocabulary has been selected, poets and storytellers can choose whether to present their signs in short, discrete segments (we saw in Chapter 11 that it is perhaps best not to call them 'lines' in sign language poetry) or in longer segments. Dorothy Miles' poems, perhaps influenced by poetic styles in written English that keep segments short, are easy to divide into smaller units, each one of which can be looked at for its poetic effect. Donna Williams, too, has a style that uses easily seg-mented signs. Richard Carter often engages in the construction of com-plex visual images and uses a style of signing in which each sign is almost inseparable from the previous one. Manual and nonmanual aspects of his poems start and end at different times from each other, so that one sign blends with the next, while facial expressions, body movements and eye gaze develop and change in a related but independent way. In his poem *The Race*, it is hard to decide when one sign ends and another begins. In his poem *Cochlear Implant*, the section in which the character considers wearing the implant is a chain of signs, each of which depends so much upon the previous one that it is hard to segment the signs without losing their meaning entirely. Paul Scott's poems, once more, present a collage of approaches to segmentation. Some of his poems are presented in short, separable segments (*Two Books* and *Blue Suit* are good examples) and others such as *No Mask like Home, Too Busy to Hug, No Time to See* and *We'll Meet Again* use long segments that blend signs almost seamlessly.

The style of interaction with the audience also varies by poet and by poem. In some poems and stories, the poet or performer appears to address the audience directly. At live events, there may be audience participation in the performance, even to the extent that the audience influences the text. Even without direct participation, though, how poets or storytellers position themselves in relation to the audience forms part of their style. We saw in Chapter 17 that poets and story-tellers can appear to be directly addressing their audience, either in the role of the Poetic-I or as the narrator of the dialogue, events and images presented. They can also present events and dialogue as part of dramatic style, in which the characters appear to act or speak for themselves (as we have seen above).

These different voices are especially shown through gaze in signed performances (recall our discussion of different gaze patterns in Chapter 17). Gaze to the audience, in the narrator's role, brings the performer and audience closer together. Almost all the signing poets and storytell-ers whose work we have studied do this to some extent, but how much they do it varies as part of their style. Dorothy Miles' style was to direct her gaze to the audience in the narrator's role as much as possible. In Richard Carter's performances, a narrator's gaze may begin with the audience but soon switches to become the character's gaze as he becomes immersed in the story that is shown to the audience. Donna Williams' gaze is often that of the Poetic-I, which does not constantly acknowledge the audience, but instead is more inward-directed. While Richard's dra-matic character gaze brings the performance to the audience, Donna's style of the Poetic-I gaze brings the audience into the poem. Each of these styles is not exclusive to any one performer and sign artists will vary the type of gaze they use. Paul Scott, for example, mixes these styles regularly so that, once again, we can see his work as a collage of the different styles.

Summary

In this final chapter, we have taken the rather different approach of using the work of five poets in an attempt to outline some styles in sign language poetry and narrative. All five poets have different styles in delivering their poetic discourse, which are partly the result of their age, education and linguistic background and partly caused by individual choice. Analysing their different styles provides us with a broader and more critical perspective of sign language poetry in general, which cannot be obtained by studying the work of a single poet, no matter how diverse and extensive that poet's work may be.

Further reading

If you want to understand more about poetic styles in general, read any introductory poetry book such as Kennedy and Gioia (2009) *An Introduction to Poetry*, 13th edition (London: Longman).

Klima and Bellugi make a brief comparison of two ASL poets in terms of their stylistic differences in *The Signs of Language* (Cambridge, MA: Harvard University Press, 1979).

Activities

1. Choose three pieces by three poets or storytellers (nine pieces in total) in a sign language that you know, and consider their narrative styles.

   (a) Identify the themes in these pieces and:

   - Compare the themes across the work by each signing artist.
   - Compare the themes across the artists.

   (b) What is the nature of the frame of the style of the pieces? Do they pursue a single linear narrative? Are two or more narrative threads interwoven? Is there a narrative at all?

   - Compare the narrative frames across the three works by each signing artist.
   - Compare the narrative frames across the three artists.

   (c) What is the 'voice' of the poet-performers? Do they seem to be addressing the audience directly or in the role of a narrator? Or are they showing the action and characters directly?

   - Compare the voice across the three works by each signing artist.
   - Compare the voice across the three artists.

   What can you say about the different narrative styles you have seen?

2. Choose three pieces by three poets or storytellers (nine in total) in a sign language that you know and consider their figurative styles. Do they appear to present their work literally or do they use figurative language and metaphor?

   (a) Compare the use of metaphor (or lack of it) across the three works by each signing artist.

   (b) Compare the use of metaphor (or lack of it) across the three artists.

3. Choose three pieces by three poets or storytellers (nine in total) in a sign language that you know and consider their signing styles.

   (a) Decide whether their language use is scholarly and lofty, formal and educated, informal and slang or colloquial. Why do you think that?

   (b) Do the signers favour 'telling' or 'showing'?

      ■ Compare the signing styles across the three works by each signing artist.

      ■ Compare the signing styles across the three artists.

4. Choose pieces by three poets or storytellers (nine in total) in a sign language that you know and consider their performance styles. How do they interact with, or appear to address, the audience?

20 Conclusion

In this book, we have introduced the notion of sign language literature and folklore, and a number of thematic, linguistic and performative features associated with them. Our overarching argument has been that visual creativity and performance influence the form, content and structure of creative sign language. Sign language literature takes the form it does because of its visual, spatial, dynamic and performative nature.

These visual qualities posed the biggest challenge for us in writing about sign language literature in a book format. Ironically for a book such as this, as soon as we translate and reproduce sign language literature in a written form, we lose the elements that create many of its effects. Ben Bahan has remarked that transcribing sign language literature loses its dynamic nature and leaves out the very elements of the performed text that make it sophisticated and valued, with the danger of making it appear simple and artless (Bahan, 2006). For this reason, we would like to emphasise once again the importance of watching the original performances of the poems or stories we discuss in this book. (Almost all of them are available on YouTube or other open-access websites, or on commercial DVDs.)

Appreciation of sign language literature requires a radical shift in the mind of viewers who are more familiar with mainstream written literature, especially the European-origin written literary tradition (who, we assume, are most of the readers of this book, since this book is written in English). Sign language literature may appear, at first glance, less sophisticated than written literature because it seems to focus on concrete topics (one person said quite frankly, 'It's so boring – it's all about trees, flowers, and animals!') and may not seem to develop complex plots or characters. Perhaps it does not contain profound metaphorical phrases as found in Shakespeare or Racine or Mishima.

These points are to some extent true, and we are not arguing that the majority of sign language literature exhibits highly complex plots or offers an intricate psychological study of characters, although some does – because ultimately it is the wrong argument. It is not helpful to explore what is not part of sign language literature in an attempt to make it comparable to written literature. Sign language literature requires its own perspective and approaches to see what is part of it. It frequently works in a fundamentally different way, and many of the expectations we have based on our experience with written literature may be betrayed. However, as we hope to have shown in this book, it sheds light on a new set of ideas and insights into human creativity. Instead of using sound-based words, deaf poets use their hands, face, body and the space as the vehicle of their artistic expressions. They are never anonymous, and develop a close rapport with the audience. They promote illustrations of concrete topics because they are far more visually appealing than abstract topics, but profound metaphorical meanings can be carefully woven into the language. All of these unique features of sign language literature challenge and stimulate our mind, and make us realise that the notion of literature is much wider than written poems and novels.

Having said that, we also need to be aware that the notion of sign language literature is constantly changing. A wealth of talent in deaf people will keep adding new ways to exploit the ingenuity of their art form. The observations and analyses made in this book are based on a small number of poems and stories in a very small number of sign languages. When more works become available in the future, they will inevitably change our understanding of artistic signing. As the number of deaf poets and their works increases, new genres are likely to emerge in sign language literature. One such is signed *renga*, a unique form of group poetry, which was introduced to the British deaf community in 2010 (by a hearing haiku poet Alan Summers who collaborated with British deaf poets) and quickly spread internationally. Exploration of language-specific features (that is, how BSL literature differs from, for example, Japanese Sign Language literature) may also point to the need for developing new analytical frameworks. Advances in technology can cast a new light upon sign language literature, as it is now possible to digitally alter recorded performances, allowing deaf poets to experiment with the editing of their 'products'.

Although deaf communities have a rich history of telling stories and passing them down through generations, studies in sign language literature started only a short time ago. (We believe this is the first comprehensive and in-depth introductory book in this field.) Most of the poems and stories we introduced in this book have been created since 2005 (although we acknowledge the debt of modern sign language poetry to the works by earlier pioneers such as Dorothy Miles and Clayton Valli), and we believe it will grow in the future. We have observed in the last few years the increased confidence and expertise among existing deaf poets, new interest among young poets-to-be, successful rooting of poetry workshops in deaf communities (and in deaf schools in particular), new university courses on sign language literature, and stronger relationships between academic researchers, poets and members of deaf communities. The number of academic researchers who are signing deaf poets and members of the deaf community is small but growing, and their input could radically alter the existing field. Greater availability of recorded materials for viewing and sharing through websites and social media will also promote this development.

Such rapid development in the quantity (as well as quality) of sign language literature means that in the near future we should be able to conduct larger surveys of any features of creative signing (themes, genres or linguistic devices). This is in contrast to previous approaches in which analyses could usually only be made as in-depth studies of one poem or of relatively small collections of work. We are very fortunate to witness this growing stage of the art form.

Sign language literature is a rich and vast research field, and we have only managed to scratch the surface of it here. We hope, however, that readers who have read this book are sufficiently intrigued by the artistry of sign language literature to explore further the visual productions created by visual minds.

References

Achebe, Chinua (1958) *Things Fall Apart* (London: Heinemann).

Arenson, Rebecca and Robert Kretschmer (2010) 'Teaching poetry: a descriptive case study of a poetry unit in a classroom of urban deaf adolescents', *American Annals of the Deaf*, 155(2), 110–117.

Attardo, Salvatore (2007) 'A primer for the linguistics of humor' in Victor Raskin (ed.) *Primer of Humor Research* (Berlin: Mouton de Gruyter).

Attridge, Derek (1995) *Poetic Rhythm: An Introduction* (Cambridge: Cambridge University Press).

Bahan, Ben (1993) 'ASL literature: the inside story' in Gallaudet University College for Continuing Education (ed.) *Conference proceedings, April 22–25, 1993* (Washington, DC: Gallaudet University Press).

Bahan, Ben (2006a) 'Face-to-face tradition in the American Deaf community' in H-Dirksen Bauman, Jennifer Nelson and Heidi Rose (eds) *Signing the Body Poetic* (California: University of California Press).

Bahan, Ben (2006b) 'Making sense of ASL literature', a paper presented at *Revolutions in Sign Language Studies: Linguistics, Literature, Literacy*, Gallaudet University, Washington, DC, 22–24 March 2006.

Barber, Karin (1991) *I Could Speak Until Tomorrow: Oriki, Women, and the Past in a Yoruba Town* (Edinburgh: Edinburgh University Press).

Bascom, William (1965) 'Four functions of folklore' in Alan Dundes (ed.) *The Study of Folklore* (Englewood Cliffs: Prentice-Hall).

Bauman, H-Dirksen (1998) *American Sign Language as a Medium for Poetry: Poetics of Speech, and Writing in Twentieth-Century American Poetics*, unpublished doctoral dissertation (State University of New York).

Bauman, H-Dirksen (2006) 'Getting out of line: toward a visual and cinematic poetics of ASL' in H-Dirksen Bauman, Jennifer Nelson and Heidi Rose (eds) *Signing the Body Poetic* (California: University of California Press).

Bernhard, Walter (1999) 'Iconicity and beyond in "Lullaby for Jumbo": Semiotic function of poetic rhythm' in Max Nänny and Olga Fischer (eds) *Form Miming Meaning: Iconicity in Language and Literature* (Amsterdam: John Benjamins).

Bienvenu, Martina J. (1994) 'Reflections of Deaf culture in Deaf humor' in Carol Erting, Robert Johnson, Dorothy Smith, and Bruce Snider (eds) *The Deaf Way: Perspectives from the International Conference on Deaf Culture* (Washington, DC: Gallaudet University Press).

Bisol, Cláudia (2001) *Tibi e Joca: Uma História de Dois Mundos* (Porto Alegre: Mercado Aberto).

Blondel, Marion and Christopher Miller (2000) 'Rhythmic structures in French Sign Language (LSF) nursery rhymes', *Sign Language and Linguistics* 3(1), 59–77.

Blondel, Marion and Christopher Miller (2001) 'Movement and rhythm in nursery rhymes in LSF', *Sign Language Studies.* 2(1), 24–61.

Booker, Christopher (2004) *The Seven Basic Plots – Why We Tell Stories* (London: Continuum).

Børdahl, Vibeke (2004) 'By word of tradition' in Vibeke Børdahl, Fei Li and Huan Ying (eds) *Four Masters of Chinese Storytelling* (Copenhagen: Nordic Institute of Asian Studies Press).

Bouchauveau, Guy (1994) 'Deaf humor and culture' in Carol Erting, Robert Johnson, Dorothy Smith, and Bruce Snider (eds) *The Deaf Way: Perspectives from the International Conference on Deaf Culture* (Washington, DC: Gallaudet University Press).

Boudreau, Kathryn (2009) 'Slam poetry and cultural experience for children', *Forum on Public Policy: A Journal of the Oxford Round Table* (www.questia.com/library/journal/1G1-216682605, accessed January 2014).

Boyes Braem, Penny and Rachel Sutton-Spence (eds) (2001) *The Hands are the Head of the Mouth: The Mouth as Articulator in Sign Languages* (Hamburg: Signum Press).

Brennan, Mary (1990) *Word Formation in British Sign Language* (Stockholm: University of Stockholm).

Bringhurst, Robert (1992) *The Elements of Typographic Style* (Vancouver: Hartley & Marks).

Carmel, Simon (1996) 'Deaf folklore' in Jan Harold Brunvand (ed.) *American Folklore: An Encyclopaedia* (New York: Garland Publishing).

Christie, Karen and Dorothy Wilkins (2006) 'Roots and Wings: ASL Poetry of "Coming Home"', *Deaf Studies Today!* 2, 227–235.

Christie, Karen and Dorothy Wilkins (2007) 'Themes and symbols in ASL poetry: resistance, affirmation and liberation', *Deaf Worlds,* 22, 1–49.

Cienki, Alan and Cornelia Müller (2008) (eds) *Metaphor and Gesture* (Amsterdam: John Benjamins).

Clark, John Lee (ed.) (2009) *Deaf American Poetry* (Washington, DC: Gallaudet University Press).

Cosslett, Tess (2006) *Talking Animals in British Children's Fiction, 1786–1914* (Aldershot: Ashgate).

Cuxac, Christian and Marie-Anne Sallandre (2008) 'Iconicity and arbitrariness in French Sign Language: highly iconic structures, degenerated iconicity and grammatic iconicity' in Elena Pizzuto, Paola Pietrandrea and Raffaele Simone (eds) *Verbal and Signed Languages: Comparing Structure, Constructs and Methodologies* (Berlin: Mouton de Gruyter).

Dexter, Colin (1977) *The Silent World of Nicholas Quinn* (London: Macmillan).

Dundes, Alan (1965) 'What is folklore?' in Alan Dundes (ed.) *The Study of Folklore* (Englewood Cliffs, NJ: Prentice Hall).

Dundes, Alan (1968) 'The number three in American culture' in Alan Dundes (ed.) *Every Man His Way: Readings in Cultural Anthropology* (Englewood Cliffs, NJ: Prentice Hall).

Ekman, Paul (1999) 'Facial expressions' in Tim Dalgleish and Mick Power (eds) *The Handbook of Cognition and Emotion* (Hoboken, NJ: Wiley).

Eliot, Thomas Stearns (1958) 'Introduction' in Paul Valéry, *Collected Works of Paul Valéry, Volume 7: The Art of Poetry* (New York: Vintage).

Fillmore, Charles (1982) *Frame Semantics* (Seoul: Hanshin Publishing).

Finnegan, Ruth (1977) *Oral Poetry: Its Nature, Significance and Social Context* (Cambridge: Cambridge University Press).

Finnegan, Ruth (1988) *Orality and Literacy* (Oxford: Blackwell).

Finnegan, Ruth (2012) *Oral Literature in Africa* (Open Book Publishers).

Fowler, David and Mark Heaton (2006) 'Onomatopoeia in British Sign Language? The visuality/sensation of sound' in Harvey Goodstein (ed.) *The Deaf Way II Reader: Perspectives from the Second International Conference on Deaf Culture* (Washington, DC: Gallaudet University Press).

Freeman, Donald (1970) *Linguistics and Literary Style* (Boston: Holt Rinehart & Winston).

Frishberg, Nancy (1988) 'Signers of tales: the case of literary status of an unwritten language', *Sign Language Studies* 17(59), 149–170.

Hall, Stephanie (1989) *The Deaf Club is Like a Second Home: An Ethnography of Folklore Communication in American Sign Language,* unpublished doctoral dissertation (University of Pennsylvania).

Herrnstein Smith, Barbara (1968) *Poetic Closure: A Study of How Poems End* (Chicago: University of Chicago Press).

Hessel, Carolina (2015) *Circulação da Literatura Surda no Brasil: análise de produções em Libras em Comunidades Surdas.* Tese apresentada ao Programa de Pós-Graduação em Educação da Universidade Federal do Rio Grande do Sul.

Hiraga, Masako (2005) *Metaphor and Iconicity: A Cognitive Approach to Analysing Texts* (Basingstoke: Palgrave Macmillan).

Holyday, Abigail (2008) *Do Deaf BSL Users Utilise Left and Right Placement in Syntactic Signing Space, to Represent Value?,* unpublished BA dissertation (University of Bristol).

Hove, Chenjerai (1996) *Ancestors* (London: Picador).

Howell, Wilbur Samuel (1961) *Logic and Rhetoric in England, 1500–1700* (Bolton: Russell & Russell).

Ichida, Yasuhiro (2004) '*Head Movement and Head Position in Japanese Sign Language,* poster presented at the 8th International Conference on Theoretical Issues in Sign Language Research (TISLR8), Barcelona, Spain, 30 September–2 October 2004.

Jackson, Judith (2006) 'Rhyming and rhythm in sign language poetry', seminar given at Centre for Deaf Studies, University of Bristol, 17 February 2006.

Jarashow, Ben (2006) 'ABC story basic principles', a paper presented at *Revolutions in Sign Language Studies: Linguistics, Literature, Literacy,* Gallaudet University, Washington, DC, 22–24 March 2006.

Kaneko, Michiko (2008) *The Poetics of Sign Language Haiku,* unpublished doctoral dissertation (University of Bristol).

Kaneko, Michiko (2011) 'Alliteration in sign language poetry' in Jonathan Roper (ed.) *Alliteration in Culture* (Basingstoke: Palgrave Macmillan).

Kaneko, Michiko and Johanna Mesch (2013) 'Eye gaze in creative sign language', *Sign Language Studies,* 13(3), 372–400.

Kaneko, Michiko and Rachel Sutton-Spence (2012) 'Iconicity and metaphor in sign language poetry', *Metaphor and Symbol*, 27(2), 107–130.

Kennedy, X.J. and Dana Gioia (2009) *An Introduction to Poetry*, 13th edn (London: Longman).

Klima, Edward and Ursula Bellugi (1979) *The Signs of Language* (Cambridge, MA: Harvard University Press).

Kövecses, Zoltan (2002) *Metaphor: A Practical Introduction* (Oxford: Oxford University Press).

Krentz, Christopher (2006) 'The camera as printing press: how film has influenced ASL literature' in H-Dirksen Bauman, Jennifer Nelson and Heidi Rose (eds) *Signing the Body Poetic* (California: University of California Press).

Krentz, Christopher (2007) *Writing Deafness: The Hearing Line in Nineteenth-century American Literature* (Chapel Hill, NC: University of North Carolina Press).

Kuntze, Marlon, Debbie Golos and Charlotte Enns (2014) 'Rethinking literacy: broadening opportunities for visual learners', *Sign Language Studies*, 14(2), 203–224.

Ladd, Paddy (1998) *In Search of Deafhood: Towards an Understanding of British Deaf Culture*, unpublished doctoral dissertation (University of Bristol).

Ladd, Paddy (2003) *Understanding Deaf Culture: In Search of Deafhood* (Clevedon: Multilingual Matters).

Lakoff, George and Mark Johnson (1980) *Metaphors We Live By* (Chicago: University of Chicago Press).

Lakoff, George and Mark Turner (1989) *More than Cool Reason: A Field Guide to Poetic Metaphor* (Chicago: University of Chicago Press).

Lane, Harlan, Robert Hoffmeister and Ben Bahan (1996) *A Journey into the DEAF-WORLD*. (San Diego, CA: Dawn Sign Press).

Leech, Geoffrey (1969) *A Linguistic Guide to English Poetry* (London: Longman).

Leith, Sam (2011) *You Talkin' to Me? Rhetoric from Aristotle to Obama* (London: Profile Books).

Li, Fei (2004) 'Performance technique and schools of Yangzhou storytelling' in Vibeke Børdahl, Fei Li and Huan Ying (eds) *Four Masters of Chinese Storytelling* (Copenhagen: Nordic Institute of Asian Studies Press).

Moffett, Helen (2014) *Seasons Come to Pass: A Poetry Anthology for Southern African Students*, 3rd edn (Cape Town: Oxford University Press).

Morgan, Gary (2002) 'Children's encoding of simultaneity in British Sign Language narratives', *Sign Language and Linguistics*, 5, 131–65.

Mukařovský, Jan (1964) 'Standard language and poetic language' in Paul L. Garvin (ed.) *A Prague School Reader on Esthetics, Literary Structure and Style* (Washington DC: Georgetown University Press).

Murch, Walter (1997) 'Walter Murch in conversation with Joy Katz', http://filmsound.org/murch/parnassus/ (accessed November 2015)

Nathan Lerner, Miriam and Don Feigel (2009) *The Heart of the Hydrogen Jukebox* (DVD) (New York: Rochester Institute of Technology).

Napoli, Donna Jo and Rachel Sutton-Spence (2014) 'Order of the major constituents in sign languages: implications for all language', *Frontiers in Psychology*, 5(376).

Napoli Donna Jo and Jeff Wu (2003) 'Morpheme structure constraints on two-handed signs in American Sign Language: notions of symmetry', *Sign Language and Linguistics,* 6, 123–205.

Olrik, Axel (1909 [1965]) 'Epic laws of folk narrative' in Alan Dundes (ed.) *The Study of Folklore* (Englewood Cliffs, NJ: Prentice Hall).

Opie, Iona and Peter Opie (1959) *The Lore and Language of Schoolchildren* (Oxford: Oxford University Press).

Ormsby, Alec (1995) 'Poetic cohesion in American Sign Language: Valli's "Snowflake" & Coleridge's "Frost at Midnight"', *Sign Language Studies,* 88, 227–244.

Paales, Liina (2004) 'A hearer's insight into Deaf sign language folklore, *Electronic Journal of Folklore,* www.folklore.ee/folklore/ (accessed November 2015).

Paxson, James (1994) *The Poetics of Personification* (Cambridge: Cambridge University Press).

Peters, Cynthia (2000) *Deaf American Literature: From Carnival to the Canon* (Washington, DC: Gallaudet University Press).

Prøysen, Alf (2000) *Mrs. Pepperpot Stories* (New York: Random House).

Reber, Rolf, Norbert Schwarz and Piotr Winkielman (2004) 'Processing fluency and aesthetic pleasure: is beauty in the perceiver's processing experience?', *Personality and Social Psychology Review,* 8(4), 364–382.

Reilly, Charles and Nipapon Reilly (2005) *The Rising of Lotus Flowers: Self-education by Deaf Children in Thai Boarding Schools* (Washington, DC: Gallaudet University Press).

Riskind, Mary (1981) *Apple Is My Sign* (Boston: Houghton Mifflin Company).

Rose, Heidi (1992) *A Critical Methodology for Analyzing American Sign Language Literature,* unpublished doctoral dissertation (Arizona State University).

Rose, Heidi (2006) 'The poet in the poem in the performance: the relation of body, self, and text in ASL literature' in H-Dirksen Bauman, Jennifer Nelson and Heidi Rose (eds) *Signing the Body Poetic* (California: University of California Press).

Russo, Tommaso, Rosaria Giuranna and Elena Pizzuto (2001) 'Italian Sign Language (LIS) poetry: iconic properties and structural regularities', *Sign Language Studies,* 2(4), 24–61.

Rutherford, Susan (1989) 'Funny in Deaf – not in hearing' in Sherman Wilcox (ed.) *American Deaf Culture: An Anthology* (Silver Spring, MD: Linstok Press).

Rutherford, Susan (1993) *A Study of Deaf American Folklore* (Silver Spring, MD: Linstok Press).

Ryan, Stephen (1993) 'Let's tell an ASL story' in Gallaudet University College for Continuing Education (ed.) *Conference Proceedings, April 22–25, 1993* (Washington, DC: Gallaudet University Press).

Scott, Paul (2010) 'Do Deaf children eat Deaf carrots?' in Donna Jo Napoli and Gaurav Mathur (eds) *Deaf Around the World* (Oxford: Oxford University Press).

Smith, Jennifer and Rachel Sutton-Spence (2007) 'What is the Deaflore of the British Deaf community?', *Deaf Worlds,* 23, 44–69.

Smith, Sandra and Kearsy Cormier (2004) 'In or out? Spatial scale and enactment in narratives of native and nonnative signing Deaf children acquiring British Sign Language', *Sign Language Studies,* 14(3), 275–301.

Sturley, Nick (2009) *Tales From Signtown* (Wheatley: DeafEducate).

Sunkuli, Leteipa Ole and Simon Okumba Miruka (1990) *A Dictionary of Oral Literature* (Nairobi: East African Educational Publishers).

Supalla, Sam and Ben Bahan (2007) *ASL Literature Series: Bird of a Different Feather & For a Decent Living* (San Diego, CA: Dawn Sign Press).

Sutton-Spence, Rachel (2005) *Analysing Sign Language Poetry* (Basingstoke: Palgrave Macmillan).

Sutton-Spence, Rachel (2010) 'Spatial metaphor and expressions of identity in sign language poetry', *Metaphorik.de* (www.metaphorik.de/19/sutton-spence.pdf; accessed November 2015).

Sutton-Spence, Rachel and Penny Boyes Braem (2013) 'Comparing the products and the processes of creating sign language poetry and pantomimic improvisations', *Journal of Nonverbal Behavior,* 37(3) 245–280.

Sutton-Spence, Rachel and Michiko Kaneko (2007) 'Symmetry in sign language poetry', *Sign Language Studies* 7(3), 284–318.

Sutton-Spence, Rachel and Ronice Muller de Quadros (2005) 'Sign language poetry and Deaf identity' *Sign Language and Linguistics,* 8, 175–210.

Sutton-Spence, Rachel and Ronice Muller de Quadros (2014) '"I am the Book" – Deaf poets' views on signed poetry', *The Journal of Deaf Studies and Deaf Education*, 19(4), 546–558.

Sutton-Spence, Rachel and Donna Jo Napoli (2009) *Humour in Signed Languages: The Linguistic Underpinnings* (Dublin: Trinity College Press).

Sutton-Spence, Rachel and Donna Jo Napoli (2010) 'Anthropomorphism in sign languages: a look at poetry and storytelling with a focus on British Sign Language', *Sign Language Studies* 10(4), 442–475.

Sutton-Spence, Rachel and Donna Jo Napoli (2012) 'Deaf jokes and sign language humor', *International Journal of Humor Research,* 25(3), 311–338.

Sutton-Spence, Rachel and Donna Jo Napoli (2013) 'How much can classifiers be analogous to their referents?' *Gesture*, 13(1), 1–27.

Sutton-Spence, Rachel and Claire Ramsey (2010) 'What we should teach Deaf children: Deaf teachers' folk models in Britain, the U.S. and Mexico', *Deafness and Education International*, 12(3), 149–76.

Sutton-Spence, Rachel and Bencie Woll (1999) *The Linguistics of British Sign Language: An Introduction* (Cambridge: Cambridge University Press).

Taub, Sarah (2001) *Language from the Body: Iconicity and Metaphor in American Sign Language* (Cambridge: Cambridge University Press).

Taub, Sarah (2006) 'Conceptual "rhymes" in sign language poetry' in Harvey Goodstein (ed.) *The Deaf Way II Reader* (Washington, DC: Gallaudet University Press).

Valéry, Paul (1958) *The Art of Poetry* (New York: Vintage).

Valli, Clayton (1990) 'The nature of a line in ASL poetry' in William H. Edmondson and Fred Karlsson (eds) *SLR87: Papers from the Fourth International Symposium on Sign Language Research* (Hamburg: Signum Verlag).

Valli, Clayton (1993) *Poetics of American Sign Language Poetry*, unpublished doctoral dissertation (Union Institute Graduate School).

Wa Thiong'o, Ngigu (1967) *A Grain of Wheat* (London: Heinemann).

Wa Thiong'o, Ngigu (1998) 'Oral power and europhone glory: orature, literature, and stolen legacies' in Ngigu Wa Thiong'o (ed.) *Gunpoints, and Dreams: Towards a Critical Theory of the Arts and the State in Africa* (Oxford: Oxford University Press).

West, Donna and Rachel Sutton-Spence (2012) 'Shared thinking processes with four Deaf poets: a window on "The Creative" in "Creative Sign Language"', *Sign Language Studies,* 12(2), 188–210.

Weyl, Hermann (1952) *Symmetry* (Princeton, N.J.: Princeton University Press).

Wilbur, Ronnie (1990) 'Metaphors in American Sign Language and English' in William H. Edmondson and Fred Karlsson (eds) *SLR87: Papers from the Fourth International Symposium on Sign Language Research* (Hamburg: Signum Verlag).

Wilbur, Ronnie (1987) *American Sign Language: Linguistic and Applied Dimensions* (Boston, MA: College-Hill Press).

Wilcox, Phyllis Perrin (2000) *Metaphor in American Sign Language* (Washington, DC: Gallaudet University Press).

Williams, Paul (2000) *The Nick of Time: Essays on Haiku Aesthetics* (New York: Press Here).

Ye, Yang (1996) *Chinese Poetic Closure* (New York: Peter Lang).

Zeshan, Ulrike (2000) *Sign Language in Indo-Pakistan: A Description of a Signed Language* (Amsterdam: John Benjamins).

Video References

(Poems by the following people – in alphabetical order – can be found at www.youtube.com/user/signmetaphor/videos. David Ellington, Donna Williams, Dorothy Miles, Johanna Mesch, John Wilson, Kabir Kapoor, Maria Gibson, Nigel Howard, Paul Scott, Penny Beschizza, Penny Gunn, Richard Carter, Siobhan O' Donovan, Vitalis Katakinas)

Acronym Paul Scott, https://youtu.be/cr4xManpNQk

Aeroplane Johanna Mesch, https://youtu.be/9mFyF6n_joI

Autumn in *Seasons* Dorothy Miles, https://youtu.be/7KDdpxs-EXY

Ball Story Ben Bahan, Available on DVD accompanying H-Dirksen Bauman, Jennifer Nelson and Heidi Rose (eds) *Signing the Body Poetic*, California: University of California Press

Bandeira Brasileira Nelson Pimenta, see *Brazilian Flag*

Being Deaf Chi Ngo, www.lifeanddeaf.co.uk/being-deaf-17

Bird of a Different Feather (ASL) Ben Bahan, Available on DVD in *Bird of a Different Feather & For a Decent Living, ASL Literature Series*, Sam Supalla and Ben Bahan, 2007, Dawn Sign Press

Bird of a Different Feather (Libras) [*O passarinho diferente*] Nelson Pimenta, Available on DVD *Literatura em LSB*, LSB vídeo, 1999, Dawn Sign Press

Black Paul Scott, https://youtu.be/HgbgGAddYuE

Blue Suit Paul Scott, https://youtu.be/tHe84JjyZqQ

Brazilian Flag [*Bandeira Brasileira*] Nelson Pimenta, Available on DVD *Literatura em LSB*, LSB vídeo, 1999, Dawn Sign Press

Bubble Measure Paul Scott, https://youtu.be/ts9cY6tqpzk

Cat in *Acronym* Paul Scott, https://youtu.be/cr4xManpNQk

Cave Clayton Valli, Available on DVD *Poetry in Motion, Clayton Valli*, Sign Media Inc.

Children's Park Richard Carter, https://youtu.be/Hpryz9d1M5E

Circle of Life Ella Mae Lentz, Lentz, Ella Mae (1995) *The Treasure: ASL Poems* (DVD-ROM), San Diego, CA: Dawn Sign Press.

Cochlear Implant Richard Carter, https://youtu.be/KskwGOyhLRQ

D not E Fernanda Machado, https://youtu.be/LF-m2l2qK2k

Deaf Nigel Howard, https://youtu.be/xitL4etCCgI

Deaf in *Acronym* Paul Scott, https://youtu.be/cr4xManpNQk

Deaf Gay Richard Carter and David Ellington, https://youtu.be/3DS5xGW8jcQ

Deaf Studies Penny Gunn, https://youtu.be/TJ4FyfsuHZU

Deaf Trees Richard Carter, https://youtu.be/o5flsMbtqIE

Defiance Dorothy Miles, Available on DVD, Miles, Dorothy (1976) *Gestures: Poetry in Sign Language*, Northridge, CA: Joyce Motion Picture Co.

Desert Wim Emmerik, https://corpus1.mpi.nl/ds/asv/?9&openpath=node:530598

District Six Brian Meyer, please contact SLED (info@sled.org.za)

Doll Paul Scott, https://youtu.be/5iM7zbis68w

Duck and Dissertation Donna Williams, https://youtu.be/CbsblW77ytI

Earthquake Johanna Mesch, https://youtu.be/m3HSnQwareQ

Elephants Dancing Dorothy Miles, https://youtu.be/Bhf6lznwUcw

England Nigel Howard, https://youtu.be/P7gnFeLbpbg

Evening in *Trio* Dorothy Miles, available on the DVD accompanying Sutton-Spence, Rachel and Bencie Woll (1999) *The Linguistics of British Sign Language: An Introduction*, Cambridge: Cambridge University Press

Evolution Kabir Kapoor, https://youtu.be/kYENPiRQOzA

Falling Leaf Wim Emmerik, https://corpus1.mpi.nl/ds/asv/?9&openpath=node:530598

Fashion Times Richard Carter and Paul Scott, https://youtu.be/DFKASTB-LHw

Five Senses Paul Scott, https://youtu.be/BKsr9JUjVEg

Flight over Rio [*Voo sobre Rio*] Fernanda Machado, https://youtu.be/YaAy0cbjU8o

For A Deaf Friend John Wilson, http://youtu.be/4GZTCBpsGVY

For My Aunt Atiyah Asmal, please contact SLED (info@sled.org.za)

For Two Special People John Wilson, http://youtu.be/Lr9mIg4ke84

Four Deaf Yorkshire Men https://www.youtube.com/watch?v=2upAsFzO9AU

Garden of Eden Wim Emmerik, https://corpus1.mpi.nl/ds/asv/?9&openpath=node:530598

Ghost Stories Christine Reeves and Rachell Bastikar, Available on the DVD accompanying Sutton-Spence, Rachel and Bencie Woll (1999) *The Linguistics of British Sign Language: An Introduction*, Cambridge: Cambridge University Press

Goldfish Richard Carter, https://youtu.be/noMoV-YB3kw

Gondola Richard Carter, https://youtu.be/4wjK0tCF20U

Graduation Vitalis Katakinas, https://youtu.be/3yEv3d4AwIE

Graduation Haiku Vitalis Katakinas, https://youtu.be/k8CmjvBeE3Q

Grass Penny Beschizza, https://youtu.be/bSG2h406K44

Grass Hairstyle Richard Carter, https://youtu.be/ZuPFN3Y5W0Q

Guilty Paul Scott, https://youtu.be/JPwKE0dXgUI

Haiku Quartets Paul Scott, Richard Carter, Johanna Mesch, John Wilson, https://youtu.be/GNqQbq-VlMc

Half Personal Poetry Sean Timon, http://www.lifeanddeaf.co.uk/half-personal-poetry/

Hands Clayton Valli, Available on DVD *Poetry in Motion, Clayton Valli*, Sign Media Inc.

Home Paul Scott, https://youtu.be/u0ZdYIqvvgk

Home John Wilson, https://youtu.be/YC_q9jSaRT0

Home Richard Carter, https://youtu.be/J_BdMWDcYOM

Homenagem Santa Maria – See *Tribute to Santa Maria*

Icon John Wilson, https://youtu.be/DqN9mk0VTfI

I Know Who (Stole My Heart) Paul Scott, https://youtu.be/6jpP3AQG43s

Identities Richard Carter, https://youtu.be/_NA7gRgdYaw

Immortal Invisible Dorothy Miles, https://youtu.be/zBZfcpvV0BE

Jack in the Box Richard Carter, https://youtu.be/cgxBPF7ljMw

Jam Richard Carter, https://youtu.be/ISutcfOSCtk

June 16th Modiegi Moime, please contact SLED (info@sled.org.za)

Just Like You Tiffany Hudson, http://www.lifeanddeaf.co.uk/just-like-you/

Kayak Johanna Mesch, http://youtu.be/5yzI5PThihA

Kettle Maria Gibson, https://youtu.be/DFGrPlWvvVg

Lifes Road Modiegi Moime, please contact SLED (info@sled.org.za)

Lift John Wilson, https://youtu.be/4NOVt3p5O-A

Little Red Ridinghood Jerry Hanifin, Available on the DVD accompanying Sutton-Spence, Rachel and Bencie Woll (1999) *The Linguistics of British Sign Language: An Introduction*, Cambridge: Cambridge University Press

Lone Sturdy Tree Clayton Valli, Available on DVD *Poetry in Motion, Clayton Valli*, Sign Media Inc.

Look at the Front Richard Achiampong, www.lifeanddeaf.co.uk/look-at-the-front/

Looking for Diamonds Richard Carter, https://youtu.be/NnjOAf6TCiE

Macbeth of the Lost Ark Paul Scott, https://youtu.be/ePj7Vwt80DQ

Make-up Theatre Richard Carter, https://youtu.be/Sd19h7jaSgw

Mirror Richard Carter, https://youtu.be/p0B8ztiVI4s

Morning in *Trio* Dorothy Miles, available on the DVD accompanying Sutton-Spence, Rachel and Bencie Woll (1999) *The Linguistics of British Sign Language: An Introduction*, Cambridge: Cambridge University Press

Morning John Wilson, https://youtu.be/OGtoU_RzEqg

My Cat Donna Williams, https://youtu.be/Z7elrYoAFvs

My Home is My Castle Donna Williams, https://youtu.be/eQxAuUL6rgs

Nature [*Natureza*] Nelson Pimenta, Available on DVD *Literatura em LSB*, LSB vídeo, 1999, Dawn Sign Press

No Mask like Home Paul Scott, https://youtu.be/0kkL0SZ7ZLc

Ocean Johanna Mesch, https://youtu.be/y7I3Fp8g-G4

Operation Richard Carter, https://youtu.be/hGxEo6g83GY

Our Dumb Friends Dorothy Miles, https://youtu.be/23Pf1rjxqZE

Owl Richard Carter, https://youtu.be/aDFTIRSKXRg

Party Johanna Mesch, https://youtu.be/s8BLY1Nm7qQ

Ping Pong Ball [*Bolinha de Ping-Pong*] Rimar Segala, www.youtube.com/watch?v=VhGCEznqljo

Pixar Kabir Kapoor, https://youtu.be/NMMkmHCn98A

Poetry Peter Cook and Kenner Lerner (The Flying Words Project), available in Nathan Lerner, Miriam and Don Feigel (2009) *The Heart of the Hydrogen Jukebox*. New York: Rochester Institute of Technology (DVD)

Phoenix Garden Donna Williams, https://www.youtube.com/watch?v=P-EVgeS0pLQ

Prince Looking for Love Richard Carter, https://youtu.be/D4hPR6DCcDA

Psychotic Memory Peter Cook and Debbie Rennie, available in Nathan Lerner, Miriam and Don Feigel (2009) *The Heart of the Hydrogen Jukebox*, New York: Rochester Institute of Technology (DVD)

Red and Green Donna Williams, https://youtu.be/O_Baj81Vr7k

Road Signs Hal Draper, available on the DVD accompanying Sutton-Spence, Rachel and Bencie Woll (1999) *The Linguistics of British Sign Language: An Introduction*, Cambridge: Cambridge University Press

Roz: Teach a Dog a New Trick Paul Scott, https://youtu.be/d9OSiB1OHvE

Sam's Birthday Richard Carter, https://youtu.be/JUBjAiSkH-4

Seasons Dorothy Miles, https://youtu.be/7KDdpxs-EXY

Shop Window Richard Carter, https://youtu.be/kPhWt2GzcNM

Sign Language Penny Beschizza, https://youtu.be/YDjx2hcjns4

Sixty-One Steps Siobhan O'Donovan, https://youtu.be/y5wxzf2Pq00

Snow Globe Richard Carter, https://youtu.be/SYY-2IGcYlI

Snowflake Clayton Valli, available on DVD, *Poetry in Motion, Clayton Valli*, Sign Media Inc.

Something Not Right Clayton Valli, *ASL Poetry: Selected works of Clayton Valli*, 1995, San Diego, CA: Dawn Sign Press

Soweto Modiegi Moime, please contact SLED (info@sled.org.za)

Speed Jerry Hanifin, available on the DVD accompanying Sutton-Spence, Rachel and Bencie Woll (1999) *The Linguistics of British Sign Language: An Introduction*, Cambridge: Cambridge University Press

Spring in *Seasons* Dorothy Miles, https://youtu.be/7KDdpxs-EXY

Spring in *Haiku Quartets* Paul Scott, https://youtu.be/GNqQbq-VlMc

Spring in *Four Seasons (Haiku)* Johanna Mesch, http://youtu.be/Xq2hiSixWeE

Street Signs Hayley McWilliams, www.lifeanddeaf.co.uk/street-signs/

Summer in *Seasons* Dorothy Miles, https://youtu.be/7KDdpxs-EXY

Surprise Apple Richard Carter, https://youtu.be/vi-uWuhARAM

Thanks Giuseppe Giuranna and Rosaria Giuranna, DVD available Giuranna, Rosaria and Giuseppe Giuranna (2000) *Seven Poems in Italian Sign Language (LIS)*, Rome: Graphic Service, Istituto di Psicologia, Consiglio Nazionale delle Ricerche

That Day Donna Williams, https://youtu.be/JsuGSFOx33w

The Bear Washing Day Modiegi Moime, please contact SLED (info@sled.org.za)

The Boy who Cried Wolf Carolyn Nabarro, http://corpus1.mpi.nl/ds/imdi_browser?openpath=MPI530401%23

The Bridge Clayton Valli, *ASL Poetry: Selected works of Clayton Valli*, 1995, San Diego, CA: Dawn Sign Press

The Cat Dorothy Miles, https://youtu.be/RZeqb_JQuCk

The Dogs Ella Mae Lentz, Lentz, Ella Mae (1995) *The Treasure: ASL Poems* (DVD-ROM), San Diego, CA: Dawn Sign Press.

The Fates John Wilson, https://youtu.be/2TS3q0vEh7A

The Lighthouse at Barra [*O Farol da Barra*] Mauricio Barreto, https://www.youtube.com/watch?v=VXcKgO-jD9A

The Painter from A to Z [*O Pintor de A a Z*] Nelson Pimenta, available on DVD *Literatura em LSB*, LSB vídeo, 1999, Dawn Sign Press

The Race Richard Carter, https://youtu.be/Zargb1vfhFI

The Staircase Dorothy Miles, https://youtu.be/GIjxVLZQTOw

The Story of the Flag David Ellington, https://youtu.be/O2VEbuB1dUk

The Ugly Duckling Dorothy Miles, https://youtu.be/oK0CyVOUNEE

Three Haiku Johanna Mesch, https://youtu.be/BY8kDN6gZHM

Three Queens Paul Scott, https://youtu.be/sbrCfrlfIRg

Time John Wilson, https://youtu.be/c_sJRF4l7Fc

Time Richard Carter, https://youtu.be/w9ekSQKPe88

Time Paul Scott https://youtu.be/se-40DjlVcs

Time Donna Williams https://youtu.be/nLS-nLwcatM

To a Deaf Child Dorothy Miles, available on DVD, Miles, Dorothy (1976) *Gestures: Poetry in Sign Language*, Northridge, CA: Joyce Motion Picture Co.

Too Busy to Hug; No Time to See Paul Scott, https://youtu.be/8OWInN15_MY

Train Journey Paul Scott, available on DVD in *Paul Scott's Poetry DVD*, Forest Books,

Tree Paul Scott, https://youtu.be/Lf92PlzMAXo

Tribute to Santa Maria [*Homenagem Santa Maria*] Alan Henry Godinho, https://www.youtube.com/watch?v=9LtOP-LLx0Y

Trio Dorothy Miles, available on the DVD accompanying Sutton-Spence, Rachel and Bencie Woll (1999) *The Linguistics of British Sign Language: An Introduction*, Cambridge: Cambridge University Press

Trip Abroad Arthur Dimmock, available on the DVD accompanying Sutton-Spence, Rachel and Bencie Woll (1999) *The Linguistics of British Sign Language: An Introduction*, Cambridge: Cambridge University Press

Tsunami Johanna Mesch, https://youtu.be/MXJDcO06WPA

Turkey Paul Scott, https://youtu.be/KXJ5eRLKm_Y

Twin Leaves Johanna Mesch, https://youtu.be/COjL2jz1zWo

Two Books Paul Scott, https://youtu.be/DQtpgVSmbOE

Two Communities John Wilson, https://youtu.be/R1P2dpk1eXo

Ugly, Beautiful Atiyah Asmal and Modiegi Moime, http://youtu.be/5dtcRIUuu1E

Veal Boycott Debbie Rennie, available in Nathan Lerner, Miriam and Don Feigel (2009) *The Heart of the Hydrogen Jukebox*, New York: Rochester Institute of Technology (DVD)

Voo sobre Rio Fernanda Machado, See *Flight over Rio*

Wartime Memories Arthur Dimmock, available on the DVD accompanying Sutton-Spence, Rachel and Bencie Woll (1999) *The Linguistics of British Sign Language: An Introduction*, Cambridge: Cambridge University Press

We Not Me Kabir Kapoor, https://youtu.be/1U01iS5FmN0

We'll Meet Again Paul Scott, https://youtu.be/zt54Xfipd2M

What's it like to be deaf? Sarah Ivy-Jayne Teacy, www.lifeanddeaf.co.uk/whats-it-like-to-be-deaf

Who am I? Donna Williams, https://youtu.be/npfpIQMHmxo

Winter in *Seasons* Dorothy Miles, https://youtu.be/7KDdpxs-EXY

World Renga I Leo Loubser, Miro Civin, Deborah Van Halle, Ashni Kumar, Megan Alexander and Mark MacQueen, https://www.youtube.com/watch?v=sFq2o-y_yso

Index of creative sign language works

245

General Index

A

ABC stories – *see* stories
Acronym, 50–51, 134–5
Adaptation, 4, 5, 36, 52, 95, 208
Aesop's Fables, 93, 108
Aesthetic, 2, 3, 28, 29, 31, 38, 62, 117, 121,124, 141, 143, 147, 157, 181, 202
Allegory, 74, 94, 95, 109, 223
Ambiguity, 79, 135–139
American Sign Language, 6, 13, 14, 24, 29, 30, 31, 44, 48–50, 58, 60, 62, 99, 113, 119, 144, 161, 169, 187, 216
Anthem – *see* national anthem
Anthology – *see also* collection, 12, 41, 61, 72, 84, 85, 99, 100, 232
Anthropomorphism, 18, 54, 68–80, 84, 108, 114, 122, 137, 195, 215, 224
ASL – *see* American Sign Language
Audience, 2, 8, 11, 14–17, 27, 28, 30–31, 46, 53–54, 58, 69, 78, 82–85, 88, 97, 98, 110, 120, 123, 124, 134, 137, 143, 161, 176, 195, 198, 207, 227
Autobiography – *see also* Narrative of Deaf Experience, 5

B

Balance – *see* symmetry
Beginning – *see* opening
Bilingualism, 93, 134, 215–216
Blending
  in anthropomorphism, 70, 72, 79
  of signs, 226 – *see also* morphing
Body posture, 60, 84, 149, 195, 202–203
  chin posture, 203
  head posture, 194, 225, 203

Borrowing – *see also* loan translation, 129, 134–135, 216
Brazilian Sign Language, 12, 49, 64, 93, 97, 100, 188, 221

C

Camera – *see* cinematic features
  as printing press, 30
Canon, 3, 24, 25, 30, 53
Caricature, 60, 211, 214
Chants, 25, 30, 150
Characters
  Deaf – *see also* Deaf Everyman, 4, 5, 36, 46, 53, 54, 93, 113, 173, 183, 210
  Hearing, 47, 111, 173, 183, 208
CHASE (Culture, History, Arts, Sign and Education), 12
Chiming, 160, 161
Chin – *see* body posture
Chinese poetry, 87, 194
Chronicles, 5
Cinderella, 36, 93
Cinematic features – *see also* Visual Vernacular, 3, 61–65, 150, 225
Cinematic stories – *see* stories
Classifiers, 7, 58, 60–63, 70, 106, 114, 121, 131, 132–138, 142, 153, 156, 187, 216, 223
Closure, 86–90
Cochlear implant, 86, 94, 96, 98, 101, 121, 153, 208, 210
Cognitive linguistics, 105, 107
Collection – *see* anthology
Comedy, (Booker's notion) *see also* Humour, 96
Conflict, 44, 46, 47, 110,
Constructed Action – *see also* roleshift, 50, 58, 60, 63, 65, 68–76, 125, 143, 201, 223, 225

249

Made in the USA
Las Vegas, NV
24 May 2021